INDUSTRIAL SOCIETY
AND THE SCIENCE FICTION
BLOCKBUSTER

# Industrial Society and the Science Fiction Blockbuster

*Social Critique in Films of Lucas, Scott and Cameron*

Mark T. Decker

McFarland & Company, Inc., Publishers
*Jefferson, North Carolina*

LIBRARY OF CONGRESS CATALOGUING-IN-PUBLICATION DATA

Names: Decker, Mark T., author.
Title: Industrial society and the science fiction blockbuster :
   social critique in films of Lucas, Scott and Cameron /
   Mark T. Decker.
Description: Jefferson, N.C. : McFarland & Company, Inc.,
   Publishers, 2016. | Includes bibliographical references and
   index.
Identifiers: LCCN 2016004314 | ISBN 9780786499113 (softcover :
   acid free paper) ∞
Subjects: LCSH: Science fiction films—History and criticism. |
   Motion pictures—Social aspects—History and criticism.
Classification: LCC PN1995.9.S26 D43 2016 | DDC 791.43/615—
   dc23
LC record available at http://lccn.loc.gov/2016004314

BRITISH LIBRARY CATALOGUING DATA ARE AVAILABLE

**ISBN (print) 978-0-7864-9911-3**
**ISBN (ebook) 978-1-4766-2387-0**

© 2016 Mark T. Decker. All rights reserved

*No part of this book may be reproduced or transmitted in any form or by any means, electronic or mechanical, including photocopying or recording, or by any information storage and retrieval system, without permission in writing from the publisher.*

Front cover: (on screen) Scene from the 1982 Ridley Scott film *Blade Runner* (Warner Bros./Photofest); theater © 2016 Photoncatcher/iStock

Printed in the United States of America

*McFarland & Company, Inc., Publishers*
  *Box 611, Jefferson, North Carolina 28640*
   *www.mcfarlandpub.com*

# Acknowledgments

Many acknowledgments begin by stating that many people have helped the author during the process of writing the book; mine will be no different. I would like to give a special thanks to Mike Levy, who first encouraged me to begin the academic study of science fiction. I would also like to thank Patrick Murphy, who gave me invaluable insight into the connection between graphic novels and blockbuster science fiction films.

Many of the arguments addressed here were first worked out in papers presented at meetings of the Science Fiction Research Association and the International Conference on the Fantastic in the Arts. Chapter 3 is a lightly revised version of an article that appeared in *Extrapolation* in 2009. I would like to thank Liverpool University Press for granting permission to reprint it here.

This book was largely written during a sabbatical granted by Bloomsburg University and funded by the Pennsylvania State System of Higher Education. During that sabbatical, office space was provided by my friend Todd Moinier; I could not have written as much as I did in such a relatively short time without his help.

I would also like to thank my wife Gayle and my children—Grace, Mary, Max, Caroline, and Rose—for supporting my efforts.

# Table of Contents

*Acknowledgments*   v
*Preface*   1

1. Big-Budget Science Fiction Film and Profitable Social Critique   5
2. Creating Cleverly Subversive Science Fiction Universes   27
3. George Lucas Battles the Empire of Unfreedom in *American Graffiti* and the *Star Wars* Films   52
4. Ridley Scott Takes On Apparently Evil Corporations in *Alien*, *Blade Runner* and *Prometheus*   74
5. James Cameron Reforms the Company Man in *Terminator* and *T2*   112
6. Cameron's Questioners: Two-Dimensional Protagonists in *Aliens*, *Titanic* and *Avatar*   134

*Afterword: The Cultural Half-Life of Subversive Blockbusters*   169
*Chapter Notes*   187
*Bibliography*   198
*Index*   207

# Preface

Blockbuster films have been a fixture of summer's—and increasingly Christmas's—commercial landscape for over four decades now. At least since Stephen Spielberg's *Jaws* (1975), action-oriented, widely released, and heavily marketed films that are seen by a significant proportion of the population come as reliably with warm weather as low interest rates, rebates on new automobiles, and Memorial Day sales at department stores. And while it would be difficult to argue that *Jaws* is best described as science fiction, some of the most commercially successful blockbusters have been science fiction films. Indeed, George Lucas' *Star Wars* (it was not widely known as *A New Hope* in 1977) solidified the blockbuster's hold on the season when it arrived in theaters two years after *Jaws* and James Cameron's *Avatar* (2009) firmly placed the science fiction blockbuster on Christmas' commercial calendar over three decades later.

Because blockbusters are the heavily financed products of wealthy corporations that expect a healthy return on their investments, it is fair to compare these films to the new cars that dealers strive to move off their lots in late summer, the new season's clothes that department stores are using to lure customers, or even the Christmas lights that hardware stores use to help their bottom line during what, for them, is a slow time of year. The aptness of this comparison is even clearer when we consider that blockbusters are sometimes little more than mindless entertainment, pleasing most audience members but leaving reviewers cold, and giving academic critics a convenient reference point for their discussions of society's myopic conceptualizations of itself.

Yet perhaps it is too easy to dismiss all blockbusters as nothing more than slick product from a multi-billion-dollar, multinational entertainment industry. Given the cultural penetration of blockbusters, if they did incorporate social critique into their themes, they could reach people who would never dream of listening to or reading an academic or public intellectual discuss society's ills. Consequently, if such films actually did contain a cogent and rhetorically powerful critique of society, some blockbusters could be a powerful conduit for delivering popularized versions of serious cultural critique to a broad audience. Because of their speculative nature, science fiction blockbusters would be particularly well suited to this task.

This book describes just such an act of cultural transmission. In the late 1960s and early 1970s, a professor named Herbert Marcuse argued that industrial society, in both its capitalist and communist forms, was estranging people from the environment, from their own desires, and from the people they loved by creating false needs for material goods. Marcuse found this situation particular reprehensible because technology could be used to free people from drudgery and create a more just society, and he was able to make this argument in bestselling books, national magazines, and in television interviews. Concepts like one-dimensional thought, false needs, and the ability of a broadly-considered Eros to help build a more just society resonated with contemporary audiences. Because of the philosopher's broader exposure, arguments that may have lived and died in classrooms and little-read scholarly books entered the zeitgeist. Not only did Marcuse become the darling of the counterculture, but his influence among the broader public drew the ire of no less a figure than Ronald Reagan, then Governor of California. And because Marcuse's ideas, or at least popularized versions of them, broke free of the academy and into popular culture, they found their way into the work of the three directors who are probably most responsible for establish the science fiction blockbuster in our cultural psyche. Extremely profitable films like 1979's *Alien*, 1984's *Return of the Jedi*, and 1991's *Terminator 2* not only entertained fans and (admittedly) enriched investors, but they also reconfigured a cultural critique that had been instrumental in the protests of the 1960s, giving it a pop-cultural half-life that extends its viability into the new century.

This book will argue that Marcuse's theories were incorporated into a critical and oppositional zeitgeist that heavily influenced blockbuster science fiction films by George Lucas, Ridley Scott, and James Cameron. This influence will be delineated by a careful reading of Marcuse's theories and a reconstruction of his place in popular culture during the height of his influence. Then, close readings of Lucas,' Scott's, and Cameron's films, as well as the filmmakers' own comments and relevant secondary sources, will reveal how their movies employ lines of argument about how the powerful often use technology to pacify rather than improve society. These readings, in turn, will demonstrate that blockbuster film can transmit serious social critique.

My interest in this topic stems from a longstanding desire to investigate the ability of popular culture to function as a means of cultural critique. In graduate school, studying canonical American literature, I read with great interest, and a healthy dose of skepticism, the contentions of mid–20th-century intellectuals like Dwight MacDonald that "middlebrow" culture dulled people's ability to think for themselves and turned them into conformists. Later, as a new assistant professor, I began to study science fiction film seriously. I noticed that there were some dismissive readings of blockbusters like Lucas' *Star Wars* films that sounded suspiciously like MacDonald's arguments. My own viewing experience, however, convinced me that popular science fiction films were often quite subversive, and as I began attempting to articulate those films' subversive content, I turned to Marcuse, whom I also first encountered in graduate school. Consequently, while this book makes a specific argument about the intellectual environment that informed the science fiction films made by George Lucas, Ridley Scott, and James Cameron as well as specific arguments about the way those films employed that intellectual environment, it also speaks to the larger issue of whether or not popular culture can be more than mindless entertainment. By demonstrating that the directors who solidified the place of blockbuster science fiction in Hollywood's business plan were also keeping a radical critique of the impact of technology and large corporations on society, this book also strongly argues that popular culture can be a powerful home for cultural critique.

*Chapter 1*

# Big-Budget Science Fiction Film and Profitable Social Critique

Pity the blockbuster movie. Or, rather, pity the artistic reputation of the blockbuster movie. It is, after all, hard to feel sorry for a product that can so well remunerate those involved in its manufacture and distribution. Yet when some of those involved in making that product have legitimate artistic pretensions, it probably gives those artistically-inclined members of the blockbuster production crew pause when their work is generally seen, as Dan McIntyre notes, to have the same cultural value "as airport fiction" (402). It is probably difficult as well for those involved in big-budget films that want to use their product to make a meaningful social commentary. Some would say that summer tent pole movies are meaningless entertainment, while others would say that such movies are actually regressive, reinforcing the worst aspects of American society. The latter of these criticisms is definitely plausible. After all, high-grossing American films have a disreputable history. Although, as Louis Menand, writing in the *New Yorker*, reminds us, "the term blockbuster dates from 1951, when Variety appropriated it from real estate jargon" to promote that year's proto-blockbuster *Quo Vadis*, D.W. Griffith's 1915 pro–Ku Klux Klan movie *The Birth of a Nation* was the first film to generate significant box office revenue, and it did this by appealing to the baser fears of the American people.

Another reason that the blockbuster lacks artistic and social credibility is that it is not a genre in the conventional sense. Instead of key themes, characters, or mise en scène being used to identify a blockbuster, these films win that designation solely by making lots of money at the box office. Even McIntyre, a linguist employing corpus analysis to argue that blockbusters share common features, is forced to base his choice of films for analysis on their success at the box office since "a selection policy based purely on box office receipts results in a strong degree of consensus" among critics (406). Since blockbuster films are literally defined by their status as a successful product, in other words, it is easy to argue that they have already been placed outside the realm of serious artistic merit or significant social commentary. Such an attitude would explain Menand's assertion that, the efforts of some academic critics notwithstanding, "there is just nothing serious to say about the larger implications of *Star Wars*." Menand further asserts that "the reason that those movies had such enormous grosses, despite terrible reviews and negative word of mouth, is that each opened simultaneously on eighteen thousand screens worldwide" in order to conclude that "blockbuster dependence is a disease" that "sucks the talent and resources out of every other part of the industry" (web).

Not everyone who has examined blockbuster films has come to such gloomy conclusions about their impact on film and culture, however. For example, William Brown finds artistic merit in 2001's *Amélie*, a film whose return on investment in light of its total global box office—over 170 million for a film with a 10 million budget—qualifies it for blockbuster status.[1] The film was also directed by Jean-Pierre Jeunet, whose credits include 1997's would-be blockbuster *Alien Resurrection*, and Brown suggests that the technology Jeunet used in creating *Amélie* allows the realization of the surrealist project. The digital effects used in that film—views of the main character's heart beating inside her chest, "photographs and bedside lamps coming alive and talking" and the protagonist turning into water and collapsing while everything else in the frame presents a realistic depiction of Parisian life— represent the achievement of the surrealist desire to depict "the fantastic *alongside* the real, such that the two cannot be told apart" (20–22).

More typical, however, is the kind of praise that takes the commercial nature of the genre at face value and openly celebrates the blockbuster's ability to make money. For example, Matthew McAllister, Ian Gordon, and Mark Jancovich, although attempting to demonstrate how graphic novels have been made into challenging or innovative films, note that because of innovations like marketing films at Comic-Con, "modern comic-book–based films have helped establish the industrial formula of the Hollywood popcorn blockbuster: fantastic action movies as cultural event" (110). Alisa Perren praises 1989's *sex, lies, and videotape* because it "ushered in the era of the 'indie blockbuster'—films that, on a smaller scale, replicate the exploitation marketing and box-office performance of the major studio high-concept event pictures" (30) and concludes that "marketing is as significant as content in the building of the quality independent blockbuster" (33).

Occasionally, critics see something socially significant in the marketing prowess of some blockbuster films. Ashley Elaine York, for example, writes that "women's films have a chance in the new millennium to compete for success among the grosses and the rankings" because of Hollywood's focus on ancillary marketing and reaching a global audience (3). Though detecting a broadly feminist theme of "validation" in the films she examines for her article (11), York seems most excited to note that women-centered films—sometimes created with significant artistic input from women directors, writers, and actors—have a chance to compete financially with male-dominated and male-centered blockbusters at the box office. For York, a female-centric film out grossing its masculinist competitors would represent evidence of a genuine—and welcome—cultural shift.

If some critics have found artistic merit in the visual aspects of some blockbusters and more critics have been able to find reasons to celebrate blockbuster's financial prowess, it is harder to find unqualified support for a blockbuster's ability to create significant social commentary. Critics who attempt to elucidate such thematics from blockbuster films often feel the need to qualify their readings with an admission that they are examining second-rate, commercial texts. One of the best and earliest examples of such criticism comes from Frederic Jameson, whose reading of Steven Spielberg's 1975 film *Jaws*—a milestone in the development of the contemporary blockbuster in terms of marketing techniques and return on investment—finds a surprisingly honest depiction of the class differences between fishing boat captain Quint, representing "the America of small business ... and the New Deal," the middle-class police officer Brody, and the upper-middle-class technocrat Hooper. Quint is literally sacrificed to the shark in the film, but Jameson sees this as a message to viewers that the more populist version of America Quint represented needed to be abandoned to make way for a partnership between the forces of law and order and technocracy. For Jameson, the significance of the ideological maneuver the film makes is not in its normalization of the new status quo, but in the social realities the film was forced to depict beforehand to set up the argument for the new status quo. In other words, in mass culture films, a "genuine social and historical content must first be tapped and given some initial expression if it is subsequently to be the object of successful manipulation and containment" ("Reification" 144). Consequently, Jameson argues that *Jaws* demonstrates "some sense of the ineradicable drive towards collectivity" is apparent, if one looks for it, even "in the most degraded works of mass culture" ("Reification" 148).

Similarly, James Hurley, though arguing that the changes in production and marketing driven by the blockbuster have created "a dark anxiety that American cinema is now systematically incapable of producing anything but bloated and infantilizing spectacle" (93), nevertheless sees a self-aware critique of the changes in the creation and distribution of Hollywood films in one of the most profitable blockbusters ever released. Hurley finds a complexly layered, though contradictory, allegorical meditation on the collapse of the Hollywood studio system and the rise of the multinational media companies that rely on blockbusters to create profitable content in James Cameron's 1997 film *Titanic*. Cameron's narrative, according to Hurley, can present this argument because the "trauma and loss that *Titanic* summons up as its world of hierarchized splendor sinks away can now be conceived as a kind of institutional melancholy" (112) for the economic and artistic realities of the old studio system.

Before proceeding, we should stipulate a few things. It is understandable that many critics see the importance of blockbusters largely in terms of the marketing that accompanies them or the revenue their release generates. It is also understandable that many critics find artistic significance largely in the way that blockbusters deploy the technology that they are so heavily dependent on. And Jameson's contention that blockbusters typically offer a subversive critique that is ultimately overwhelmed by the grain of their narrative is often true, but not always. Social commentary found in a big-budget movie may in fact be a coherent aspect of the film's theme. The construction of the category "blockbuster film" on financial criteria does mean that some blockbusters and blockbuster franchises are purely commercial enterprises employing characters, themes and dialog that do little more than validate popular ideologies. But since financial prowess is the only criterion in use, the category "blockbuster" does not preclude thematically rich texts. Popularity and profundity are not always already mutually exclusive. Popular culture is not always already ideologically degraded. Using a blockbuster film to present a relatively unmitigated critique of society is possible, and the broad reach of a big-budget summer or holiday tent pole makes it much more likely that a social critique found in a blockbuster movie will penetrate society. Furthermore, the long pop-cultural half-life of blockbuster characters and plots—witness the seemingly endless recreation of superhero franchises like Batman and Spider Man, the profitable and sequel-guaranteeing resurrection of obscure graphic novel protagonists in Disney/Marvel's *Guardians of the Galaxy* (2014), or the multi–billion-dollar valuation of George Lucas' rights to the *Star Wars* properties—ensures that remnants of a blockbuster's social critique will remain in popular culture for decades.

This is not to say that direct social critique was a key concern when the blockbusters themselves were greenlighted; that the major studios are in the market for unique and challenging reading of their contemporary society. This, at least for mass entertainment, would be a very bad business decision. Instead, some of the directors, writers, and producers who create blockbusters are incorporating existing critiques of society that had already become popular and, in the process of giving the audiences familiar ideas in new packages, mobilizing the utopian potential of those critiques by bringing them more fully into the popular conscience. For example, if Ridley Scott's *Alien* (1979) speculatively portrays the multinational corporations that arose with late capitalism in the first world as murderously indifferent to their employees, it should not surprise anyone that the reaction of the employees of those corporations to Scott's film was something along the lines of "it figures." After all, these employees had probably already learned this over the course of their own careers.

Yet more importantly when investigating thematic influences, thinkers like Karl Marx, Max Weber, Emil Durkheim, Thorstein Veblen, C. Wright Mills, and, as we will discuss extensively below, Herbert Marcuse, had been collectively warning of the dehumanization of administered, capitalist, industrialized society for decades before *Alien* debuted. These warnings were seconded by radical political figures—American examples would include Emma Goldman, Eugene V. Debs, and a late-life Martin Luther King, Jr.—who echoed some or all of these critiques in their political activism, further embedding those ideas in the popular conscience. And it wasn't just those on the left fringe of politics who helped popularize critiques of capitalism—after all, key elements of Roosevelt's New Deal was at least implicitly structured on the assumption that capitalists would not or could not take care of their workers.

Since it would also be a bad business decision to directly reference and slavishly follow radical cultural and economic theorists, however, we should not see these filmmakers as immediately influenced by, say, Marx. After all, the tagline for *Alien* was "In space, no one can hear you scream," not "A speculative rendering of Marx's theories of surplus value and alienation." Of course, movie posters aren't usually seen as venues for political analysis, but they are only a small part of the marketing effort surrounding a blockbuster. Often, as part of the marketing blitz surrounding the release of a blockbuster or in the ongoing effort to keep a franchise in the public eye, directors discuss their influences. Consequently, it is suggestive that there is precedence for filmmakers to accentuate their narratives' resonance with more apolitical literary and cultural theory. George Lucas' frequent claim of the *Star Wars* film's debt to Joseph Campbell's *The Hero with a Thousand Faces* is perhaps the most obvious example of this. Yet while Campbell's work does much to explain both the popularity and the structure of Lucas' first three films, we will see below that there is much more going on in the director's narrative than the repetition of the patterns that Campbell so ably describes.

This is not to say that Lucas or other directors deliberately obscure a direct debt to radical political and cultural theorists when they discuss their influences. Instead, directors and writers participate in what is best conceptualized as a structurally obscured chain of popularization of radical critiques. There is no direct influence. Instead, when the zeitgeist is imbued with a critique of society, that critique sometimes finds its way into a director's narrative without an immediately obvious structure of transmittal. The writers do not compose scenes with a given theorist's work open at their sides. The director has not been mentored by one of the radical theorists whose ideas find reflection in the director's work. The director does not directly credit the radical theorists when she or he discusses the film with the press, and the studios market the film as would any other of their products. Indeed, the writers and director may not even be aware enough of the contours of the critique they are borrowing to name the theorist that is most associated with that critique. And sometimes, blockbuster films transmit the ideas of a theorist who is deeply suspicious of both capitalism and popular culture and therefore would be upset to see her or his ideas used to make money for the multinational conglomerates that make up the entertainment industry. Nevertheless, elements of the theorist's critique becomes integral to the director's narrative because a version of that critique was already available in popular discourse. This understandable inclusion of already popularized critique, in turn, helps further cement the critique's place in popular thought and can ensure that a critique outlives the popularity of the thinker who first articulated it.

The best way to describe how the structurally obscured transmission of radical critiques takes place can be found in the writings of Michel de Certeau. The cultural anthropologist and historian argues that storytellers frequently play on the extra elements they hide in commonplace, stereotypical tales in order to make small, reformist changes in broadly-held ideologies. According to de Certeau, these changes are possible because commonplace tales get their affective power from the associations they trigger in people's memory. Since memory is so protean, according to de Certeau, "mobilization is inseparable from an *alteration* ... memory derives its interventionary force from its very capacity to be altered" (86, italics author's). Commonplace tales, in other words, are far from stable but instead are always already available to be re-remembered as something else. Accordingly, the "significance of a story that is well-known, and therefore classifiable, can be reversed by a single 'circumstantial' detail" inserted into a familiar framework that makes the commonplace produce other effects (87). This "subtle manipulation of 'authorities' in every popular tradition," according to de Certeau, causes the ideology of the established order to change over time (ibid).

As we will discuss below, films like 1977's *A New Hope*, 1979's *Alien*, and 1984's *The Terminator* are not terribly original. Lucas' film clearly borrowed from sources as diverse as Akira Kurosawa and Leni Riefenstahl. Scott's film owes a debt to classic science fiction tales like A. E. van Vogt's *The Voyage of the Space Beagle* and films like *It! The Terror from Space*. James Cameron was legally required to add Harlan Ellison's name to his film's credits after the writer claimed that *The Terminator* plagiarized two episodes of *The Outer Limits* that Ellison wrote. This is not to say that these three directors are plagiarists, however. Instead, these directors were successful because they were very good at what de Certeau describes: adding extra elements to popular stories. And one of those extra elements available in the zeitgeist during the late 1970s and early 1980s was the already-popularized version of Marcuse's critique of industrial society.[2]

Though generally hostile to popular culture, Marcuse was not above de Certeau's process. Indeed, the theorist himself was popular—how many leftist philosophy professors write bestselling books, after all—because he creatively reconfigured and articulated critiques of capitalism and industrial society that had been circulating, in one form or another, for more than a century. When scholars describe Marcuse's debt to figures like Marx and Freud, they typically use a more reverential tone than scholars who describe how Scott's film was influenced by A.E. van Vogt's stories, but there are key similarities in both acts of appropriation. And while scholarly conventions dictate that Marcuse can be far more open in his borrowing from Marx than, say, Cameron is in his borrowing from Ellison, the philosopher is nevertheless creating popular and timely versions of Marx's and Freud's critiques of society as Cameron is creating a more popular and timely version of Ellison's tale.

With the foregoing in mind, it will hopefully be easy to see how this monograph can establish the ability of blockbusters to critique society by means of de Certeau's process through presenting a case study of the Marcusian elements of Lucas, Scott, and Cameron's critiques. This case study will investigate how a rigorous and widely influential left critique of industrial society that engaged student protesters and suburbanites alike during the turbulent 1960s was gradually transformed into the thematic underpinnings of the work of three directors who created several highly profitable science fiction films beginning in the late 1970s and continuing, in one rebooted form or another, to the present day. This allowed a critique created by an academic whose reputation is now arguably in eclipse to provide the foundation for no less than four different "universes" involving, among other things, sequels created by other directors, television adaptations, graphic novels, and films—again by other directors—based on the graphic novels.

Specifically, this monograph will argue that George Lucas, the Henry Ford of science fiction blockbusters, wove a popularization of Herbert Marcuse's critique of repressive, contemporary industrial society in his first film, 1971's *THX-1138*. After the failure of that film, he relied more heavily on Marcuse's utopian vision of a more caring civilization that technology could create when envisioning both 1973's successful, mainstream film *American Graffiti* and the *Star Wars* films. In part because of all of those films' astonishing cultural penetration and staggering return on investment, the Marcusian themes that Lucas began addressing in 1977's *A New Hope* then begin surfacing, with greater or lesser intensity, in other blockbuster science fiction films created by Ridley Scott and James Cameron in the years after Luke, Han, and Leia dominated the box office in 1977. Furthermore, Scott and Cameron, like Lucas himself, continued creating films with a Marcusian critical bent well into the new millennium and long after the philosophical darling of the New Left's work was relegated to specialized graduate seminars in philosophy and literary criticism.

Because of his amply documented hostility to popular culture[3]—and Marcuse's lack of positive commentary on the films under consideration here that were released during his lifetime—it may initially seem counterintuitive to apply the theorist's work to blockbuster science fiction films. Marcuse, in the last few decades of his life, could easily have been taken for yet another curmudgeonly professor whose scholarly reticence about popular culture limited the appeal of his ideas to his colleagues a few eager graduate students. Yet while Marcuse did toil in relative obscurity when he was a member of the Frankfurt School in Germany in the 1930s and when he was a wartime government official in the United States in the 1940s, by the 1960s and 70s, he had become well-known outside of academia. Espen Hammer notes that Marcuse was the only member of the Frankfurt School to achieve genuine popularity with not only the left but also broader society (1071–2). Tom Bourne reminds us that in the late 1960s, mainstream periodicals like *Time* and *The Saturday Evening Post* called him the "father of the New Left" (36). He was interviewed at length on KCET Los Angeles in 1968. In 1970, *Playboy* called Marcuse "the nation's hottest political philosopher" (175). Perhaps Barry Katz best captures what happened to Marcuse in his last decades when Katz observes that after a life of academic and governmental anonymity, "in a great American tradition, Herbert Marcuse moved to California and became a star" (18). This popularity was only fueled when Marcuse received death threats from the Ku Klux Klan and frequently squabbled with California governors like Ronald Reagan and the administrators of the University of California at San Diego until he was forced to retire in 1975.[4]

If Marcuse attained some measure of celebrity—or notoriety—with the American public, he achieved something like rock star status with the young radicals of the New Left. According to Raymond Aron, the signal feature of the "New Left"—what separated it from the old left—was its temporal location at "the end of the postwar period." Most of the members of the New Left were members of a generation whose worldview was not dominated by the exigencies of World War II and its aftermath (304). By the late 1960s, leftist students and other radicals were looking for a new theorist who could express their dissatisfaction with capitalism in a way that did not seem tainted by the problematic support of the Soviet Union that characterized the old left. They wanted to theorize modernity in a way that would transcended Cold War binaries and lead to genuine change for the entire world. Many members of the New Left found what they were looking for in the works of Marcuse. As Charles Reitz notes, "there is no question that Marcuse's original impact was connected closely to the intellectual and political campus-based turmoil of the 1960s, and derived from his theoretical leadership in the very definition of the cultural and educational issues involved" (web). To understand the way the counterculture of the 1960s impacted the popular culture of the next several decades, then, it is very helpful to understand what Marcuse was saying.

Many aspects of Marcuse's thought represent the hopes and desires of the New Left. Espen Hammer, for example, calls *Eros and Civilization* "an embodiment of the *zeitgeist* of the 1960s" (1071–72). Perhaps Marcuse's most important theoretical contention, however, was his creation of a Marxian critique that did not posit an efficient socialism that would eventually replace capitalism. Instead, he argued that despite the clear difference in articulated political ideologies, in practical terms the East and the West were converging. In "Protosocialism and Late Capitalism," for example, Marcuse argues that, because of the need to catch up, "socialism adopts the consumption model of the highly-developed capitalist countries" (28). Consequently, both systems employed an increasing reliance on technology to keep populations docile and this convergence in strategy was effectively negating the difference between socialist and capitalist countries. The powers that be—whoever they were—remained in power and everyone else became more and more dependent on the powers that be. As Marcuse argues in *One-Dimensional Man*, in both economic systems the "enslavement of man by the instruments of his labor continues in a highly rationalized and vastly efficient and promising form.... The more the rulers are capable of delivering the goods of consumption, the more firmly will the underlying population be tied to the various ruling bureaucracies" (43).

Because Marcuse's approach gave young radicals the new way to critique contemporary society and conceptualize utopia, the late 1960s saw the theorist achieving an unprecedented influence among the campus leftists who were at the same time engaging in a historically significant series of protests. According to Sam Keen, after the events of May 1968 in France, "students in rebellion all over the world" claimed "Herbert Marcuse as an ally and major prophet of their hoped-for 'New Age'" (35). K.L. Julka notes that Marcuse "shot into prominence in the 1960s in the wake of student unrest in the US, France, and Italy" (13), and George Katsiaficas contends that in "1968, students and young radicals the world over read and discussed the three M's: Marx, Mao, and Marcuse" (web). Aronowitz observes that Marcuse's "writing and his political intervention animated the generation of 1968 like no other social theorist" (133–34) and called *One-Dimensional Man* the text that, "whether they read it or not, those who identified with the 'movement' took its descriptions of the flattening of everyday existence as a personal testament" (144). With all this in mind, it is easy to see why Eliseo Vivas called *One-Dimensional Man* "part of the holy writ of the New Left" (140).

Because of his widespread notoriety among the general public and because of the wide dissemination of his ideas as well as his intense personal popularity among the radical student left, Marcuse became part of popular culture. So even though Marcuse himself may not have advised the creation of tales like *Star Wars, Alien,* or *The Terminator* as a means of social critique—though there is reason to believe he would have appreciated *THX-1138*—popularized versions of his ideas were in circulation because he was able to turn some of his ideas into bestselling books and because his involvement in the student movements and social upheavals of the 1960s brought media attention. Therefore, Marcuse's ideas—or at least reasonably accurate popularizations of those ideas—were available to clever storytellers like George Lucas, Ridley Scott, and James Cameron. These storytellers were free to expand on Marcuse's critique of industrial society, as well as refining each other's use of Marcusian critique.

With the foregoing in mind, it is easy to see how George Lucas was influenced by the Marcusian moment in the student movement and broader American culture. After all, if, as Brad Rose has observed, Marcuse "influenced a generation of radicals and New Left politicos" (55), why couldn't he also have influenced a generation of New-Left-fellow-traveling filmmakers? And if we look at the context from which Lucas emerged, we realize that Lucas, a lifelong Californian, was in film school at USC when Marcuse's associations with radical student groups and battles with the UCSD administration made the nightly news. Furthermore, according to Stephen Farber, when Lucas "was in Junior College," in the mid–1960s, around the time that *One-Dimensional Man* became a best-seller, his "primary major was in social sciences" because he has always been "interested in America and why it is what it is" (6). Biographer Dale Pollock further notes that during the director's student days at USC during the late 1960s, Lucas "supported civil rights, was against the war in Vietnam and Lyndon Johnson, and in favor of all the right liberal causes" (59). While Pollock does not make this contention, it's fairly easy to assert that people familiar with all the right liberal causes in graduate school in California in the 1960s would have been at least passingly familiar with the concepts articulated by Marcuse's critique of industrial society. And while Ridley Scott and James Cameron would have seen less direct Marcusian influence, they have both claimed that *A New Hope* profoundly influenced their careers and would therefore have closely studied Lucas' popularization of Marcuse's concepts. Furthermore, Scott, a working adult in Europe during the events of May 1968, would have had to have deliberately turned a blind eye to current events—not a very wise move for an advertising executive—in order to be unaware of Marcuse. Similarly Cameron, who lived in California during the height of Marcuse's early-1970s notoriety, would have had to be deliberately obtuse to be completely unaware of Marcuse's critique.

If this study assumes the mediated and selective rather than the direct and strictly constructed influence of Marcuse's thought on blockbuster science fiction film, then it is much easier to detect parallels between the theorist's writings and the way the storytellers made use of popular notions of Marcuse's critique. Two aspects of Marcuse's thought will be instructive as we examine the idea that a popular filmmaker can in fact generate pointed social critique that could actually lead to social change: the role of an intellectual elite in helping educate the working and middle classes about the perils and benefits of industrial society and the role that art plays in this educational process. Even though Marcuse himself would not have suggested that they do so, filmmakers could indeed serve as the intellectual elite who could help people envision and alternative to industrial society, and we will therefore discuss the aspects of Marcuse's thought that make it amenable to popularization in blockbuster science fiction films.

Perhaps unsurprisingly for a Marxist professor, Marcuse placed a great deal of faith in the ability of intellectuals to, as K. L. Julka argues, educate the "new working class" of knowledge workers (20) as well as the industrial working class. In "Liberation from the Affluent Society," Marcuse argued that the "intelligentsia has a decisive preparatory function" (189) that would pave the way for the revolution. Marcuse was aware of the social and educational distance between the intelligentsia and the middle and working classes, but in his more theoretical writings he downplayed the difficulty the intelligentsia would face in connecting with the masses. For example, in *The Aesthetic Dimension* Marcuse argues that the "fact that the artist belongs to a privileged group negates neither the truth nor the aesthetic quality of his work" (18). Similarly, in "Letters to Chicago Surrealists," Marcuse asserts that the "historical link between art and social privilege cannot be broken by manipulation of art ... but only by the abolition of established social division of labor" (41). Furthermore, Julka notes that Marcuse believed that education may create "a revolution in man's consciousness" (22), allowing the intelligentsia to have more influence in society. Clearly, Marcuse was not thinking of Hollywood when he writes of a committed group of revolutionary artists standing outside of the social hierarchy and creating difficult art. But, as we will see below, it was easy for aspiring filmmakers to see themselves as members of an intelligentsia not unlike Marcuse's artists.

Because Marcuse did not believe that the role of the intelligentsia was to help the workers seize the means of production, but rather to see past the means of production, their primary role was not to provide leadership for a hierarchical movement, but rather to create art that had a liberating potential. As Agger has noted, "Marcuse in his later work came to regard art as the last refuge of critical insights in a totally mobilized society" ("Aesthetic" 329). Schoolman argues that for Marcuse, the "transcendent and critical functions of art" are in "its ability to serve as the vehicle for fantastic recreations of the social and political universe" even though art "tacitly" affirms the social reality (56). Marcuse himself argues in the *Aesthetic Dimension* that

> a work of art can be called revolutionary if, by virtue of the aesthetic transformation, it represents, in the exemplary fate of individuals, the prevailing unfreedom and the rebelling forces, thus breaking through the mystified (and petrified) social reality, and opening the horizon of change.... In this sense, every authentic work of art would be revolutionary, i.e. subversive of perception and understanding, an indictment of the established reality, the appearance of the image of liberation [xi].

Marcuse also felt that a work of art would shift "the locus of the individual's realization from the domain of the performance principle and the profit motive to that of the inner resources of the human being: passion, imagination, conscience" (4–5). Art would function as "a dissenting force" (8) that creates "a counter-conscious: negation of the realist-conformist mind" (9). In *Eros and Civilization*, Marcuse similarly argues that art "is perhaps the most visible 'return of the repressed,' not only on the individual but also on the genetic-historical level. The artistic imagination shapes the 'unconscious memory' of the liberation that failed, of the promise that was betrayed" (130). In "Letters to Chicago Surrealists," Marcuse further solidifies the image of art as a trigger for radically re-examining the status quo when he argues that real art can "invoke the images of liberation as those of a possible reality" (41).

Factoring out Marcuse's cultured, early–20th-century, European notions of art—notions that would probably not find a place for highly visual and heavily marketed mass entertainment like 1980's *The Empire Strikes Back* or even relatively low-budget, independent productions like *The Terminator*—there is much here for a would-be science fiction auteur to latch on to. Science fiction is a wonderful genre for depicting the struggles of a thinking individual against a conformist, technologically-driven society. Science fiction, furthermore, probably lends itself best to storytellers who want to argue for the resurgence of human qualities in a high-tech capitalist society because the genre is best suited to take dehumanizing, high-tech capitalist society to its logical conclusion. So while Marcuse himself may not have been comfortable with artists who wanted to create Terminators, Jedi, or Replicants, an aspiring filmmaker living in the moment when Marcuse was achieving his improbable fame would have felt nothing but validation in the arguments about art that the philosopher was feeding into the zeitgeist.

Towards the end of his life, Marcuse, who notes the movement's "apparently elitist character" (8) in "The Movement in a New Era of Repression," began to admit to himself that his hoped-for artist's revolution was not likely to appear. In "Failure of the New Left?" Marcuse speculates that the movement failed, among other reasons, because it was elitist, though paradoxically that elitism was necessary to develop a genuinely radical consciousness (5). Creating such a consciousness is difficult because the left intelligentsia is "isolated from the conservative mass of the population" (9). Perhaps, however, the movement did not fail as much as it was continued by other means. Filmmakers, compromised as they are by their association with the wealthy investors and multinational corporations that finance blockbuster films, nevertheless attempted to create images of liberation that would touch the conservative mass of the population.

The attractiveness of Marcuse's theories about the place of the artist in society to would-be auteurs would not have led to marketable films if Marcuse's theories about society had not been compelling thematic fodder for insertion into familiar narratives. It would be facile to simply suggest that the best-seller status of *One-Dimensional Man*—rare for an uncompromising critique of society written by a philosophy professor—proves that Marcuse had connected with a non-academic audience. An examination of the assertions made during Marcuse's unlikely career as a public radical, however, will demonstrate a critique that, for all its Marxist and Freudian roots, would appeal to anyone thoughtfully engaged with contemporary society. This discussion will first examine three aspects of Marcuse's work found in texts that were directed, in one way or another, to the broader public. These arguments encapsulate the core of the Philosopher's critique of industrial society that found broad acceptance in American culture. First, Marcuse made a strong argument that industrial society was seducing the masses into an unquestioning acceptance of the status quo. Second, Marcuse redefined Freud's concepts of Eros and Thanatos to describe a broadened conception of sexuality that included the human creative drive. And finally, Marcuse offered a utopian vision of work that allowed people to express their interests while giving them maximum freedom from alienated labor.

We will then examine contentions about society and technology that make Marcuse's arguments friendly to blockbuster science fiction films. First, Marcuse, for all his opposition to the Vietnam War, was not a pacifist. Instead, the veteran of the German army who had served during World War I often spoke in favor of what he called defensive violence—the legitimate use of force to resist oppression. Since blockbuster science fiction tends to depict the use of force by protagonists as defensive violence—burning up a xenomorph who is trying to use you to incubate its young, blowing up a space station that can destroy a planet—directors can place a Marcusian critique of society within their violent tales. Second, Marcuse was an instrumentalist rather than a Luddite in his attitude toward technology. He believed that technology had the potential to do great harm, but that in an ideal society people would use technology to greatly reduce the amount of alienated labor.

Consequently, his ideas are well-suited for films that tend to depict technologically dystopic settings being disrupted by individuals using sophisticated technology. A third, related aspect of Marcuse's thought is his use of the environment as a means to critique a society that had become overly dependent on the products advanced technology created. This is similar to the way blockbuster science fiction films tend to contrast stark technological dystopias with images from nature—a thematic that permeates science fiction blockbusters ranging from *A New Hope* to Cameron's *Avatar* (2009).

Marcuse employed several concepts to explain how industrial society was tying the masses to the ruling elite. Perhaps the most important concept is one-dimensional thought, which Marcuse would have us understood as a type of nondialectical thought which refuses to question the status quo. In a way, one-dimensional thought is understandable, since, as Marcuse argues in *One-Dimensional Man*, "there is no reason to insist on self-determination if the administered life is the comfortable and even the 'good' life" (49). Marcuse further reminds us that, because of one-dimensional thought, often "the intellectual and emotional refusal 'to go along' appears neurotic and impotent" (9).

Because of one-dimensional thought, according to Marcuse, the ruling elite in capitalist and communist countries typically does not need to use force to control populations that are not in the habit of questioning the status quo. Instead, the elite use dependence on the goodies industrial society delivers to keep people in line. Marcuse explains the paradox involved in what he calls soft repression in *One-Dimensional Man* when he observes that "the most effective subjugation and destruction of man by man takes place at the height of civilization, when the material and intellectual achievements of mankind seem to allow the creation of a truly free world" (4). Thus, the elites control "centrifugal social forces with Technology rather than terror, on the dual basis of an overwhelming efficiency and an increasing standard of living" (xlii). Marcuse was careful to argue that soft repression was an incredibly powerful motivator to stay in line since, as he argues in "Letters to Surrealists" it is "not 'ideology' or 'false interest'" to be invested in the status quo "if the worker has a relatively human place to live in, adequate food, apparel, some vacation, television, etc." (41).

Of course, soft repression would not be possible if people did not value the material goods created by industrial society more than their freedom. Marcuse called this desire for the bounty of industrial society false needs. In "The Movement in a New Era of Repression," Marcuse defines false needs as a form of domination "through steered satisfaction and steered aggression" (6). Consequently, even though people are aware of "the world of alienated labor, misery, and repression," they acquiesce because "capitalism, at its present stage, creates a world of ease, gadgets, enjoyment, and surpluses, in which increasing numbers of people participate" (7). In *Eros and Civilization*, Marcuse finds evidence of false needs in "the promotion of thoughtless leisure activities" and "the triumph of anti-intellectual ideologies" (86).

One-dimensional thought, soft repression, and false needs lead to a condition that Marcuse calls unfreedom. In *One-Dimensional Man*, Marcuse explains that unfreedom, "humanity's repressive subjection to the productive apparatus," is often "perpetuated and intensified in the form of many liberties and comforts" (32). Thus, since "all liberation depends on the consciousness of servitude, and the emergence of this consciousness is always hampered by the predominance of needs and satisfactions which, to a great extent, have become the individual's own," people are not able to agitate for freedom in a meaningful way (7).

Marcuse did not see the gently coercive power of industrial society being limited to the affective impact of the material goods and living conditions being produced. Marcuse also argued that contemporary consumer society limited the ability to be truly creative and engaged in life by limiting our instinctual drive towards self-fulfillment and altruism. Marcuse conceptualized this loss by means of his reading of Freud's conceptualization of "Eros," so in order to fully grasp the way the philosopher deploys this highly charged term, we need to turn to *Eros and Civilization*. Here, Marcuse defines Eros as the *"life instinct"* (21) and notes that Freud called it "the great unifying force that preserves all life" (25) and argued that "the drive toward ever larger unities belongs to the biological-organic nature of Eros itself" (39). Consequently, Marcuse himself could argue that the "sex instincts," broadly considered, "are *life* instincts: the impulse to preserve and enrich life by mastering nature in accordance with the developing vital needs is originally an erotic impulse" (114). Marcuse then notes, as he aims for genuine breadth of sources, that in the New Testament the "message of the Son was the message of liberation: the overthrow of the Law (which is domination) by Agape (which is Eros)" (63). In Marcuse's just society, then, the Law would be overthrown by Eros as people followed their better impulses without interference from industrial society.

When Marcuse employs words like "Eros" and "erotic" in a nuanced way, however, it becomes easy to deliberately misunderstand him and portray instinctual liberation leading to, as the philosopher sarcastically notes "a society of sex maniacs." Marcuse makes it clear, however, that his vision "involves not simply a release but a *transformation* of the libido: from sexuality constrained under genital supremacy to eroticization of the whole personality" (ES 184). Marcuse speaks of Eros as a drive to create that encompasses, but is not exclusively conceptualized as, sexuality and physical reproduction. Thus, it is easier to conceptualize Eros "as a life instinct" that is best understood as "a larger biological instinct rather than a larger scope of sexuality" (ES 187). As Marcuse further clarifies,

> nothing in the nature of Eros justifies the notion that the "extension" of the impulse is confined to the corporeal sphere. If the antagonistic separation of the physical from the spiritual part of the organism is itself the historical result of repression, the overcoming of this antagonism would open the spiritual sphere to this impulse.... There is an unbroken ascent in erotic fulfillment from the corporeal love of one to that of the others to the love of beautiful work and play and ultimately to the love of beautiful knowledge [193].

Properly understood, then, Eros is a joyful approach to life that includes sexuality but is better understood as encompassing all creative activity. As Myriam Malinovich, an associate of the philosopher who often disagreed with his assessment of society, argues, for Marcuse, "freedom and happiness have little if anything to do with unfettered sexuality and have all to do with the fulfillment of true rather than false needs" (172).

If Marcuse's discussion of Eros ranges far beyond sexuality, then it should surprise no one that his discussion of repression addresses not only the deferral of sexual gratification but also the deferral of all creative gratification. In *Eros and Civilization*, Marcuse admits that reason has "conquered and shaped the historical world," mostly for the good, but has "done so in the image of repression, internal and external" (52). Some repression is necessary, then, but the modern world Marcuse detects what he calls surplus repression or "the restrictions necessitated by social domination. This is distinguished from basic repression, the 'modifications' of the instincts necessary for the perpetuation of the human race in civilization" (32). Consequently, Marcuse goes beyond Freud when he contends that "the pleasure principle was dethroned not only because it militated against progress in civilization but also because it militated against a civilization whose progress perpetuates domination and toil" (36). For Marcuse, surplus repression is a great obstacle to a just society since, under non-repressive conditions, sexuality tends to "grow into" Eros" (203) while under repressive conditions sexuality can be used as another lever of social control.

In the introduction to the 1962 edition of *Eros and Civilization*, Marcuse refines his discussion of surplus repression by introducing the concept of repressive de-sublimation, which he defines as the "release of sexuality in modes and forms which reduce and weaken erotic energy" even though this sometimes means "sexuality spreads into formerly tabooed dimensions and relations" (ix). Instead of sexuality growing into Eros, in other words, industrial society is allowing people to experiment sexually and thus dispel the energy that could be turned to creative expression. In 1964's *One-Dimensional Man*, Marcuse expands his discussion of repressive de-sublimation when he notes that the "mobilization and administration of libido" characterizes advanced industrial societies. Both reproductive technology and a popular culture that enforces normative sexual behavior leads to a type of sexual satisfaction "which generates submission and weakens the rationality of protest" (75) because that satisfaction prevents sexuality from growing into Eros.

Concurrently, because of the repression of Eros, Marcuse sees the growth of Thanatos, the destructive drive that opposes Eros. In *Eros and Civilization*, Marcuse describes Thanatos as the desire to "return to the Nirvana of the womb" (50) and "the regressive impulse for Peace" (69)—of course, "peace" here meaning a general lack of conflict or opposition and not the absence of war. Indeed, Thanatos often leads people to destroy what Eros would have them interact with. Instead of the creative engagement with the world that Eros would engender, then, Thanatos leads to retreat from the world by means of the destruction of the world. Because people turn to Thanatos when Eros is thwarted, Marcuse sees modern civilization marked by "the progressive weakening of Eros" and the "growth of aggressiveness and guilt feelings" (125). The combination of repression and the growth of Thanatos leads to what Marcuse calls "the fatal dialectic of civilization: the very progress of civilization leads to the release of increasingly destructive forces" (49).

Marcuse's discussion of Eros and Thanatos accompanies a related discussion about work in industrial society versus work in a society that allowed Eros to flourish. In *Eros and Civilization*, Marcuse describes the performance principle, in which "society is stratified according to the competitive economic performance of its members" (41). Accordingly, "efficiency and repression converge: raising the productivity of labor is the sacrosanct idea of both capitalist and Stalinist Stakhanovism" (141). It is interesting here that instead of speaking of Taylorism, Marcuse employs its Soviet counterpart, Stakhanovism—named after a Russian worker who exceeded his quota and was promoted as a shining example—in order to emphasize how the performance principle pervades society.

Yet Marcuse hoped that repression through performance would be replaced by something more humane. In *Eros and Civilization*, the philosopher discusses the hope that "the elimination of surplus labor would *per se* tend to eliminate, not labor, but the organization of human existence into an instrument of labor." While the opposite has happened—human existence has become an instrument of labor—because of one-dimensional thought and repressive de-sublimation, Marcuse's revolutionary optimism rests on the assumption that "the emergence of a non-repressive reality principle would alter rather than destroy the social organization of labor" (140). This alteration would center on work becoming a function of Eros, of the individual's drive to engage in activities that would improve life. According to Marcuse, "in a genuinely humane civilization, the human existence will be play rather than toil, and man will live in display rather than need" and work would be transformed "into play" (171, 176). Perhaps Ben Agger sums up

Marcuse's desire to redefine work when he notes that "at the root of Marcuse's reinterpretation of the Marxian concept of praxis is his vision that work and play might converge in such a way that human beings could be seen to engage in constructive, useful work without abandoning their creative individuality" ("Work" 192). This new kind of work could not help but create a more just society. In "Marxism and Feminism," Marcuse hints at this when he asserts that "the rule of functional rationality," which he sees as gendered masculine, discriminates "against emotions," so the performance principle could be undermined by qualities gendered feminine like "receptivity, non-violence, tenderness" (283). Feminism, in other words, offers a possible way to subvert the performance principle and create a truly equitable society.

Hopefully, the thematic appropriateness of Marcuse's contentions about one-dimensional thought, repressive de-sublimation, and the performance principle to a filmic critique of society is apparent. But there are other aspects of Marcuse's thought that lend themselves quite well to the type of social critique found in science fiction. Since sci-fi movies tend to depict violence, we will first look at Marcuse's discussion of defensive violence.

In a letter to fellow Frankfurt School member Theodor Adorno which is designed to chastise his former colleague for calling the police on protesting students, Marcuse states that, in principle, "if the alternative is the police or left-wing students, then I am with the students." Marcuse then goes on to list several examples of when he would call in the police or otherwise avail himself of violent means. For example, Marcuse would call the police if his "life is threatened or if violence is threatened against my person and my friends, and that threat is a serious one" (125) or if "if there is a real threat of physical injury to persons, and of the destruction of material and facilities serving the educational function of the university" (129). Marcuse also implicitly justifies violence of resistance when he castigates Adorno for his request that Marcuse denounce the Viet Cong's use of torture by refusing to accuse "those who desperately fight against this hell, by whatever means they can" of using violence inappropriately (129). Marcuse concludes his argument about the appropriate uses of violence by noting that social theorists like himself and Adorno "should have the theoretical courage not to identify the violence of liberation with the violence of repression" (134–35).

It could be asserted that Marcuse's arguments are little more than an isolated example found in one letter and not in one of the theorist's major works. Yet Marcuse had made very similar assertions in *Eros and Civilization* when he argued that individuals should respond to a perceived threat of danger by reasoning that either "our safety is really threatened, in which case our wish to destroy is a sensible and rational reaction; or we only 'feel' it is threatened, in which case the individual and supra-individual reasons for this feeling have to be explored" (248). In most blockbuster science fiction films, wishes to destroy on the part of the protagonist are presented as sensible and rational reactions to real danger. Furthermore, it is not uncommon for that danger to emanate from an oppressive technological dystopia. Marcuse's thought, then, does not conflict with perhaps the central plot device in most of the films under consideration.

Because he uses the phrase "industrial society" to describe forces in contemporary society that limit human potential, it would be easy to misread Marcuse as something of a Luddite. Marcuse saw no inherent evil in technology itself, however, and instead viewed it as something of a misused tool. In an interview in *Psychology Today*, the philosopher noted that he had "been criticized for being against technology" before calling that assertion "utter nonsense" (62). Instead, Marcuse saw a great deal of potential freedom in the power technology gives man to escape from alienated labor, and made this argument in several places. In "Liberation from the Affluent Society," Marcuse argues that the "technical and material resources for the realization of freedom are available" (183). In the *Aesthetic Dimension*, the philosopher posits that the "radical possibilities of freedom" are "concretized in the emancipatory potential of technical progress" (27). In *Studies in Critical Philosophy*, Marcuse asserts that because of technological advances "the historical Subject appears capable of building a society in which the imperatives of self-preservation and growth can become the imperatives of freedom," a "reconciliation of necessity and liberty," though capitalism "undermines" these prospects (213, 215). In the introduction to the 1962 edition of *Eros and Civilization*, Marcuse offers that a non-repressive society is possible, though highly unlikely "as an extension of the achievements of science and technology" (vii), and goes on to argue that the "achievements of this civilization seem to make the performance principle obsolete, to make the repressive utilization of the instincts archaic" (160). Marcuse's thought, then, is quite compatible with science fiction narratives that portray technology as a tool that can be turned to good or evil—something that preoccupies the films we will discuss below.

Marcuse's contentions about the environment also accord with commonplace themes in blockbuster science fiction stories. Marcuse sees humanity as an integral part of nature, and argues that people find the greatest self-fulfillment when they are working with, and not against nature. In *Studies in Critical Philosophy* Marcuse posits that man "is not *in* nature; nature is not the *external* world into which he first has to come out of his own inwardness. Man *is* nature" (17). Consequently, "nature is ultimately not a limitation on or something alien outside him to which he, as something other, is subjected" (25) and men and women need to work in harmony with nature in order to attain happiness. Because of the link between the kind of creative work Marcuse championed and an individual's sense of place in nature, the philosopher saw the environmental degradation inherent in industrial society as an indication of the encroachment of Thanatos into society. Since, as Kellner observes, "in his major writings, Marcuse consistently followed the Frankfurt School emphasis on reconciliation with nature as an important component of human liberation" (web), it cheered the philosopher when people resisted the damage the performance principle was visiting upon the earth. In "Ecology and the Critique of Modern Society," for example, Marcuse argues that the ecology movement and its fight against the destruction of the environment is a manifestation of Eros, proving that "men and women can be computerized into robots" but they "can also refuse" (38). In "Protosocialism," Marcuse similarly argues that "rebellious human and external nature" can halt late capitalism (43). All of these contentions about the impact of nature—or the lack of nature—on the human psyche lend themselves well to discussions of science fiction tales that deal with the consequences of removing humanity from contact with nature.

In a rapidly technologizing culture, then, Marcuse's ideas spoke to those who bothered to think about the long term social and cultural impact of a rapidly rising standard of living. Concepts like one-dimensional thought, false needs, and repressive de-sublimation did much to explain the emerging lived environment in the late 1960s and early 1970s. Furthermore, even though Marcuse himself gave little thought to science fiction, several key assumptions Marcuse makes echo typical preoccupations of science fiction film or allow for their use in science fiction film. It is easy to see, for example, in Lucas' sterile and technologically-dominated empire, with its desire to destroy all that opposes it, the marriage between industrial society and Thanatos. And Scott and Cameron's apparently evil corporations—Weyland-Yutani, Cyberdyne Systems, and RDA—can clearly be seen as embodying Marcusian ideas like soft repression and the performance principle.

In order to develop the relationship between Marcusian critique and the blockbuster science fiction films of the last 40 years, subsequent chapters will trace the filmic portrayal of Marcuse's theories in the relevant works of Lucas, Scott, and Cameron. In the case of Scott, the most prolific director here, this means that many of his critically and financially successful films will not be addressed since he has worked in a wide range of genres with an equally wide range of critical perspectives. Lucas and Cameron, on the other hand, primarily released science fiction films with Marcusian content and this will be reflected in this monograph's analysis of their films, though both directors' greatest mainstream success—Lucas' *American Graffiti* and Cameron's 1998 *Titanic*—will be discussed. Because the argument attempts to track the use of Marcusian tropes in science fiction film over time, the discussion will move in a modified chronological manner, with the release of the first film under consideration dictating the placement of the director's chapter. Additionally, the chapters will group films by director, assigning ultimate creative responsibility for the narrative to that person. Chapter 3 will focus on Lucas' construction of a Marcusian critique of society in *THX-1138, American Graffiti* and the *Star Wars* films. Chapter 4 will examine Ridley Scott's Marcusian discussion of the apparently evil corporation and the possibilities of resistance to it in *Alien*, 1982's *Blade Runner*, and 2012's *Prometheus*. Chapter 5 will examine Cameron's transformation of a company man built by the ultimate evil corporation into a two-dimensional thinker in the first two *Terminator* films. Chapter 6 will explore how the director furthered his Marcusian critique by depicting protagonists who challenge the received wisdom of industrial society in 1986's *Aliens*, 1998's *Titanic* and 2009's *Avatar*.

In this volume, the term "blockbuster" is defined in economic terms. For the purposes of this study, a blockbuster cannot simply be intended to make money; it must actually have provided a good return on its backer's investment. Consequently, most of the movies included in this study made lots of money. According to boxofficemojo.com, all of the films treated at length in this study were, with two exceptions, among the top ten grossing films in American theaters during the year they were released. Many of the films—all of the *Star Wars* movies except for 2002's *Attack of the Clones*, 1991's *Terminator 2, Titanic,* and *Avatar*—were the highest grossing movies in the year they were released. Furthermore, many of the films discussed here belong to series marked by multiple box-office champions.

The three films under lengthy consideration that are not blockbusters— one film for each director—are included because of their centrality to the filmic project of their directors. Of course, James Cameron's *The Terminator*'s 21st place finish in 1984 was very strong for an R-rated, non-sequel science fiction film. Furthermore, given the film's $6.4 million production budget and its $78 million worldwide box office total, its return on investment would probably make an accountant use the term "blockbuster." Ridley Scott's *Blade Runner*, with a $33 million worldwide box office on a $28 million production budget, was a flop in financial terms and did not become a force in popular culture until people started watching it on home video. *THX-1138*, which ultimately grossed about $2.5 million on a production budget of just under $800,000, has not achieved broad recognition for being anything other than Lucas' first film. We will examine this qualified blockbuster and these two financial disappointments because these films predated their director's blockbusters, and both films, directly or indirectly, outline the themes that will drive the later, more successful films.

Before turning to individual directors and the blockbuster franchises they were involved with, however, Chapter 2 will explore the process of narrative appropriation that combines familiar science fiction tales with widely available cultural critiques to create newer, timelier versions of those familiar tales. This will involve an extended examination of de Certeau's description of the way storytellers modify existing narratives by inserting extra elements to make new arguments about society. We will then use an extended discussion of the *Alien* universe that Scott's *Alien* and Cameron's *Aliens* created to provide a case study of de Certeau's theories.

*Chapter 2*

# Creating Cleverly Subversive Science Fiction Universes

As products of their historical moment and cultural location, all blockbuster films make some kind of comment on the society that produces them—even if it is a craven statement about what the filmmakers think will do well at the box office. Tracing serious social commentary in narratives that are ostensibly light entertainment, however, requires a theoretical approach that allows for the detection of socially aware thematic strands in popular texts that are similar to socially aware thematic strands found in other popular texts. Because he felt that popular culture was actually part of the problem, however, Marcuse's work does not provide the means for decoding popular texts. Instead, in order to detect blockbuster films' employment of broadly available Marcusian critiques, we must return to Michel de Certeau's *The Practice of Everyday Life*.

The outlines of the central concept of de Certeau's description of the mechanism of popular narratives—that storytellers recreate familiar tales by adding extra elements that resonate with their audiences—was discussed in the introduction. With de Certeau's contentions in mind, we can see how a clever storyteller can take recognizable science fiction plot, genre, and stock characters and make something new yet entirely familiar by inserting the extra element of social critique. George Lucas did not invent the space opera, but by adding—among other things—popularly available versions of Herbert Marcuse's contentions about industrial society to the space opera, Lucas created a narrative that at first blush appeared new, but was actually something very familiar that was making a new argument. De Certeau correctly points to the ideological nature of these kind of narrative reconfigurations, but we need to fully appreciate the rhetorical impulse behind them. The circumstantial detail(s) inserted into texts are themselves appealing to the audience for those texts because these circumstantial details have a great deal of affective power. The Marcusian critique of society that found its way into blockbuster science fiction had already gained traction in popular culture and therefore many who saw those films were already willing and able to be pleased by the reconfigured space operas that Lucas presented, the haunted house in space that Scott created, or the incredibly violent company man Cameron sent after Sarah Connor.

De Certeau's contentions about the malleability of popular narratives as well as the rhetorical impact of the changes made to those popular narratives are supported by Raymond William's discussion of dominant, residual, and emergent cultural artifacts. According to Williams, "in cultural production both the residual—work made in earlier and often different societies and times, yet still available and significant—and the emergent—works of various new kinds—are often equally available as practices" (204). Science fiction tales that had been established in the golden age pulps, films, or pioneering television shows like *The Outer Limits* and Marcuse's critique of society—sometimes roughly contemporary but never separated by a significant historical distance—were sometimes reflective of different ideas about society and technology. Yet they were both available to Lucas and then later Scott and Cameron as they created retrofitted narratives capable of commenting on the iteration of society that they were making films for.

Given de Certeau's assertions about the way storytellers create new narratives, it is now possible to conceive of some blockbuster science fiction films having a sort of shared thematic DNA that allows them to make cogent commentary on contemporary society while at the same time employing the already-popular narratives that give them a chance of making money at the box office. Before exploring how the science fiction directors under consideration here added elements of Marcusian critique to commonplace science fiction tales, however, we need to document how common this practice is. We will illustrate this process with a case study that focuses on the persistence of Marcusian elements in the post–Scott and Cameron *Alien* universe—a review that will also include comic-book adaptations and a look at the *Aliens vs. Predator* films.[1]

Sometimes—here, Lucas' *Star Wars* films—the arc of a series of films is so completely under the control of one director that this director can sell the universe the films created to an entertainment conglomerate for billions of dollars. Of course, control is a problematic term when it is applied broadly. Lucas wrote and directed some, but not all, of the *Star Wars* films, and let his closely controlled company oversee the array of novels, comic books, video games, and television shows that became the *Star Wars* universe. Consequently, Lucas can best be understood as creating the role of project manager as auteur. Nevertheless, Lucas clearly had creative control over the first six *Star Wars* films and it is easy to assert that the director was a clever storyteller inserting the extra element of Marcusian critique into his science fiction tales.

This kind of beginning-to-end artistic and thematic control is not always granted to directors, however. James Cameron was clearly in charge of the *Terminator* films in the beginning, directing and co-writing both 1984's *The Terminator* and 1991's *Terminator 2: Judgment Day*. And when we consider that one of his co-writers was his long-term collaborator and short-term wife Gayle Anne Hurd, we can see a creative vision that compares with that of Lucas. The twelve years that passed between *Terminator 2* and 2003's *Terminator 3: Rise of the Machines*, however, saw Cameron relinquishing the director's chair and only receiving a courtesy writing credit for creating the characters. Cameron did not direct 2009's *Terminator Salvation* and received no writing credit on that film. According to imdb.com, he received another courtesy credit for creating the characters for 2015's *Terminator Genisys*. Clearly, Cameron has lost control of that franchise—though it's hard to feel sorry for the man who also directed *Aliens* and went on to direct *Titanic*, and *Avatar*. When using that series to depict Cameron as a storyteller who reimagines popular tales, then, we can only focus on *The Terminator* and *Terminator 2*.

If there are some blockbuster franchises that begin as the intellectual property of a writer/director only to later either be sold when that director retires or to slip away from that director, it is best to remember that the narratives contained in the films are not like the narratives contained in novels—the product of no more than a handful of people even if you consider editors and author's confidantes. The concept of authorship in a multimedia environment is much more problematic. Films are the products of scores of people with varying amounts of creative and/or financial control, and while most directors are clearly responsible for the creative qualities of the finished product, once they have created a film that catches the public's imagination they can become replaceable. If a sports analogy can be forgiven here, directors can be like goalkeepers in football or quarterbacks in American football—in control of the team when they are on the pitch or the field, but easily replaced during the off-season at the discretion of the moneymen and women who are actually calling the shots. Consequently, it should surprise no one that there are also franchises that, because of changes in directors and other key personnel as they develop, come to resemble a large-scale project that, instead of coming under the guidance of a project manager, is being driven by an unruly and ever-changing committee made up of filmmakers, rabid fans, comic book authors and artists, and video game designers.

At this point, an apparent methodological contradiction needs to be addressed. It is plausible to assert that Lucas had overriding thematic designs for the *Star Wars* films. It is also possible to assert that the first two *Terminator* films largely bear Cameron's thematic imprint. And *Blade Runner* clearly belongs to Ridley Scott. It appears to be deeply problematic to find a source for any thematic imprint found across the chaotic jumble of the *Alien* films, which had no less than 11 different writers and directors even if we do not consider the *Alien vs. Predator* films. As Kim Newman says of the *Alien* films, it could easily be thought of as "one of those masterpiece-by-committee films, fathered by writers, producers, designers and cast as well as" a director "who was attached to the project after it was well along" (web). This makes it very difficult to assert that an auteur had a grand vision that included inserting a Marcusian critique of society beneath the films' entertaining surface. Indeed, even in the relatively controlled worlds that Lucas created, there is so much input from other creative professionals that we simply cannot treat the films like novels. Fortunately, this is not what this monograph is asserting, even in the case of the *Star Wars* films. Instead, this argument posits that both science fiction narratives and Marcuse's critique of society were available in the broader culture as Lucas created the *Star Wars* films. Lucas' creation, in turn, was available to other storytellers along with the source material—the science fiction canon and Marcuse's popularized critique—which he drew from. These individuals often chose to add Marcusian elements to the stories that they were reworking. This is a discussion of a process that continued the popularization of Marcuse's critique by other means and not a story about how a handful of geniuses used the work of another genius to create masterpieces of social commentary—even though the intentions of individual directors are an important part of the story.

The process of reconfiguring existing science fiction tales by means of adding extra elements from Marcuse's social thought is best illustrated by examining the development of the universe of films, comic books, and other ancillary products that emerged from the first *Alien* film. After all, Andrew Osmond, reviewing 2007's *Aliens vs. Predator: Requiem* in *Sight and Sound* observes that "the *Alien* quadrilogy feels like four contrasting takes on one premise" (54) instead of a coherent whole that moves through a discernible narrative arc. This does not mean that the quadrilogy is flawed, however. Indeed, according to Karin Littau, who was arguing that a Darwinian model best explained the emergence of this sprawling universe from the first film, because it is reconfigured in every iteration, "the figure of the Alien thematizes adaptation" (22). Littau's contentions about Darwin are apt and productive, but her observations also work when put in the context of de Certeau's contentions because the anthropologist is also discussing a type of adaptation that both occurs over time and helps the "creature" in this case, narratives involving the xenomorphs first seen in Scott's 1979 film—function in different media environments. Consequently, the figure of the Alien, as well as the figure of the Predator who becomes the Alien's antagonist in some of the narratives, thematizes the transformational process de Certeau describes.

The status of the Alien as a representation of the process of retelling familiar tales becomes apparent when we examine the first film. Ridley Scott directed, but did not write, 1979's *Alien*, which was penned by Dan O'Bannon and Ronald Shusett. After the film's release, science fiction writer A.E. van Vogt sued, claiming that *Alien* was based on both "Black Destroyer," which was published in *Astounding* magazine in July of 1939, and "Discord in Scarlet," which was also published in *Astounding* in December of that same year. The stories were later published as part of a book titled *The Voyage of the Space Beagle*. Both stories feature an alien creature that is brought on board a spaceship and begins killing crewmembers, but in "Discord in Scarlet," the monstrous antagonist, Ixtl, lays eggs in crew members and waits for the larvae to hatch "inside each man's stomach" and eat their way out of the bodies of the crew members (145). Since both *Astounding* and *The Voyage of the Space Beagle* were foundational texts in the science fiction canon, van Vogt's attorneys felt justified in arguing that O'Bannon and Shusett were likely influenced enough that they needed to share credit.

Parallels were also drawn with Edward Cahn's 1958 film *It! The Terror from Beyond Space*, which, like *Alien*, featured a difficult-to-kill alien who sneaks aboard a ship and menaces a gender-mixed crew who are shown eating meals together. The monster, which is also shown hiding in ventilation shafts, was able to board the ship as they were trying to rescue the crew of another ship that had crashed. Eventually, the monster is killed when the remaining crewmembers, having donned spacesuits, open an airlock and drain all the oxygen out of the ship. Interestingly the writer of *It!*, Jerome Bixby—Cahn died in 1963—probably did not join in van Vogt's litigation because Bixby's script itself borrows heavily from van Vogt's "Black Destroyer." van Vogt's tale features a creature called the Coeurl that tricks the crew of the *Space Beagle* into taking it aboard. The beast is a remnant of a dying civilization who lives by plunging "its mouth" into the "warm body" of his victims and "letting the latticework of tiny suction cups" drain the lifeforce from their bodies (12). The monster in *It!*, which sneaks aboard the rescue ship *Challenge 142*, is a remnant of Mars' dead civilization. It sustains itself by draining oxygen and water from its victim's bodies.

This instance of borrowing from classic science fiction and from an earlier movie that had also borrowed from classic science fiction would by no means indicate that Scott and his collaborators are somehow unique—after all, James Cameron was forced to add an acknowledgment to Harlan Ellison after the author sued contending that *The Terminator* borrowed heavily from two episodes of *The Outer Limits* that Ellison wrote: 1964's "Demon with a Glass Hand" and "Soldier." Science fiction tales tend to build on previous science fiction tales. But van Vogt's somewhat successful assertion of plagiarism against Scott and his writing team seemed to move *Alien* into a sort of creative fair use zone, signaling that it had become a text that was available for reinterpretation and repurposing. The sequels to the first movie illustrate this well. Directing and lead writing duties were turned over to James Cameron for 1986's *Aliens*, which presented audiences with an interesting combination of high Victorian sentiment—a woman battling evil to save a small child—and a marines-in-space action narrative that was very much of a piece with *Rambo II*, which Cameron had recently co-written with Sylvester Stallone. *Alien*[3] from 1992 was directed by David Fincher and written by Vincent Ward, David Giler, Walter Hill, and Larry Ferguson. This film added the gritty despair of prison films to the *Alien* narrative, and featured a downbeat ending worthy of Greek tragedy. The creative team changed again for 1997's *Alien: Resurrection*, which was directed by Jean-Pierre Jeunet and written by Joss Whedon. The final installment in the film series, which featured a cloned Ripley and a cloned alien queen, deals with issues of identity and humanity similar to those addressed in *Blade Runner*.

The above overview should provide some illustration of the extent to which the initial version of a popular narrative can be altered in subsequent versions, at least on the level of plot. Ridley Scott, Dan O'Bannon and Ronald Shusett either directly reworked tales like *The Voyage of the Space Beagle* and *It!* or were so immersed in golden-age science fiction stories and later science fiction films that they created a character like Ixtl and put that character in a film that was plotted remarkably like *It!* When other writer/director teams took over, they riffed on Scott, O'Bannon, and Shusett's tale by adding their own extra elements as described above and created new tales that were different from, but clearly of a piece with, not only Scott, O'Bannon, and Schusett's creation, but also the broader corpus of science fiction films about dangerous aliens. The writers also amplified the rudimentary attempts at scaring audiences seen in *It!* by more explicitly transplanting elements from horror films into their narrative. Yet it can be argued that the extra ideological element added by Scott, O'Bannon, and Shusett—the Marcusian critique of one-dimensional thought which will be discussed thoroughly in Chapter 4— was the genuinely compelling element that made *Alien* so appealing to audiences in 1979. In order to clearly see the ideological shifts that the addition of the extra element of Marcuse's critique brings to the many iterations of the already-told space monster tale that inhabit the *Alien* universe, it will be helpful to first examine the ideological shift that occurs between "Black Destroyer" and *It!* before tracing the use of Marcuse's contentions about the performance principle across the films and graphic novels that came after the first two *Alien* films.

There seems to be an implicit approval of the New Deal in *The Voyage of the Space Beagle*—unsurprising for a text that is a compilation of stories mostly written between 1939 and 1943 and published before 1950. After all, the hundreds of scientists and technicians aboard the ship are not seeking to monetize the universe at the behest of some all-powerful Weyland-Yutaniesque corporation. Instead, they are on a voyage of discovery for the sake of gaining knowledge and they appear to be funded by the government. van Vogt seems to suggest a kind of technocratic version of programs like the Federal Writer's Project—something an American writer working in the 1930s would no doubt have been at least familiar with—behind the *Space Beagle*'s voyage. But there is more in "Black Destroyer" than implicit approval of Roosevelt's public works projects. There is also an extended commentary on a profound change that, in the 1930s, had recently taken place in the American workforce: the rise of the trained professional.

Curiously, at least for modern readers, van Vogt's story invokes his invented interdisciplinary science of Nexialism to argue for the need to bridge the gaps in knowledge created by the hyperspecialization inherent in the way people are trained in the modern university. Indeed, van Vogt's protagonist, Grosvenor, is the only Nexialist on the *Space Beagle*, and he usually manages to save the ship by applying the principles of Nexialism. In order to make sure that no readers miss his propagandizing on behalf of interdisciplinarity, van Vogt concludes *The Voyage of the Space Beagle* by depicting Kent, Grosvenor's primary antagonist, taking "his first notes on the science of Nexialism" (215). While interdisciplinarity remains important, van Vogt's preoccupation with it and his clumsily-named "science" is more than a charming quirk that limits the appeal of the narrative to serious science fiction fans. It is also an indication of an ideological intervention into a historical moment that has now passed.

In America in the 1850s, the middle class was made up of small landowners, shopkeepers, and a handful of attorneys and physicians. The rise of the state-funded public university and corporate capitalism, however, had created by the 1930s a new version of the middle class that included many, many more trained experts. There were now, for example, civil and mechanical engineers, managers of all stripes, and corporate attorneys working in the new workplace corporate capitalism had created. Given the entrenched position of the older version of the middle class, the rise to prominence of the new professionals was not inevitable, and, as Donald Stabile suggests, this new segment of the middle class was "forced to bolster its claims for legitimization through the application of science in service of society" (56) because of its relative lack of political and economic clout. Members of this new class fragment sung the praises of a scientifically managed society, though they made the scientific managers look like natural heirs of the existing middle class's values and therefore expanded the cachet of the existing middle-class ideology. For example, Charles Horton Cooley, an early American sociologist and proponent of the manageability of the social sphere, attempted to calm the fears of all who were not part of America's managerial revolution when he posited that the "'rise of the expert,'" was not "undemocratic," but instead "a phase of that effective organization of the public intelligence which real democracy calls for" (148).

With the foregoing in mind, we can see that while Cooley's version of the value of a specialized society had carried the day by 1939, van Vogt is offering a pointed critique of the new middle class' claims that society was best guided by a specialist technocracy. Grosvenor's Nexialist seems to exist, at least on an ideological level, to show up the specialists and, by constantly saving the ship, to imply that society needed to rely less on specialization if it wanted to save itself.

Jerome Bixby's 1958 reconfiguration of van Vogt's "Black Destroyer," though written only a few decades after the stories that make up *The Voyage of the Space Beagle*, adds ideological elements that address the new world that had emerged between the late 1930s and the late 1950s. On the level of plot, however, Bixby also adds the extra element of the hardboiled police procedural to the narrative, with members of the rescue crew interrogating Colonel Edward Carothers about what happened to the rest of the crew of the *Challenge 141*, the wreck that the crew of the *Challenge 142* had been sent to salvage, before the bodies begin to pile up and everyone realizes that Carothers did not kill his crewmates. The addition of some of the trappings of another popular genre makes the surface of Bixby's narrative appear different than that of van Vogt's tales, but there are more changes than initially meet the eye.

The more interesting elements Bixby added to the film are the slight shift in pro-big-government ideology and the abandonment of the arguments on behalf of interdisciplinarity. The absence of a Tyrell corporation prototype and clear signals that the government is in ultimate control of the two missions to Mars featured in *It!*—the film is practically bookended by two press conferences in the Capitol offices of the Division of Interplanetary Exploration's Science Advisory Committee—directly state *It!*'s political sympathies. Much had change in the twenty years between the publication of van Vogt's short story and the theatrical release of *It!* The Great Depression and the Cold War both featured an American government that was styled by its supporters as a benevolent guide, but the context of that guidance was very different. So while *It!* does not explicitly comment on cold-war tensions between east and west, it does present an existential threat that the government needs to protect its citizens from. In the closing press conference scene, the government official informs the gathered reporters that there will be no more trips to Mars because "another name for Mars is death." If van Vogt's New Deal era government could fund open-ended research projects because it was eager to let scientists use their talents to discover new things, then Bixby's Cold

War era government was eager to tell its citizens what they must do to avoid destruction. Furthermore, none of the crew of the *Challenge 142* are Nexialists, or anything remotely resembling a Nexialist, probably because in the atomic-age 1950s it appeared unwise to question the wisdom of specialization.

Clearly, van Vogt and Bixby both added the extra element of ideological commentary to their narratives, with van Vogt quietly supporting the assumptions behind the New Deal and loudly advocating for a turn away from specialization by means of his portrayal of Nexialism and Bixby so fully invoking the reverence for the government and military that pro–cold-war rhetoric depended on that the film's tone is reminiscent of the era's now–oft-parodied duck and cover films. Yet the important thing to note here is that the ideological extra elements clearly shifted to reflect the different preoccupations of the different eras that produced each text.

The two decades that passed between the release of *It!* and the release of *Alien* and *Aliens*—which will be discussed at length in chapters 4 and 6— saw both Marcuse's rise into pop-culture prominence and a growing discomfort with the lived reality of industrial society. Although Marcuse was active in the Frankfurt School's efforts to critique society in the 1930s and *Eros and Civilization* was first published in 1955, his ideas—and other critiques of industrial society—had yet to gain widespread support outside of the academy when van Vogt or Bixby's texts were released. Furthermore, in mid-century, America had not reached the level of disenchantment with the technocratic utopia progressives and engineers had been promising since the turn of the 20th century. By the 1970s, however, Marcuse's ideas had become popularized and influential and nothing resembling a technologized utopia had appeared.

In *Alien*, Scott, O'Bannon, and Schusett were also able to pluck Marcuse's critiques from popular culture and add them in as key extra elements in *Alien*'s take on the space monster tale that can be traced to van Vogt's stories. As control of the *Alien* universe passed from Scott, O'Bannon, and Schusett, subsequent directors would continue to riff on some or all of the Marcusian themes found in *Alien* while adding extra elements of their own. As we will see in chapters 4 and 6, Scott, O'Bannon, and Schusett portray Warrant Officer Ripley as a two-dimensional questioner of her corporatized status quo, and James Cameron's *Aliens* continues that critique—though he adds the extra, seemingly sentimental element of a woman protecting a defenseless child—with Ripley displaying open contempt for the one-dimensional thought that would lead people to avoid questioning a corporation that is seemingly obsessed with turning a dangerous life form into a weapon.

There are other Marcusian critiques that make their way into the *Alien* films, and in order to flesh out our portrayal of how elements of social critique can be incorporated across a sprawling, multimedia science fiction universe, we will explore how one such aspect of Marcuse's thought migrated across many of the other *Alien* narratives. Even the most theoretically uninformed viewer of the *Alien* films, or reader of the *Alien* graphic novels, will note a thematic and structural preoccupation with not only the Weyland-Yutani corporation itself, but with the idea of the evil, pan-galactic corporation. Such a theoretically uninformed viewer or reader would probably also notice the stark difference in tone between *Alien*'s fear-your-corporate-overlords thematics and the trust-your-government thematics of *It!* This obsession with the apparently evil corporation per se indicates the incorporation of Marcusian critique into much of the *Alien* multimedia universe. Consequently, by following the ways in which scores of writers, directors, and other artists depict the machinations of the Weyland-Yutani Corporation, we can see how the extra element of Marcusian critique continues to reappear in various versions of the tale.

The centrality of Ripley's other antagonist—her employer—allows for several of Marcuse's critiques of industrial society to appear in the *Alien* universe. Along with the critique of one-dimensional thought discussed in chapters 4 and 6, another Marcusian theme that consistently appears in the various iterations of the *Alien* tales is the philosopher's critique of the performance principle. According to Marcuse, writing in *Eros and Civilization*, industrial society is marked by a nonreflexive pragmatism that leads to social stratification "according to the competitive economic performance of its members" (41). Furthermore, "efficiency and repression converge: raising the productivity of labor is the sacrosanct idea" (141). While this all-consuming focus on productivity is perhaps best illustrated when Ripley twice finds out that, in the eyes of Weyland-Yutani, the lives of the crew of the *Nostromo* or the marines aboard the *Sulaco* are far less important than retrieving a potentially very valuable xenomorph, the depictions of the ruthless pragmatism of the performance principle continue in *Alien³*.

While *Alien³* was not a commercial failure—earning almost $160 million on a budget of about $50 million—it was definitely not the blockbuster its creators hoped it would be. About two thirds of the box office came from overseas, though its domestic take gave it a respectable 28th place in 1992. Critical reception was equally mixed, with the film currently receiving a 42 percent fresh rating on rottentomatoes.com. The *New York Times*' Vincent Canby, repeating his assessment of *Alien* as an entertaining but predictable horror–sci fi hybrid, notes that although the second sequel is enjoyable, lead Sigourney Weaver's performance "also never suggests that the movie is anything more than a haunted-house movie for the space age."[2] The *Washington Post*'s Hal Hinson was more dismissive, arguing that "once the creature makes its entrance, the movie simply becomes a grisly game of monster tag."

While there has been little direct academic criticism, of the film, it mostly echoes the psychoanalytic and feminist tone of many of the assessments of

*Alien* and *Aliens*—suggesting that a Freudian exploration of gender and birth is another extra element that Scott, O'Bannon, and Schusett added to Cahn and Bixby's space monster tale.[3] The depiction of the performance principle coexists with a thoughtful portrayal of gender anxiety and the postmodern abject, however, in *Alien³*. If *Alien* depicts Weyland-Yutani sacrificing the *Nostromo*'s crew of working-stiff space truckers to the needs of the bottom line and if *Aliens* depicts the sacrifice of a platoon of marines who probably enlisted because they needed the college money and thought, in their more poetic moments, that they might cover themselves in glory, *Alien³* fully illustrates the logic of the performance principle by depicting the sacrifice of inmates living on Fiornia "Fury" 161, a combination prison and lead refinery on a barely inhabitable planet that is owned by Weyland-Yutani, to the bottom line. After all, while the *Nostromo* was interrupted in the middle of delivering a presumably valuable shipment of ore and while the marines aboard the *Sulaco* had apparently been successfully involved in several bug hunts—the individuals aboard, in other words, had value to Weyland-Yutani—the inmates in *Alien³* are tending a refinery that has been shut down for years, presumably because it was not profitable to operate it. They are barely valuable people keeping a barely valuable asset from turning into a complete loss. And while the inmates believe that the company has allowed them to remain in the refinery in deference to their religious beliefs, events that develop reveal that the company was holding their nonperforming assets and personnel in reserve for a suicide mission since both the refinery and the men could be easily written off.

The full extent of the performance principle's application to all the inhabitants of Fury 161 begins to become apparent when what's left of the android Bishop tells Ripley that the alien was with them all the way from the *Sulacro* to the crash landing and that the company knows everything that happened to her in the escape pod because everything goes into the computer and gets sent back to Weyland-Yutani's network. This explains why after Ripley's arrival, Fury 161 suddenly starts receiving direct, non-routine communication from Weyland-Yutani for the first time in decades. Previously, the company had simply sent a supply ship and regularly rotated out the warden and his assistant. After realizing that a valuable bioweapon was present on Fury 161, however, direct orders arrive telling the warden to quarantine Ripley and, in a scene that did not make it into the theatrical version of the film, denying permission to kill a captured warrior alien.

These scenes strongly imply that the performance principle was behind Weyland-Yutani's inexplicably indulgent decision to keep the prisoners on as caretakers for a refinery that they apparently no longer needed; that the company had created a sort of reserve army of the expendable. In case anyone missed this, however, Ripley spells out the critique of the performance principle when she notes that if the queen gets off the planet, it will kill everything, but the company doesn't care about that. It just wants the queen for their bioweapons division. Furthermore, while Ripley's suicide clearly makes sense in terms of the film's plot, it could also function as a symbolic rejection of a society that is dominated by the performance principle. After all, Ripley is not only destroying herself, but she is also destroying that which made her so valuable to the company: the embryo alien queen—over the vociferous objections of Charles Bishop Weyland.

Ripley's death at the end of *Alien³* gives the impression that the series and the character had completed a logically consistent arc. Ripley would return once more, however, in 1997's *Alien Resurrection*, a film that seems to take advantage of its status as an appendix to the trilogy and push the *Alien* franchise's extra elements to their logical conclusions. It's clear from scenes like those depicting the alien queen giving birth to an alien-human hybrid and Ripley jokingly telling a man who is incubating an alien warrior that she is the monster's mother that the film invests a great deal of energy exploring the first three film's discussions of gender, pregnancy, and birth. *Alien Resurrection*, however, also continues *Alien³*'s critique of the performance principle.

With its domestic gross of just under $48 million on a budget of $75 million, *Alien Resurrection* could not be considered a blockbuster. Unsurprisingly, critical reaction was mixed, with the film receiving a 52 percent fresh rating on rottentomatoes.com. Roger Ebert, who gave favorable reviews to the first three films, finds the fourth installment "a geek show designed to win a weekend or two at the box office and then fade from memory." Some critics, however, were genuinely impressed with the self-aware approach Jenuet and Whedon brought to *Resurrection*. The *Washington Post*'s Stephen Hunter, for example, thought he would be reviewing an action-oriented science fiction film, but was pleasantly surprised to find "an art film with bugs that explode out of people's chests" that is also surprisingly "funny."

Academic critics were far more favorably disposed to *Alien Resurrection*, however, primarily because they appreciated the way the film furthered the series' implicit and explicit discussion of gender, reproduction, and identity. They were impressed, in other words, that it was an art film featuring bugs that explode out of people's chests.[4] While Jenuet does playfully extend the series' discussions of reproduction, gender, and otherness, he also continues their critique of the performance principle. In the first three films, Ripley is a worker treated like the personal property of the Weyland-Yutani Corporation. *Alien Resurrection*, although it loudly jettisons the conceit of the Weyland-Yutani Corporation, takes the logic of the earlier films to its natural conclusion by making her literally a product. Set 200 years after Ripley dives into molten lead to save humanity from the alien queen in her chest, *Resurrection* opens with a cloned Ripley undergoing surgery to remove the alien queen she was carrying. When other characters discuss this event, they make it clear that Ripley's value rests solely in what she is able to do for them. While the government scientists tactfully yet problematically refer to her as "the host," the General in charge of the project refers to her as a meat byproduct. The scientists are also impressed that Ripley heals so quickly after the alien is removed from her chest, telling her that she will make them all proud, presumably because of her value as a genetic human-alien hybrid. Ripley later reiterates this point when she tells Call that she is being kept alive because she is the latest thing.

A critique of the performance principle also comes with the depiction of the actions of the crew of the *Betty*, an unregistered freighter that is little better than a pirate ship. At the behest of the General in charge of the project, the crew hijacks a ship full of workers that was headed for a nickel mine—an interesting riff on the equally sacrificial crew of the *Nostromo*—and sells them, still asleep in stasis, to the mad scientists aboard the *Auriga* without asking any questions. The miners are then used to provide hosts for the alien eggs the newly harvested queen has laid. While the outlaws are later humanized when they attempt to save Larry Purvis, the last of the infected workers who is still alive, their initial sale of Purvis and his colleagues is clearly driven by the logic of the performance principle: these relatively unskilled workers are far more valuable as incubators for the latest bioweapon than in whatever role it was they were going to fill at the nickel mine, and the horrors they will be forced to endure are not even part of the equation.

As noted above, *Alien Resurrection* makes an offhand reference to the demise of the Weyland-Yutani Corporation, which viewers of the director's cut on DVD learn was bought out by Wal-Mart. Initially, this may seem like a rejection of the previous film's use of the performance principle and other Marcusian concepts to critique industrial society. As we will see, however, while Jenuet does add an interesting extra element in his shift away from a critique of corporate malevolence and toward government malevolence, the performance principle is not dependent on the location of the pressure to produce results.

It is important to note, however, that *Alien Resurrection* makes the government—though given the film's setting hundreds of years in the future, it's now the United Systems instead of the United States—the heavy. Interestingly, the return to depictions of an all-powerful government funding scientific research expeditions—even if those expeditions are black operations that threaten the survival of the human race—harks back to the portrayal of the government in *It!*, albeit in a backhanded way. Of course, as the Cold-War-era trust of the government was a timely addition to *It!*, a turn to the portrayal of the government as something possibly worse than Weyland-Yutani also fit well with *Alien Resurrection*'s late-1990s release. In the United States, the 1990s saw mistrust of the government increase because of alleged and actual scandals and because of the way the government was portrayed in popular culture. During the Clinton Administration, many of the president's political enemies used conspiracy theories in an attempt to discredit him. This tactic began in earnest in 1993 when the suicide of White House counsel Vince Foster was alleged to be an assassination and culminated in 1998 when Independent Counsel Kenneth Starr released evidence of Clinton's affair with Monica Lewinsky. While this was going on, more and more Americans were watching what became the longest-running science fiction show on American television, *The X-Files*. This program, which featured numerous episodes depicting government conspiracies, was arguably at the peak of its cultural influence during the late 1990s After all, fellow Fox network '90s touchstone *The Simpsons* aired a parody of *The X-Files* in early 1997. Given what was going on politically and in popular culture, even a French director could understand the mood of his intended American audience.

If Jenuet's shift from vilifying corporations to vilifying the government looks less original when removed from the context of the series and placed in the historical context of the film's release, it is nevertheless important to the tale he and Whedon tell in *Alien Resurrection*. The change is not merely implied, but instead it is heavily underlined in a scene early in the film where Ripley is talking to Dr. Wren and Dr. Gediman in the ship's mess hall. After Ripley learns that the queen was successfully harvested, she tells the scientists that everyone in the company is going to die. When she is told that that things have changed since she was last alive, she replies that she doubts that is true. When the scientists attempt to clarify and note that the operation is being run by the United Systems Military and not some greedy corporation, Ripley responds that it won't make any difference. Marcuse argued that in industrial society there was little actual difference between socialism and capitalism because maladies like the performance principle were supported by government policy and corporate decisions. Ripley seems to be making the same argument. Nothing has really changed and it genuinely does not matter if the uniforms of the expendable crewmembers read Weyland-Yutani or United Systems Colonial Marines. Jenuet thus both incorporates his historical moment's assessment of the government and cogently argues that a change in the source of a repressive insistence on performance does not make that repressive demand for performance any less dangerous to humanity.

*Alien Resurrection* has been seen as the conclusion to a relatively coherent—at least in terms of chronology—quadrilogy, though Scott's *Prometheus*, which will be discussed in Chapter 4, problematizes this assertion. Yet the fourth *Alien* film was by no means the end of the *Alien* universe. In the mid–1980s, Dark Horse Comics purchased the rights to produce graphic novels based on the *Alien* films, as they did for other filmic properties. These comics, along with the video games they helped inspire and the films they directly inspired, riffed on the ideas presented in the *Alien* films while generally maintaining the elements of Marcusian critique found in those films. Investigating the way that the clever storytellers who created these graphic novels and films chose to employ the extra element of a negative portrayal of the performance principle will not only help us understand how the *Alien* film franchise was impacted by the graphic iterations of the tale, but it will also—and much more importantly—further illustrate how the process of retelling familiar narratives that contain the extra element of social critique functions in popular culture.

It would require another book to completely map and untangle all of the iterations of the *Alien* narrative that appeared across all of the films, graphic novels, video games, and other ancillary materials generated since Dark Horse started publishing comics that—sometimes incorrectly, as it turns out—answered the question "What happened after the end of *Aliens*?" in 1988. Consequently, we will confine our examination to the thematic deployment of the performance principle that emerge in some of the Dark Horse graphic novels about aliens, predators, and aliens fighting predators, along with the critique of the performance principle that can be found in both the *Predator* and *Alien vs. Predator* films, further demonstrating that popularized versions of Marcuse's ideas were available for incorporation into science fiction narratives.

Two Dark Horse graphic novel series that clearly employ a critique of the performance principle similar to that found in the first four films: 1992's *Alien Apocalypse* and 1998's *Aliens Versus Predator Eternal*. *Alien Apocalypse* features Daniel Grant, a pharmaceutical company CEO who offers to give the military an "uninterrupted supply" of his performance-enhancing drug Xeno Zip—which is made from an alien queen's royal jelly—if they attack the aliens' homeworld. Apparently, the Xeno Zip Grant is able to produce is of inferior quality and has caused some of its users to go berserk and destroy themselves and whoever happens to be near them. Since a dangerously inferior product usually spells the end of the company that makes it, Grant wants the military to stage this suicide mission in order to secure an unlimited supply of quality jelly for his manufacturing operation. While it is readily apparent that the graphic novel is critiquing a favorite corporate villain by having a drug company owner serve as a deeply flawed—though ultimately likeable—protagonist, the focus of that critique is clearly on Grant's enthrallment to the performance principle. After all, he sees the marines only as a means to an end and the marines' commanding officers in turn are eager to sacrifice their own so that the corps as a whole will perform better. Furthermore, the overall marketability of Xeno Zip, his company's product, depends on a cultural investment in the performance principle: people are willing to take a potentially deadly supplement because they know they will be more valuable if they can run faster, work later, or otherwise outperform their unmodified self.

Thematically similar to *Alien Apocalypse*, 1998's *Aliens Versus Predator Eternal* tells the story of Gideon Lee, an industrialist who has survived for centuries because he found a wrecked predator ship and realized that eating predator body parts would extend his life. Lee, who made his fortune selling products derived from predator technology, employs a small army of mercenaries clad in predator gear to help him kill the predators that come to Earth to hunt him. This immortal capitalist is clearly a typical-for-the-*Alien*-universe evil corporate overlord who lives and dies by the performance principle, buying and selling those who are valuable to him and risking everyone else's lives in search of profits and his own peculiar fountain of youth. *Eternal* provides an interesting counterpoint to Lee in the form of journalist Rebecca McBride, however. Initially, McBride, though she sees herself as a crusading reporter, is much like Lee. She is indirectly responsible for her cameraman's death when she persuades him to help her get a ratings-grabbing story in the middle of a war zone. After the cameraman is killed, her only regret is that her personal reputation takes a hit. After Lee kidnaps her and persuades her to write his biography by offering her lots of money and appealing to her absence of morals, however, she has a change of heart when she sees the lengths Lee goes to in order to keep himself alive. The series concludes with McBride using the money Lee had given her to fund an investigative reporting institute and to support her cameraman's extended family. McBride's personal development, combined with the negative portrayal of Lee and his death at the hands of angry predators, clearly argues against the performance principle.

*Aliens Versus Predator Eternal* is also of interest because it demonstrates how the critique of the performance principle found in the *Alien* universe survives the expansion of that universe through the co-optation of the characters and situations found in another science fiction tale. Of course, this combination of aliens and predators was not introduced in *Alien Versus Predator Eternal*. Aliens were first hunted by predators in a comic series released by Dark Horse in 1990 in a narrative set on a desert colony planet where settlers raise dinosaur-like creatures called Rhynth for export to slaughterhouses on more populous planets. Clearly, the new element added here is the allusion to Western narratives, with the third panel of the comic noting that "the terror came at high noon," just in case readers couldn't draw the right inference. Before the predators and aliens attack as the settlers are preparing to ship Rhynth for the first time, however, there is an extended discussion of the performance principle similar to the one found in *Aliens Versus Predator: Eternal*.

The narrator of *Aliens vs. Predators* is Machiko Noguchi, incoming manager of the Chigusa corporation's colony on Ryushi. Placing a colony whose sole purpose is to provide food for people who live elsewhere on a scorching hot planet whose two suns provide 19 hours of daylight in a 33-hour day strongly suggests that Chigusa operates under the performance principle. Bringing in a hard-charging manager like Noguchi, who has alienated the entire colony by the time the tale begins with her inflexible demands for greater production, further suggests that Chigusa is of a piece with Weyland-Yutani. Hiroki Shimura, the outgoing manager, however, tries to remind Noguchi not to forget that "these are human beings you're dealing with." He suggests working with the Rhynth ranchers in the field and later, Noguchi herself asks the company that a greater share of the profits from the Rhynths be given to the ranchers. These actions create a brief period of détente, which is of course greatly disrupted by battles with predators and aliens. Nevertheless, the subplot concerning Noguchi's personal growth clearly makes a negative comment on the performance principle.

Although the foregoing is a small sample of the graphic novels that make up the *Alien* universe, it nevertheless suggests that Scott, O'Bannon, and Schusett's discussion of the performance principle recurs with some frequency in the texts inspired by their film. The examination of the films generated by the *Alien vs. Predator* graphic novels suggests that the critique of the performance principle survives into this third generation of *Alien* tales.

In 2004, fans of the comic books and video games as well as fans of the original film series were treated to the release of *AVP: Alien vs. Predator*, which was directed and written by Paul W.S. Anderson. The relative success of *AVP*—a worldwide gross of $173 million on a budget of $60 million—lead to a sequel, 2007's *Alien vs. Predator: Requiem*, which was directed by Colin and Greg Strause and written by Shane Salerno, who had helped Anderson write *AVP*. After this film's relative failure—its $130 million worldwide gross barely verged into respectability—there seems to have been an amiable, at least by Hollywood standards, divorce between the aliens and the predators. As we explore this hybrid universe—including the first two *Predator* films—we will realize three things. First, 1987's *Predator* and its 1992 sequel contained elements of social commentary best understood as a critique of the performance principle, probably because Lucas, Scott, and Cameron had already made this type of critique available in the first three *Star Wars* films, the first two *Alien* films, and *The Terminator*. Second, the *Alien vs. Predator* films feature a more direct employment of the critique of the performance principle, seemingly using the *Alien* storylines to clarify what the *Predator* films had hinted at. And finally, while 2010's *Predators* seeks to distance itself from the social critique found in all of the previous films, the stark nature of this distancing makes the performance principle the present absence in that film.

*Predator* (1987) was not only a financial success, but its 78 percent fresh rating on rottentomatoes.com suggests that it was something of a critical success as well. As with *Predators* 23 years later, however, most of the favorable reviews seemed to be praising the film for providing the derivative yet compelling action its audience was seeking. Roger Ebert, though calling the film an enjoyable distraction, observes that it "begins like *Rambo* and ends like *Alien*" a backhanded compliment for being inspired by "more than one blockbuster." The *Chicago Reader*'s Pat Graham, less impressed by the film's frenetic action, argues that *Predator* is an "equatorial transposition" of John Carpenter's remake of *The Thing*. Academic critics who looked on the film favorably made similar arguments, seeing the film as a good example of the action genre. For example, classics professor David Frauenfelder sees the film is "a retelling of the superhunter story pattern" that would help his students understand the adventures of Hercules (212). David Wright notes that the main character "Dutch survives much of his ordeal due to his superior physical capabilities" (26) and argues that Dutch eventually comes to represent "the truest image of pure masculinity" (28). Not all academic critics were so willing to heap the film with faint praise, however. Kevin Frank, reminding us that the film's DVD commentary designates the predator as a "Rastafarian warrior," argues that "the predator's meaning combines a fear of racial Otherness" and therefore makes a supportive comment about the American government's involvement in Central America in the 1980s (57).

The film largely bears these readings out. It is a well-told action movie very much like *Rambo*—muscular men running through dense foliage and shooting large-caliber weapons with one hand—that makes a vague and therefore problematic comment on American involvement in Central America from a right-populist perspective. The new elements added to this story appear to be the science-fiction aspects. It is in the film's comment on the American presence in Central America, however, that we can see the storytellers who created *Predator* also added two brief critiques of the performance principle to the narrative's well-established action-film narrative.

Given the right-wing politics of the film, those in thrall to the performance principle are government workers and not representatives of faceless corporations—though Marcuse, who was quick to remind his readers of the complicity of both capitalist and socialist governments with industrial society, would have been comfortable with the arguments the film makes. If the *Alien* films in existence by 1987 had featured space truckers and then marines as the workers who were valued only for their ability to add to the company's bottom line, *Predator*'s depiction of a team of elite mercenaries as the workers who were only valued for their ability to forward a government's policy decisions seems like a clever riff.

The government's performance-based valuation of the mercenaries becomes apparent in both the way the mission is presented to the mercenaries and in what happens after the mission goes badly. Dutch, the leader of the combat team, thinking that he and his men are going to rescue civilian hostages, tells his CIA handler that his men are rescuers and not assassins. The hostages are in fact Russian military advisors and CIA agents, however, and Dutch's team is being sent in to interfere with the operations of a rebel group deemed hostile to the United States. The convenient lie told to Dutch by his CIA handler implies that the only consideration for the government is how well Dutch's men perform under fire. After all, the crew of the *Nostromo* were told that they were responding to a distress signal and not that they were picking up a deadly bioweapon. Further parallels between Dutch's team and Captain Dallas' crew emerge after the mission begins to fall apart. At this point, Dutch's CIA handler, sounding an awful lot like Mother, the *Nostromo*'s computer, tells him that he is an expendable asset. While a major reveal in *Alien*, there is a curiously perfunctory quality to this pronouncement in *Predator* as the events leading up to Dutch's mano a mano confrontation with the predator quickly leave this thematic strand behind. In the 1990 sequel, however, the critique of the performance principle is made more explicit.

*Predator 2*, from 1990, by most measures, was not as successful as its predecessor. There has been no significant academic discussion of the film, even though it seems to double down on the problematic connection of dreadlocked villains and the racial other. Not only does the film feature dreadlocked predators, but one of the most vicious urban gangs is Jamaican, and the members of this gang are heavily influenced by voodoo. The movie's 25 percent fresh rating on rottentomatoes.com suggests that nonacademic critics were also not captivated by the film. For example, the *New York Times*' Janet Maslin called the film "the most mindless, mean-spirited action film of the holiday season." The *Washington Post*'s Desson Howe, equally unimpressed, described the movie as "a blithely unoriginal, megadeath blitzkrieg" and also correctly notes "a blatant theft of the set-piece finale from *Blade Runner*." Credit should be given to director Stephen Hopkins and writers Jim and John Thomas, however, for not simply revisiting the events of the first movie but for transplanting the new film's action not only to a new place but also into a new subgenre.

If the first *Predator* movie was, at least on the surface, an action movie about commandos with an alien injected into it, the second *Predator* movie is an action movie about cops patrolling a decaying city with an alien injected into it. An easy way to understand this shift in subgenre is to look at the shift in lead actors. Arnold Schwarzenegger, though no stranger to science fiction thanks to his turn as the Terminator, was at that point in his career also known for his roles as a warrior—either the sword-wielding Conan the Barbarian from that eponymous 1982 film and its sequel or Kalidor from 1985's *Red Sonja* or the machine gun toting John Matrix from 1985's *Commando*. Pred-

*ator 2*'s Danny Glover, whose Lt. Harrigan was the predator's main antagonist, was in the middle of his run starring opposite Mel Gibson's Officer Martin Riggs as Officer Roger Murtaugh in the *Lethal Weapon* films (1987–1998). Although Murtaugh was the soul of caution in the two top-10-grossing *Lethal Weapon* films which appeared before *Predator 2*, his presence signaled the arrival of the themes and concerns of the blockbuster cop film.

The unmistakable shift in subgenre is not the only important addition to the *Predator* narrative that the sequel makes, however. *Predator 2* brings the franchise thematically closer to the *Alien* films by increasing *Predator 2*'s borrowing from the critique of the performance principle found in the Alien franchise. The sequel also features the attempt by industrial society to bring everything it encounters into its network of production and consumption. Similar to the Queen in *Alien*,[3] the predator is being chased by federal agents who want to harvest and weaponize its technology. They set up an elaborate trap for the predator and track its movements in a way that visually recalls the tracking technology used to search for the xenomorph on the *Nostromo*. Of course, given the conservative politics of the *Predator* series, the government once again takes the place of the Weyland-Yutani Corporation, but the blind devotion to securing a better product is remarkably similar. Throughout the film, government operatives routinely ignore the violence of near-future Los Angeles as they make their preparations to catch the predator and repeatedly warn Glover's character that police interference with their predator hunt will not be tolerated. If the first *Predator* film depicts commandos as sacrificial victims to the performance principle, *Predator 2* continues the series' riff on the critique of the performance principle found in the *Alien* films as cops become the latest in the parade of tough-as-nails workers who are sacrificed to the bottom line.

Clearly, then, there was a degree of thematic overlap between the *Alien* and *Predator* series. By the time the sequel to *Predator* had been released, however, the two series seemed to inhabit two logically segregated universes. After all, if aliens and predators did interact, and if predators had been hunting humans for hundreds of years, wouldn't the crew of the *Nostromo* have more concrete speculations about just what they had found on LV-426? Nevertheless, *Predator 2* did provide a hint of the union that was more or less simultaneously occurring in graphic novels when *Predator 2* depicted Lt. Harrigan seeing an alien skull in the predator's underground lair. Leaving aside speculative plot- and continuity-based questions, e.g., what would the predators have done if they had found out that Weyland-Yutani was attempting to imprison an alien queen?, we can profitably ask what happened to the more productive thematic elements of both series. The *Alien* and *Predator* films both employed a Marcusian critique, though that critique was far more integral to the *Alien* films. An analysis of the *AVP* films reveals a consistent employment of a strong Marcusian critique of the performance principle before that critique was blatantly repudiated in *Predators*.

Neither of the *Alien vs. Predator* films was well-received critically though, as pointed out above, the first film made enough money to justify a sequel. *AVP* is 21 percent fresh on rottentomatoes.com, with most of the critics expressing some dismay that the *Alien* and *Predator* franchises had sunk to such a low point. *The Village Voice*'s Ed Halter, for example, describes the film as the underwhelming result of "the most convoluted revenue-stream daisy chain to date: It's a film based on a video game series that in turn drew inspiration from a string of comic books and novels (!) that were themselves retreads of two separate sci-fi movie franchises." Perhaps some of Halter's ire can be explained by the release of *AVP* a year after the release of the superficially similar slasher nostalgia film *Freddy v. Jason* which, especially without fairly considering the impact of the graphic novels, makes the film appear to be an egregious instance of creative bankruptcy. The *San Francisco Chronicle*'s Mick LaSalle is similarly unimpressed by the film's pedigree, arguing that its director "takes a pair of exhausted sci-fi franchises from decades past and cobbles together a story" that is not a movie but "something unfortunate on film."

While academic criticism of the film is sparse, one of the few essays on the film is surprisingly positive. Sandra Jackson approvingly notes that *AVP* features an African American female protagonist who is not only a competent enough explorer to be hired by Charles Weyland to lead the team of explorers into an Antarctic pyramid, but also a resourceful enough warrior not only to avoid being killed by the predators and xenomorphs that infest the pyramid but also to actually help a predator battle xenomorphs. For Jackson, Alexa's status as the last woman standing and the honor accorded to her by the Predators suggests that blacks, and black women in particular "will be present in the future; they will survive"—something also noted favorably by Halter, who discusses Alexa's "revelatory bad-assism" (251).

While largely agreeing with the B-movie status assigned to *Alien vs. Predator*, we can also assert that is clear from Jackson's article that Alexa represents a reimagining of Ripley that de Certeau would heartily approve of. Ripley herself was reputedly supposed to be a male character until Twentieth Century–Fox Chair Alan Ladd suggested adding the extra element of making Ripley female. Anderson's decision to make his protagonist an African-American version of Ripley represents a productive riff on Ladd's initial extra element. Furthermore, confirmation of honorary warrior status by the predator Alexa fights with is an implicit homage to the character that Sigourney Weaver created. Of course, finding another version of Ripley in a film that openly proclaims itself to be directly inspired by *Alien* should surprise no one. Nevertheless, it is interesting to note that there is no correlative to *Predator*'s

Dutch in *AVP*. The protagonist, then, suggests that thematically *AVP* is more of a sequel to the *Alien* films than the *Predator* films.

The film does resemble *Predator* more in terms of plot, with a focus on the battle between Alexa, a relatively human-friendly predator, and the aliens. But the way the stage is set for that battle represents a relatively transparent continuation of the performance principle critique found in the *Aliens* films. When the movie opens, audiences witness the discovery of an Antarctic pyramid that will later be found to contain xenomorph eggs by pre-merger Weyland satellites. Lance Henriksen, who played the android Bishop in *Aliens* and *Alien³* (as well as the voice of Bishop in the recent *Aliens: Colonial Marines* game), plays industrialist Charles Bishop Weyland, who takes out his checkbook and assembles a team of scientists and explorers to investigate said pyramid. We begin to understand that Weyland may be interested in something other than knowledge for the sake of knowledge when he essentially bribes his team of explorers and scientists to enter the pyramid after Alexa tells them that it is too dangerous. It turns out that Weyland is interested in weaponizing the predator's technology, something that is no great surprise to the intended audience for this film. On a thematic level, however, audiences are greeted with something slightly new. Previously, they had seen a future iteration of Weyland's company sacrificing tow vessel crewmembers, marines, and violent prisoners to obtain a product that will greatly boost the bottom line. In *AVP*, Weyland sacrifices a high-priced team of experts to help obtain products that will greatly boost his company's bottom line. Both the *Alien* and *Predator* films have clearly established that people have an intrinsic worth that goes beyond what they can do for the company or the government, and *AVP* is no different. After all, Weyland's death at the hands of the predators, who see him as completely useless in their alien hunt, would only be less subtle if Matthew 26:52—all they that take the sword shall perish with the sword—scrolled across the bottom of the screen.

Such clearly-signaled thematic additions to films that essentially serves to justify a battle between aliens, humans, and predators continues in *AVP Requiem*. The Strauss brothers' 2007 film was poorly received, with a 12 percent fresh on rottentomatoes.com and a near-total lack of published academic criticism. Most critical reactions featured more heavily qualified praise than outright condemnation. *Entertainment Weekly*'s Chris Nashawaty, for example felt that it worked as an unrepentant B movie, "a brisk, gooey bit of schlock" that fans of sci-fi and horror would enjoy if they weren't expecting anything too cerebral. *Variety*'s Joe Leyden offers similarly qualified praise when he notes that the film "moves at a reasonably brisk clip" and predicts that it will "blast off" commercially when it is released on video for *Alien* and *Predator* fans who didn't want to pay full theater price.

Though arguably accurate, attaching the B-movie designation to *AVPR* is somewhat unfortunate since the brothers Strauss were at least attempting to revitalize the franchise in interesting ways. Their film, as viewers would expect, is a hybrid science fiction/horror film. The directors, however, decided to add as many extra elements as they could, producing a film that is marked by rapid shifts between subgenres—*AVPR* starts out as a criminal redemption story and then shades into a teen love triangle with elements of forbidden romance broadly similar to *Romeo and Juliet* before verging into a topical-for-2007 treatment of a wife and mother who's just returned from deployment in Iraq before shifting again to become a teens-find-the-spacemonster film reminiscent of the 1950s before finally returning to the criminal redemption story it began with.

While this rapid genre tour probably doesn't work, it makes it even more interesting to note the thematic consistency regarding the performance principle. Instead of coming before the battle between humans, predators, and aliens, however, the scene directly addressing the performance principle comes after all the shooting (and nuclear explosions) are over. During the battle, reformed con Dallas Howard is able to secure and use the predator's shoulder-mounted weapon. After Dallas and *AVPR*'s Riplyesque female protagonist Kelly O'Brien escape from the predator-infested town in a medevac helicopter, soldiers perhaps understandably confiscate this weapon. Later, however, in the film's last scene a high-ranking Army officer gives the weapon to Ms. Yutani—presumably because Charles Bishop Weyland died in the last film and perhaps in an effort to give backstory to the merger. Behind this hat tip to series mythology, however, lies the very familiar argument that human suffering, up to and including the nuclear annihilation of a small town, is a small price for the government or an apparently evil corporation to pay if it leads to better weaponry or an increase in the bottom line.

*AVPR*'s disappointing box office performance led to the financially understandable decision to separate the fused franchises. While *Alien* director Ridley Scott would craft something between a prequel and a reboot for his original film five years later in *Prometheus*—which will be discussed in Chapter 4—the third direct installment of the *Predator* franchise, *Predators*, arrived in theaters in 2010, just three years after *AVPR*. Perhaps seeking distance from the Strauss Brother's poorly-received film, or perhaps seeking distance from all the *Alien* films, *Predators* pointedly abandons a critique of the performance principle in exchange for an emphasis on self-reliance. Given the context of all of the previous films, however—even the politically right-leaning *Predator* films warned against seeing individuals as assets—the rejection itself reminds viewers that the critique of the performance principle is no longer there and that the previous films prominently featured such a critique. *Predators*, in other words, is haunted by the absence of the Marcusian elements in the other films.

Directed by Nimrod Antal and written by Alex Livtak and Michael Finch, *Predators* was reasonably well received by critics, earning a 64 percent fresh rating on rottentomatoes.com. Most of those reviews, however, simply praised the film for providing what its intended audience was expecting in a package that other viewers would find watchable. After comparing it favorably to the first film, for example, the *New York Post*'s Lou Lumenick calls it "a fun ride" that will please fans. Similarly, the *Minneapolis Star-Tribune*'s Colin Covert damned *Predators* with faint praise by anointing it an example of B-movie Nirvana designed to please fanboys. There are significant differences between this B movie and the B movies that inspired it, however.

If it is important to add a new elements to familiar tales in order to successfully reboot them, it is probable that Antal, Livtak, and Finch decided to reject a critique of the performance principle and insert a rebooted Social Darwinism. After all, this reconfiguration befits the film's clearest fictional precedent, Richard Connell's 1924 short story "The Most Dangerous Game" and, perhaps, the 1932 film version of that story. Consequently, there is no evil corporation or government entity trying to weaponize the Aliens' bodies or the predators' technology. Instead, a group of morally compromised people whose lives revolve around killing others have been transported to a planet by the predators, who are stocking their own private game preserve. The predators' intended victims must put all other considerations aside for survival, and are punished when they forget this. For example, a Russian heavy machine gunner mistakenly befriends another member of the group and then pays for this mistake with his life. Additionally, an Israeli sniper kills what appears to be a wounded man to avoid falling into a predator trap but then almost dies when she stays behind to help a man who appears to be a hapless physician but turns out to be a serial killer determined to sacrifice her to show the predators that he is really one of them.

This radical rejection of the critique found in the previous *Predator* films does make the story new, potentially making it appealing to fans of all three series. Yet thematically, the loud rejection of the earlier films' discussion of the performance principle and the investment in the performance principle that both large corporations and large governments find necessary in industrial society places that concept under erasure for both viewers and critics who are familiar with the earlier films—a group that probably represents a near-total majority of potential ticket buyers. While the critique is no longer there, it is nevertheless noticeable because it used to be there and because the film seems to be indirectly but insistently saying that the critique of the performance principle has been banished. It is as if the filmmakers had decided, for example, to replace predator dreadlocks with buzzcuts, though on a thematic rather than visual level.

By examining both the persistence of the performance principle as well as the persistent borrowing from older science fiction tales found in the graphic novels and films that make up the *Aliens, Predator* and *Aliens vs. Predator* universes we realize that popular storytelling functions as De Certeau would suggest. Popular tales and the rhetorical appeals of those popular tales reemerge in slightly altered forms in subsequent iterations of those tales. This is how narratives like science fiction blockbusters function, and this is why Marcuse's ideas could reemerge in films like 1981's *The Empire Strikes Back* and 2009's *Avatar*, not because a dedicated cadre of Marcuse's students decided to infiltrate popular culture with their mentor's ideas, but because popular culture works by repackaging popular narratives by adding extra elements and details to them. And in order to fully understand how Marcuse's thought became so widespread that it could easily spill over into the ancillary universe created by two blockbuster science fiction films, we need to examine how George Lucas first used the theorist's work to enliven the space opera.

*Chapter 3*

# George Lucas Battles the Empire of Unfreedom in *American Graffiti* and the *Star Wars* Films[1]

If de Certeau is to be believed, the best way for a text directed at a popular audience to participate in social critique is for it to subtly reconfigure an existing narrative by adding the extra element of cultural commentary, helping its audience develop new memories of familiar tales that give them a new way to look at their society. Following this line of reasoning, it would be easy to assert that social commentary found in unfamiliar narratives—i.e., an overtly Marcusian attack on industrial society that assumed a comprehensive familiarity with the theorist's writings—would be more likely to fail to connect with an audience, since those narratives would not produce the re-remembering that is so crucial for popular acceptance. Consequently, a successful Marcusian critique would have to be carefully blended with a familiar narrative; the narrative could not simply be a lightly fictionalized version of Marcuse's contentions.

The career of one of the world's most commercially successful directors bears out the assumption that cultural critique is best blended with familiar, popular narratives. This director's first movie had been moderately successful with critics but a disaster at the box office, probably because this film was a deliberately difficult and non-commercial critique of American Society, a movie remembered decades later by no less an arbiter of commercialized popular culture than *Entertainment Weekly* as "a head-scratcher of a science-fiction flick" (Nashawaty 94). In light of that director's later success with high school nostalgia and then a decidedly non–head-scratcher variety of science fiction—with the kind of familiar narratives that tend to sell movie tickets—it would be easy to see the first movie as a rookie idealist's mistake, and that director's later, more commercial and more commercially successful work, as either a sign of someone who has entered reality or as a sign of someone who has sold out.

The above scenario describes the general arc of George Lucas' career and, at first glance, explains why biographer Dale Pollock calls Lucas a "conservative businessman from Modesto."[2] His first film, *THX-1138*, did poorly at the box office. And while some critics approvingly noted Lucas' critique of contemporary society, the film has not exactly become a key text in film studies courses. Lucas' second film, *American Graffiti*, a seemingly straightforward idealization of Lucas' own immersion in cruising and top 40 rock 'n' roll during his adolescence in California, was reviewed well in the popular press,[3] received five Academy Award nominations and made lots of money.[4] The film's entrance into pop culture's broad collective memory, as evidenced by its presence on several "best of" lists also suggests that *American Graffiti* was designed to please American moviegoers rather than critique American society.[5] Academic critics, when not dismissing the film as "a collection of teenage stereotypes" (Bernardoni 28), have tended to see it as ideologically problematic. Frederic Jameson famously anointed *American Graffiti* as the "inaugural" example of a "new aesthetic discourse": the nostalgia film. For Jameson, this discourse is characterized by a "desperate attempt to appropriate a missing past" that has been "refracted through the iron law of fashion change" (*Postmodernism* 19).[6]

Of course, *American Graffiti* allowed Lucas to return to science fiction, albeit in the more commercially palatable form of the *Star Wars* films, which also made lots of money, won praise from critics and awards committees, and penetrated popular culture in a way that would have been unthinkable for *THX*. According to boxofficemojo.com's chart of domestic grosses adjusted for ticket price inflation, the six *Star Wars* films made close to $3.5 billion in American theaters alone.[7] Furthermore, the popularity of the franchise as a whole increased so much over the more than three decades since the release of *A New Hope* that in 2012 Disney purchased the rights from George Lucas for a reported $4.05 billion. Mainstream critics were generally approving of Lucas' films, though 1999's *The Phantom Menace* and *Attack of the Clones* were not well received. In addition to winning numerous science fiction awards, all the films received at least one Academy Award nomination, with *A New Hope* winning six Oscars and *The Empire Strikes Back* winning one.[8] And while the films may never again achieve the phenomenal popularity *A New Hope* experienced during the late 1970s, an ever-expanding "universe" of books, direct-to-DVD-films, and video games combined with Disney's aggressive agenda of reboots and spinoffs will keep the universe Lucas created in the public eye for years to come.

While the Star Wars films have achieved roughly the same financial and mainstream critical success as *American Graffiti*, they have not been summarily dismissed by academic critics. Indeed, a critical consensus has not emerged. Unsurprisingly, some of the criticism labels the films as "family adventure movies" (Kramer, "Big Pictures" 127), as "an intergalactic fairy tale" with "sexless" heroes (Holte 188, 189), or as a collection of "adolescent rites-of-passage films" (Gordon, "Power" 196). Most of the criticism, however, sees the films as either very important or very dangerous, with some critics praising the films' status as a modern-day myth or as a stealth critique of technology while other critics have charged that the series is more ideologically conservative product from Lucas' nostalgia factory. Lucas himself frequently and publicly acknowledged the influence of Joseph Campbell's *The Hero with a Thousand Faces*[9] after Andrew Gordon anointed *A New Hope* "a modern fairy tale, a pastiche that reworks a multitude of old stories" ("Myth" 73). Gordon stressed that this fairy tale was necessary because "we are in a period in which the heroes have been cast down through such national catastrophes as Vietnam and Watergate" ("Myth" 82).[10] But if the Campbellian reading is the most influential positive assessment of the series, other critics have seen more concrete social critique, suggesting that "the films explicitly and implicitly criticize faith in technology at every possible turn"[11] because, as David Begor argues, acting "like a machine is, after all, the first stage in losing one's humanity" (web). This critique of technology may also illustrate Heidegger's distinction between ready-to-hand technology that is more or less in harmony with nature and the environmentally destructive, unbalanced present-at-hand technology of the Empire and present-day industrial society.[12]

Critics who find the films problematic usually do so for reasons that echo Jameson's dismissal of *American Graffiti*: the film presents "an America locked into some false nostalgic past" that is "conservative and populist" (Lewis 73, 77), the film "creates an ideologically conservative future" by means of a rebellion that "in no way challenges gender, race, or class relations" (Lev 30, 33), or it fetishizes "advanced and fantastic technology" making global capitalism "less threatening by effacing all evidence of the mode of production that makes such wonders possible" (Silvio 57, 54), or it participates in an American neomedievalism designed to teach boys traditional masculinity (Henthorne 79) and is therefore an embodiment of the "imperial myth" of the nuclear family (Kuiper 79), or it argues that "in the face of massive technology, you can only expect to win with religion" (Wright 124).

The sum of these critical readings of *THX*, *American Graffiti*, and the *Star Wars* films gives Lucas' career the same shape that popular culture does: the filmmaker released a difficult first film that delivered a strident critique of society only to retreat to highly marketable nostalgia before returning to science fiction films with decidedly mixed results. While this chapter will not directly take issue with individual readings of individual films, it will strongly argue that the picture that emerges from those readings does not capture the essence of the auteur's project. A close consideration of Lucas' major films reveals that after using *THX* to conduct a Marcusian attack on industrial society, the director seemed to learn the practical lesson embedded within de Certeau's work: critique works best when blended with familiar, popular narratives. Lucas then created rhetorically deft critiques of industrial society in *American Graffiti* and the *Star Wars* films that cleverly continued the Marcusian critique found in *THX* by means of a narrative that embedded both a familiar coming-of-age tale and carefully-timed nostalgia and then creating a series that return to the space opera that had driven science fiction films for decades.

Lucas, who has always maintained that the *Star Wars* films had been written shortly after *THX* and *American Graffiti*,[13] told Pollock that he was committed to not making the same mistakes he had with *THX*. He had learned that "you have to come at things sideways" and not directly critique society if you want people to watch your films (140). In an interview conducted shortly after *American Graffiti* had become a commercial and critical success, Lucas admits that he "was considered a cold, weird director, a science-fiction sort of guy who carried a calculator" after *THX*. Consequently, Lucas decided to "do something exactly the opposite," reasoning that if "they want warm, human comedy, I'll give them one just to show them that I can do it. *THX* is very much the way that I am as a film-maker. *American Graffiti* is very much the way I am as a person" (Farber 5). Outwardly, these are the words of a director who realizes that "they"—the people who purchase movie tickets—don't want to see their society depicted as a stark technological dystopia. Instead, "they" want to be told how much fun technology is in a movie that glorifies, for example, fast cars and loud music. The subtext here, however, is a simple declaration that he is changing tactics. As Marcuse might have said, Lucas decided that if audiences want unfreedom and one-dimensional thought, a director might have to give them an unadulterated dose of unfreedom and one-dimensional thought along with any credible critique of industrial society.

Marcuse, after all, was not entirely dismissive of positive social change coming from within the system. Instead, he hoped that if people could think critically about society they might be able to make it more humane. In his introduction to *One-Dimensional Man*, Marcuse openly admits to vacillating between "two contradictory hypotheses: (1) That advanced industrial society is capable of containing qualitative changes for the foreseeable future; (2) that forces and tendencies exist which may break this containment and explode the society" (xlvii). Thus, by focusing on the resistant forces and tendencies, it is possible to create a rhetorical critique that will not make audiences feel powerless but will instead suggest that there are alternatives to blindly accepting the status quo. The protagonist of a narrative informed by Marcusian critique does not have to reject industrial society wholesale, as THX does. She or he can also remain as a questioning participant, as *American Graffiti*'s Curt does or as Luke Skywalker—and perhaps ultimately Anakin Skywalker—does. In order to fully understand the critical enterprise that informs these outwardly dissimilar films, we must look at all of them through a Marcusian lens, beginning with Lucas' pointed yet problematic first film and then following Lucas' refinement of his critique through the film that saved his career and the series that made his name.[14]

While it is always difficult to clearly understand why a given filmic or literary narrative fails to connect with a popular audience, *THX-1138*'s commercial failure—before the success of *Star Wars* created legions of Lucas fans who watched the auteur's first film on VHS or DVD—is difficult to understand. One could argue, after all, that Lucas was employing familiar narratives that audiences should have felt comfortable with. The film seems of a piece with much mid-20th-century dystopian science fiction and has been described as having a premise "classic in SF: an individual asserting himself against the social machine" (Pye and Myles 117). Its technologically driven, totalitarian, conformist society is reminiscent of novels like George Orwell's *1984* and Aldous Huxley's *Brave New World*. And Lucas' tale of technologies that enervate the human spirit in the name of comfort and security resembles the world imagined by E.M. Forster in "The Machine Stops." Furthermore, *THX*'s depictions of computerized compulsion in a completely managed environment resonate with other filmic portrayals of coercive technology. Though there are broad thematic similarities with early science fiction films like Fritz Lang's *Metropolis*, the ominous and nearly constant background drone of official announcements and police scanner chatter remind viewers of the increasingly menacing pronouncements of HAL 9000 in Stanley Kubrick's and Arthur C. Clarke's *2001: A Space Odyssey* which, given its box office take of over $50 million on a $12 million production budget, was something of a blockbuster. The extensive social control of the panoptic technological network is mirrored in the nuclear-armed, colluding Soviet and American supercomputers found in the film *Colossus: The Forbin Project*. Clearly, Lucas' first film had the potential for broader audience appeal, and there is some speculation that Warner Bros.' inability to properly market the film may have contributed to its lack of success.[15]

Yet the film's relentless assault on contemporary society combined with its lack of any familiar source narrative beyond a love story is a much more likely explanation for its audience's discomfort. After all, dystopia is usually a tough sell, and Lucas' dystopia was a particularly unrepentant one. Because of its claustrophobic portrayal of technologized dystopia, it would be easy to argue that the film is simply asserting that technology is bad, something that Michael Ryan and Douglas Kellner essentially do when they note that the "technophobic theme is most visible in the early 1970s in" *THX-1138* (59). Yet Lucas, like Marcuse, had a more nuanced discussion of technology in mind. When interviewed by the *San Francisco Chronicle* a few months before the film's March 1971 release, the director cast his first feature-length project in immediately allegorical terms. According to Lucas, the film was not a speculative warning about what society might become, but was instead an "abstraction of 1970." In clarifying this observation, Lucas further explained that in THX's world, "nobody was having any fun, but no one was unhappy. A lot of people live that way now."[16] Interestingly, Marcuse also felt that the early 1970s were a time when the industrial society could be recognized by most people, offering in an interview in *Psychology Today* that 1971 was a time of "organized counter-revolution" (65) because of a growing awareness of technology's threat to individual agency.

Almost 35 years later, on the occasion of the release of the director's cut DVD, Lucas reiterated these contentions, noting that "*THX-1138* is how I saw 1970.... It was designed as a metaphor for the way we were living at the time. The world has taken a strange twist from there, but I think the ideas we examined in *THX-1138* are still valid in the 21st century" (Snider 1E). Much more explicitly than its contemporaries, then, Lucas' film not only asks "what if" but also creates an allegory of the all-consuming, technologically-driven totality that Lucas feared American society had already become.

When the film was initially reviewed, not everyone agreed that Lucas had fully realized his abstraction of 1970. The film was praised for its ability to "select, compress, and organize elements of social relationships and architecture that already exist among us" (Callenbach 63). Yet most mainstream critics were not impressed with the film's dystopia. For example, the *New York Times*' Roger Greenspun argued that "whatever horror lies ahead, I don't think that anybody now seriously imagines that it will take the form of a de-emotionalized asexual society enslaved by its own models of technical efficiency." Social scientists found Lucas' film more plausible, however, because it made predictions that sounded familiar to them. In a review of *THX-1138* published in the social science journal *Trans Action*, Bernard Beck notes that the portrayal of technological dystopia is not only common in science fiction, but is also "a commonplace" of the mass society theorists who were so influential in the 1960s and early 1970s (62). Seeing this parallel leads Beck to make the backhanded compliment that the film is best seen as an "extrapolation from the conventional wisdom of sociology about the structural uniformities of all industrial societies" (63). And while this extrapolation helps illustrate Lucas' employment of the intellectual milieu that Marcuse was a dominant part of, it also could explain the films disappointing box-office performance. After all, few theatergoers actively look for fictionalized social theory when selecting a movie.

The potential for audience alienation notwithstanding, *THX*'s sociological bent also squares well with Lucas' initial positioning of himself as the kind of thinker who would be familiar with academic critiques of industrial societies. Lucas once told an interviewer that when he "was in Junior College," his "primary major was in social sciences" because he has always been "interested in America and why it is what it is" (Farber 6). The filmmaker was also coming from the same political space as the social critics alluded to by Beck. According to Pollock, during his student days at USC, Lucas "supported civil rights, was against the war in Vietnam and Lyndon Johnson, and in favor of all the right liberal causes" (59). Clearly, Lucas was partaking in the same cultural moment that made a celebrity out of Herbert Marcuse while living in the same state. This makes it easier to see that the storyteller and the philosopher were attempting, in their own way, to describe industrialized society in the 1960s and 1970s as worlds where nobody was having any fun, but no one was unhappy. As we will see below, *THX* follows some of the same lines of argument about the repressive potential of the desire for comfort so crucial to Marcuse in works like *One-Dimensional Man* and *Eros and Society*. Like the director, the social theorist sees a society that conquers "the centrifugal social forces with Technology rather than terror, on the dual basis of an overwhelming efficiency and an increasing standard of living" (xlii). Thus, nobody has any fun, but nobody is unhappy.

Lucas begins his examination of comfortable yet imprisoning consent in the opening moments of *THX*. The auteur juxtaposes carefully altered scenes of a chapter of the Buck Rogers serial titled "Tragedy on Saturn" in which the announcer claims that Buck, an ordinary fellow, lives in the *20th* century, an exciting "world that sees a lot of our scientific and mechanical dreams come true." Lucas then undercuts this implicit utopia with images of the stark conformity and mindless activity of a world that has become one self-perpetuating machine because of the realization of scientific and mechanical dreams, a world in which totalitarian domination is largely dependent on the consent of the dominated. Interestingly, with these images Lucas is directly rejecting the kind of familiar narratives that might have helped his audience embrace his social critique.

Like all dystopias, THX's world has many utopian aspects—no war, want, or worries—and it is therefore unsurprising that most of its citizens cooperate. Of course, the price of this contentment is the abandonment of any individuality—almost everyone wears white and shaves their head—and the ability to question the system. This illustrates the paradox that Marcuse calls unfreedom: humanity's repressive subjection to the productive apparatus "is perpetuated and intensified in the form of many liberties and comforts" (32). Lucas' all-encompassing dystopia, which is buried far underground, also calls to mind the concept of Thanatos that Marcuse develops in *Eros and Civiliza-*

*tion*. After all, if Thanatos is best considered as the desire to "return to the Nirvana of the womb" (50) and "the regressive impulse for Peace" (69) defined by the absence of conflict, then an unfree society that exists in an enormous steel womb where people live a peacefully numb existence makes a fair filmic portrayal of the logical endpoint of Thanatos. Furthermore, since Thanatos often leads people to destroy what Eros would have them interact with, the complete absence of nature from THX's world neatly represents a retreat from the world by means of the effective destruction of the world.

In addition to its depiction of unfreedom and Thanatos, *THX* agrees with *One-Dimensional Man*'s reading of contemporary society in several key areas. First, both texts, despite their Cold War status, collapse communist and capitalist modes of production into the category of industrial society, arguing that differences in political ideology pale before the reality of life in a technological society. Further, Marcuse and Lucas describe technological society with three shared assumptions about how it gains the acquiescence of its citizens: through the creation of false needs, through actively turning the sublime aspects of life into quotidian non-events, and through the encouragement of one-dimensional thought.

Marcuse's discussion of industrial society attempts to transcend the competitive divide between capitalist and communist systems and instead examine the real conditions of people living in societies increasingly dependent on technology. Though heavily influenced by Marxist thought, Marcuse saw little real difference between the Sino-Soviet bloc and the capitalist nations, arguing that in both economic systems the "enslavement of man by the instruments of his labor continues in a highly rationalized and vastly efficient and promising form.... The more the rulers are capable of delivering the goods of consumption, the more firmly will the underlying population be tied to the various ruling bureaucracies" (43). Lucas creates THX's world similarly, focusing on the impact of industrial technology and deliberately blurring what could have been obvious ideological markers in a film produced during the Cold War. Instead, Lucas leaves small clues that THX's city contains the worst elements of both systems. When the robot police interrogate THX, they ask him, "Are you now, or have you ever been?" omitting the direct reference to membership in the communist party yet clearly invoking Wisconsin senator Joseph McCarthy and the anticommunist paranoia that marked the United States in the 1950s. Nevertheless, from all available evidence THX lives in a one-party welfare state that has no visible division between public and private property and that presents itself as a technological utopia. This communist/capitalist mélange is best exemplified by the advice given by OM, a computerized Jesus/Buddha figure that personifies the state religion. When OM hears a confession, he imparts "blessings of the state and blessings of the masses"—sounding like a member of the comintern—but also implores the supplicant to "be grateful we have commerce: buy more and be happy"—sounding like a member of the chamber of commerce.

Marcuse argues that industrial societies create an addiction to what he calls false needs in order to keep the populace invested in the status quo. Of course, these false needs dampen dissent since, according to Marcuse, "all liberation depends on the consciousness of servitude, and the emergence of this consciousness is always hampered by the predominance of needs and satisfactions which, to a great extent, have become the individual's own" (OD 7). Lucas makes the addictive nature of industrial society clear by making mandatory drug use a signal feature of THX's world. As THX learns, however, the total industrial city does not fully trust its workers to acquire the right habits. Consequently, failure to be properly sedated leads to criminal charges for drug evasion. There are also more quotidian examples of the addictive consumerism Marcuse speaks of. We see the workers devoting their spare time to consuming goods of dubious utility in a vast shopping mall, as when THX purchases a seemingly purposeless red polygon, carries it home, and then discards it.

Marcuse calls industrial society's efforts to subvert any aspect of culture or the human experience that would evoke an alternative to the banality of daily existence repressive de-sublimation. While Marcuse spends much time discussing the repressive de-sublimation of art and literature, he also focuses on sexuality, arguing that the "mobilization and administration of libido" characterizes advanced industrial societies. Both reproductive technology and a popular culture that enforces normative sexual behavior leads to a type of sexual satisfaction "which generates submission and weakens the rationality of protest" (75). This observation finds ironic confirmation in *THX* when a talking head on the holographic television opines that the "economic advantages of the mating structure far surpass any disadvantages in increased perversions." When we remember that in THX's society living selection is computerized and roommates are called mates, we realize that the city's asexual mating structure has made it normal for THX to masturbate to the erotic dance of a hologram created by the fantasy bureau but a perversion for him to make love to his roommate. Indeed, this scene seems to echo the contention in *Eros and Civilization* that a society in thrall to false needs would be characterized by "the promotion of thoughtless leisure activities" (86). Yet THX and LUH do fall in love, and the sublime irrationality of their relationship helps THX realize that he needs to critique the world he lives in. And since THX's and LUH's relationship ends in a tragedy that compels THX to escape from the mechanized dystopia that he inhabits, it is clear that Lucas is not giving his audience a simple love story but an argument that supports Marcuse's contentions that Eros is "a life instinct" that is best understood as "a larger biological instinct rather than a larger scope of sexuality" (EC 187).

Marcuse believes that intellectual life in industrial society is characterized by one-dimensional thought, which can best be understood as a nondialectical thought which refuses to question the status quo. In a way, one-dimensional thought is understandable, since "there is no reason to insist on self-determination if the administered life is the comfortable and even the 'good' life" (49). Many of Lucas' characters behave in ways suggesting an inability to imagine an alternative to the status quo, as when THX's fellow prisoner SEN cannot bring himself to escape the city but instead returns to confess his sin of nonconformity to OM and beg for another chance. Also, during foreplay before THX and LUH make love for the first time, THX tells his "mate" that he was happy and then asks her, "Why get me involved?" While this statement may seem odd considering the obvious zest with which THX is exploring his roommate's body, Marcuse reminds us that often "the intellectual and emotional refusal 'to go along' appears neurotic and impotent" (9).

While we may never know if Marcuse's theories exerted a direct influence on Lucas as he crafted his first film, it is clear, at the very least, that the theorist and the filmmaker had drawn similar conclusions about their era. Unfortunately, at least from a commercial standpoint, most ticket buyers were not looking for a visually disturbing popularization of what academic social critics were saying about industrial society. Audiences might have forgiven Lucas' grim depiction of the impact of technology on the human experience if he had provided a happy ending. Yet the ending of *THX-1138* is, at best, ambiguous. Although viewers are treated to what initially appears to be a rousing escape featuring a stolen jet-powered car reaching speeds of over 200 miles per hour, THX does not outrun or outwit the police. Instead, the police meekly retreat when the budget for the chase has been exceeded—an understandable event in a society that is a metaphorical expression of Thanatos and therefore features no growth, no creativity, no conflict—but not exactly what movie audiences are expecting. And when THX finally climbs out of the concrete tube leading out of his underground city, he emerges not into a natural paradise, but into an apparently sterile landscape dominated by a setting sun. Although he raises his arms to signal victory, audiences are left to wonder just what he has won. Perhaps the police were right not to waste money chasing someone who could not survive the oncoming night? And perhaps there really is no way out of a society that controls through false needs and repressive de-sublimation? It has been argued that the film depicts "tensions that most of our ideological representations, particularly our film narratives, typically work to dissolve or dismiss" (Telotte *Science Fiction Film*, 134). Of course, those tensions are typically dissolved because audiences are paying money to see just that dissolution.

Since it came on the heels of an intellectually challenging commercial failure, it would be easy to categorize *American Graffiti* and its stunning success at the box office as Lucas' hasty retreat from both deep social critique and discomfiting ambiguity. Yet it could also represent Lucas' demonstration that he has learned de Certeau's implicit lesson: clever storytellers who want to critique society work with familiar narratives. Despite the outward dissimilarity between both the films and their reception, some critics have seen parallels, reminding us, for example, that Lucas maintained that "we are living in cages with the doors open" and then arguing that in "*THX*, the cage was the electronic labyrinth his society had constructed around him. In *American Graffiti*, the cage is "life in the small California town."[17] But the connection between the two films goes beyond the director's reconfiguring of his own escape from small-town life. Instead, the thematic similarities point to a reconstruction of the critique presented in *THX* by means of a more muted, more commercially responsible, yet nevertheless similarly powerful, depiction of Eros, Thanatos, unfreedom and one-dimensional thought. Lucas also shifts from the depiction of industrial society as an unstoppable totality to a set of economic and cultural relationships that can be questioned from within and perhaps, in time, be overcome or at least be reconfigured.

It will be easier to see Lucas' reconfiguration after first quoting Marcuse at length on why one-dimensional thinking makes constructive critique impossible:

> I ride in a new automobile. I experience its beauty, shininess, power, convenience—but then I become aware of the fact that in a relatively short time it will deteriorate and need repair; that its beauty and surface are cheap, its power unnecessary, its size idiotic; and that I will not find a parking place. I come to think of *my* car as a product of one of the Big Three automobile corporations. The latter determine the appearance of my car and make its beauty as well as its cheapness, its power as well as its shakiness, its working as well as its obsolescence. In a way, I feel cheated. I believe that the car is not what it could be, that better cars could be made for less money. But the other guy has to live, too. Wages and taxes are too high; turnover is necessary; we have it much better than before. The tension between appearance and reality melts away and both merge in one rather pleasant feeling [OD 226].

It doesn't look like Marcuse will be driving his '57 Chevy down to Mel's Drive-In any time soon. Yet a careful reading of this passage reveals an important subtext: cars are not bad in and of themselves, but that they are one of the many products of industrial society that could be questioned and improved but are instead used to make people acquiesce to the powers that be. It is possible to ask for a better car, or wonder why cars aren't better, and in doing so critique the system in a small but important way while still using that car for transportation.

It is important to emphasize here that Marcuse saw no inherent evil in technology itself, instead viewing it as something of a misused tool with a great deal of potential freedom in the power technology gives man to escape from alienated labor. As the philosopher notes in "Liberation from the Affluent Society," the "technical and material resources for the realization of freedom are available" (183) because of technology. In the *Aesthetic Dimension*, the philosopher posits that the "radical possibilities of freedom" are "concretized in the emancipatory potential of technical progress" (27). In *Studies in Critical Philosophy*, Marcuse asserts that because of technological advances "the historical Subject appears capable of building a society in which the imperatives of self-preservation and growth can become the imperatives of freedom: reconciliation of necessity and liberty" (213). Automobiles, in and of themselves, in other words, are not the problem. The way that industrial society values them, however, is the best way to understand how industrial society engenders co-optation.

To understand the Marcusian critique of industrial society found in *American Graffiti*, then, we must look at the character that is the least invested in car culture. If we do this, we will find the one person who consistently—and somewhat successfully—questions the status quo by rising above the unfreedom of technologized consumer society and engaging in two-dimensional thought. That character is Curt, *American Graffiti*'s doppelganger of THX-1138 and the core of Lucas' revised Marcusian critique of industrial society.[18] As we will see, Curt seems curiously un-nostalgic because he is gradually placing himself in opposition to a system that everyone else embraces. The best place to appreciate Curt's gradual distancing from the cage that is popular youth culture is his relationship with the automobile.

At first glance, all of the male characters in *American Graffiti* are defined by their relationship, or lack of a relationship, with an automobile. Although Terry the Toad ineptly rides a small Vespa scooter, he spends most of the film pretending that Steve's car is his and lying about the other automobiles he owns. Obviously, Milner's identity is intertwined with, if not completely defined by, his Deuce Coup. Steve's relationship with his Impala becomes clear as he recites instructions for its care to Terry as he prepares to turn this beloved object over to his friend for a semester. In short, each of these young men finds, as Marcuse would say, his soul "in his automobile" (9). Curt, however, does not. He drives what appears to be a Citroen 2CV, a car that, in the late 1950s and early 1960s, featured an engine with an output of 10 horsepower and a top speed of about 50 miles per hour. This is a stark technological contrast with Steve's 1958 Chevrolet Impala coupe which, when it left the assembly line, would have an engine making about 200 horsepower, though Steve's car has obviously been modified and may very well have a much more potent powerplant. Sitting next to the hulking and gleaming American cars in the parking lot of Mel's, Curt's Citroen looks as ridiculous as Terry's Vespa. Yet Curt, unlike Terry, does not seem to feel any less of a person because his car is barely capable of maintaining highway speeds. Instead, his choice of transportation and his lack of concern about the social implications of that choice reveal his ability to casually place himself outside the widely-shared assumption of his social circle that equates manhood with horsepower.

This ability to distance himself calmly yet effectively from prevailing assumptions, while at the same time enjoying the technological advantage that automobiles provide, emerges in almost every scene Curt is in, and it is this ability to engage in Marcusian two-dimensional thought without seeming like a paranoid or a killjoy, that allows him to critique a popular culture that is the product and promoter of industrial society without alienating the film's viewers. Indeed, viewers are most likely rooting for him when, at the end of the film, he climbs aboard a Magic Carpet Airlines flight and escapes his cage by flying into a rising, and not a setting, sun. It would also not be too much of a stretch to imagine that most audience members were sympathetic when they read during the closing credits that Curt had become a writer, a position of possible social critique that would also allow him to engage in the kind of fulfilling work Marcuse hints at in *Eros and Civilization* when he argues that there "is an unbroken ascent in erotic fulfillment from the corporeal love of one to that of the others to the love of beautiful work and play" and ultimately "to the love of beautiful knowledge" (EC 193). As proof of his status as someone who has fled false needs to find fulfillment in beautiful knowledge, the credits inform viewers that Kurt had fled to Canada during the Vietnam war—perhaps the most grotesque example of industrial society creating a false need that engendered one-dimensional thought.

If we keep in mind that a critical distance from technology is an important part of *American Graffiti*'s critique of the false needs and one-dimensional thought created by industrial society, Curt emerges as a pattern for the Jedi's transcendence of technology—and therefore industrial society—in *A New Hope, The Empire Strikes Back*, and *Return of the Jedi* and as the antithesis of the seduction of the Jedi by technology—and therefore industrial society—in *The Phantom Menace, Attack of the Clones*, and *Revenge of the Sith*. Because of statements Lucas has made about the moral and instructive nature of the *Star Wars* films, it has been easy for critics like those cited above to construct those films as conservative in one way or another.[19] But morality and conservatism or reaction should not be so swiftly equated. Marcuse's critique, in its insistence on the primacy of the human soul over the products of industrial society, is deeply moral. According to Pollock, Lucas wanted to imbue his films with "the message that technology cannot replace mankind ... the human element must ultimately prevail" (138). As we will see below, Luke Skywalker's elevation of the human element above technology and Anakin Skywalker's envelopment by technology after the loss of his humanity are best understood in Marcusan terms.[20]

Initially, Luke is afflicted by one-dimensional thought. In one sense he is much like *American Graffiti*'s Steve: hot rodding around a small desert town—is a T-16 skyhopper so different from a '58 Impala?—and dreaming of escape. More disturbingly, however, Luke's dreams of escape involve going to the Imperial Academy to become, presumably, a TIE fighter pilot. A visual reference to THX's emergence from the underground city comes when Luke emerges from the underground garage to watch the twin suns set just before R2-D2's escape, suggesting that his own plans, at least at that point, are problematic. When destiny offers him a more oppositional way to leave Tatooine, however, he feels the kind of misgivings with questioning the status quo Lucas had previously depicted when THX asked LUH why she got him involved. When Obi-Wan Kenobi asks him to come with him on his quest to bring the Death Star plans to the Alliance and to begin his training as a Jedi, he initially protests that he can't because it would upset the status quo of his Uncle's farm and only agrees after his adoptive family is slaughtered by stormtroopers. He is not motivated by an intellectual critique of industrial society, but instead by a more viscerally felt—and more easily understood by audiences—desire to avenge Aunt Beru and Uncle Owen's deaths.

Luke's journey initially seems like the kind of supercharged adventure that a would-be fighter pilot would dream of: escaping Imperial pursuers by blasting out of a spaceport and jumping to hyperspace in a souped-up pirate starship, then rescuing a princess from a heavily armed space station followed by a successful assault on that same space station in a high-performance starfighter. Yet Luke's journey does much to change his perspective on technology and help him realize that it might not be wise to worship the products of industrial society. After witnessing the sobering aftermath of the destruction of Alderaan, Luke finds himself aboard the Death Star, whose stark interiors look very much like those of THX's underground city. After surviving the perils of this killing machine, and witnessing the death of his mentor Obi-won at the hands of the monstrous cyborg Darth Vader, Luke finds temporary safety at the Rebel base on Yavin 4, which is set in a dense jungle.

At this point it should be obvious that Lucas associates the Alliance—as much as possible for an organization that routinely employs starfighters and deep space combat ships—with the natural world. Unsurprisingly, this depiction dovetails neatly with Marcuse's contention that humanity is an integral part of nature, and, consequently, people find the greatest self-fulfillment when they are working with, and not against nature. In *Studies in Critical Philosophy* Marcuse posits that man "is not *in* nature; nature is not the *external* world into which he first has to come out of his own inwardness. Man *is* nature" (17). Consequently, "nature is ultimately not a limitation on or something alien outside him to which he, as something other, is subjected" (25). Because it is a depiction of the kind of technologically-enabled but not technology-worshiping society that would resonate with Marcuse's thought, then, The Alliance is less dependent on the products of industrial society and therefore better able to critique it and avoid the horrific excesses of the Empire.[21]

This critical distance from the products of industrial society is best illustrated by the climax of the film: Luke, who must feel a gleeful mastery of technology as veteran pilots compliment him for his "nice shooting" during the assault on the Death Star, switches off his targeting computer at the urging of the disembodied voice of Obi-Wan. He is then able to allow the Force—an Eros-like energy field that, as Yoda will soon tell Luke, life breeds and makes grow, and therefore a science fiction metaphor for the forces Marcuse hoped could hold industrial society in check—to guide him as he releases the torpedoes that will shatter the Empire's technological monstrosity.

In *The Empire Strikes Back* Luke becomes less and less of a fighter pilot, taking part in the battle on Hoth—flying out of another rebel base that is set in nature; though this time it is carved out of ice and not jungle—but then never flying another combat sortie. And during that mission Luke has as much success against the Imperial AT-ATs with his lightsaber as his snowspeeder. After this battle, Luke engages in Jedi training on Dagobah, which has massive life form readings but no cities or technology and where his X-wing spends a great deal of time at the bottom of a swamp. Here he meets a chastened Yoda—more on that below—who instructs him in the ways of the Force, primarily by having Luke test his physical abilities against the harsh, swampy wilderness. This is a subtle but important contrast to the Jedi training that Yoda performed before the rise of the Empire in the Jedi temple on Coruscant—a planetwide city featuring every technological convenience as well as an ultimately successful plot against the Jedi by a resurgent Sith—that is best understood by a turn to Marcuse.

In "The Realms of Freedom" Marcuse argues that the "instinctual root of freedom in the individual would generate a biological need for silence, solitude, peace: a need for the beautiful and the pleasant" (24). After viewing all six films, it would be natural to see Yoda's state as fallen. He has, after all, moved from the center to the periphery of political power and civilization and Luke at first does not believe that the small green creature before him could be a great Jedi master. Yet Yoda, after the grave errors he makes in the first three films because he is blinded by his seat at the center of power, has found solitude and peace, along with what probably could be construed as pleasant and beautiful for a being with his biology. The freedom that Dagobah gives him makes him a much more formidable opponent for the dark side than the manufactured comfort of Coruscant.

That Yoda's efforts to get Luke to rely on the Force are also an attempt to encourage him to critique technology become apparent when his apprentice enters a cave under a tree that is strong in the Dark Side of the Force. Yoda tells his pupil that he will not need his weapons, but Luke ignores his mentor. While in the tree, the future Jedi has a vision of a lightsaber duel with Darth Vader. At the end of the struggle, Luke beheads Vader, only to reveal his own face staring up at him from the detached helmet. At this point, Luke should have learned that confronting technological monstrosities head-on with what you hope is superior technology will only lead to your envelopment in the soul-crushing built space of industrial society. But Luke does not understand the import of this vision, so when he discerns that his friends are menaced by Vader he sets off to save them, ignoring Yoda's protests and once again thinking one-dimensionally. He brings along the weapons that cannot help him transcend the Dark Side. In a battle significantly set in a city floating in the clouds, Vader tells Luke that he is his father and offers him the chance to overcome the Emperor and rule the universe as father and son. While Luke's rejection of the dark technological empire Vader offers signals the degree to which he has embraced Yoda's teachings, he does loses his hand, which is replaced by a robotic prosthesis, in the struggle. Thus he becomes less human, heightening his fears that he is to become like his father.

At the beginning of *Return of the Jedi*, Luke seems to have learned his lesson. When he confronts Jabba the Hutt over the return of Han Solo, he does so unarmed and offering to purchase his friend's release, only resorting to lightsabers and blasters when those negotiations fail. After learning from a dying Yoda that he had indeed become a Jedi Knight, however, Luke seems to fall back into old habits. He volunteers to go with Han and Leia to destroy a shield generator on Endor's forest moon so that the alliance can destroy the Empire's second Death Star. While on the moon, Luke participates in a speeder bike battle against Imperial scouts and prepares for the impending attack. But Luke abandons a role not entirely unlike the one he played in the destruction of the first Death Star when he leaves his comrades behind after realizing that Vader can sense his presence and that he is therefore threatening the success of the mission.

By rejecting his role as space commando, Luke sets up a confrontation that will ultimately demonstrate that he understands what Yoda was trying to teach him better than the venerable Jedi Master himself. Luke does not want to kill Vader, even though Obi-Wan and Yoda, who believe their former friend is irredeemably evil, seem to want him to. In this, the two Jedi masters are thinking like the Emperor, who tells Vader that Luke's "compassion for" his father "will be his undoing" and who is confident that the conversion or destruction of Luke will erase the Jedi from the Galaxy. They all see the confrontation one-dimensionally: kill or be killed. Violently seize control of the technologically monstrous Empire or be destroyed by it. Luke, however, knows that his only hope lies in the human connections that predate and therefore transcend industrial society, in a turn to a Marcusian Eros evidenced by a powerful devotion to life. He believes that if his father can truly see him as his son, he will stop being the evil cyborg Darth Vader. Of course, this is not an easy task and for a time, it looks like Luke will give in to the Dark Side and destroy his father. In an almost Jamesian renunciation—if Henry James had ever written space operas—of technology, however, Luke eventually abandons his lightsaber, even though he has just used it to defeat Vader, and instead uses his human connection to whatever is left of Anakin to encourage him to save his son and in so doing to defeat the Emperor. Here, it is significant that Anakin does not use a weapon to destroy Palpatine, instead throwing his former master into the Death Star's reactor core.

While such an act of renunciation may superficially resemble other refusals of social expectations in literature, Luke's rejection of one-dimensional violence and Thanatos on the new Death Star has a specifically Marcusian sense. Julka argues that Marcuse's "negative dialectics is linked up with his concept of the great refusal, a complete transcendence of one-dimensional society" (15). This concept of the revolutionary power of refusal can easily be found in the philosopher's work. For example, in *Studies in Critical Philosophy*, Marcuse argues that "the revolutionary imperative assumes the form of a negation: to reject the needs and values which increase the social wealth while strengthening 'voluntary servitude' among the privileged populations of the metroples" (221). In *Eros and Civilization* Marcuse offers that the "Great Refusal is the protest against unnecessary repression" (136). Luke's humane appeal to Eros rather than to his skill with a lightsaber and the seductive Thanatos of Emperor Palpatine represent a brilliant illustration of the power of Marcusian refusal for a mass audience.

Luke's journey from an immature speeder jockey on Tatooine who cannot see beyond the Imperial Academy to the calm and humane individual who fully transcends his reliance on the goods of industrial society above Endor's forest moon finds a surprising parallel in the transformation of Han Solo. The smuggler initially appears, as Marcuse might say, to finds his soul in the "hot rod" that is the *Millennium Falcon*, which he believes to be one of the fastest ships in the Galaxy.[22] In some ways, Han is much like Anakin Skywalker, who, according to J.J. Abrams, will eventually become Han's father-in-law: both are arrogant hotrodders whose overreliance on technology leads to their being either literally or metaphorically frozen in metal. Han's path leads away from Anakin's, however, because much like Luke, he learns to think outside the one-dimensional claim by industrial society that technology solves all problems. In *The Empire Strikes Back*, the mighty *Millennium Falcon*, the storied ship that saved Luke from Vader so that he could destroy the first Death Star, repeatedly breaks down. Han's inability to fix the hyperdrive is so chronic that it becomes a source of humor, at one point prompting Leia to ask if it would "help if" she "got out and pushed." Although Han finally escapes the Imperial star destroyers by hiding in the trash they dump before they jump into hyperspace and limping to Bespin, he finds no shelter in his friend Lando Calrissian's technologically astounding city. Boba Fett is waiting in the cloud city to freeze Han in carbonite and return him to Jabba the Hutt.

Having learned the hard way that technology, however powerful, cannot solve all of your problems, Han lets Lando fly the Falcon during the assault on the second Death Star featured in *Return of the Jedi*. Instead, Han volunteers to lead the decidedly more low-tech mission to Endor's forest moon designed to destroy the shield generator protecting the new Death Star. Unlike Luke, Han does not completely abandon hi-tech weaponry and use human feeling to bring the shield down. But though he does lead with his blaster, Han's participation in the battle on the forest moon needs to be understood in terms of the way *Return of the Jedi* visually invokes the Vietnam War, clearly one of the most pernicious excesses of the industrial society Marcuse wrote against. It has been noted that the Jedi are often aided by more primitive species in their successful and legitimate battles against evil,[23] but on Endor's forest moon that aid was depicted in a way that should have been familiar to anyone who was paying attention to America's then-most-recent imperial conflict. During that war, the Viet Cong harassed American troops with many different primitive booby traps. Some of the more common were punji sticks, sharpened sections of bamboo driven into the ground and then smeared with excrement so that wounds would quickly become infected, and toe poppers, bullets buried just below the ground that would be driven into nails and made to fire by the tread of GI's boots. There were also numerous tripwire devices that would make weapons fire or cause bamboo logs to come crashing down on the heads of American soldiers. While these devices rarely killed anyone, they also did much to hinder combat operations and could not have been beneficial for American morale. Undoubtedly, these booby traps furthered the Viet Cong's agenda of slowly wearing down the American will to fight.

While shots of Imperial shuttles hovering like helicopters over a landing zone cleared of dense vegetation serve as an immediate visual link with American troops in Vietnam, the tactics of the Ewoks leave little doubt what historical allusion Lucas is making. The first Ewok Leia meets stabs the stormtrooper who is trying to arrest her in the leg. While there were no punji sticks or toe poppers on display, audiences do see the Ewoks employing primitive booby traps to harass and sometimes kill what the Emperor calls "my best troops" during the battle for the shield generator. Interestingly, in most of the battle scenes, tripping and tripwires are a common motif. Many times a heavily armed but ultimately unstable two-legged AT-ST becomes tangled in wires or wobbles over logs or boulders tied together with rope—a hyperbolic recreation of the well-equipped and well-trained GIs who were felled by shit-smeared sticks. Of course, the Ewoks, much like the Viet Cong, are clearly outgunned and many of them die. Indeed, the battle on Endor's moon is actually won when Chewbacca steals an AT-ST and guns down unsuspecting imperials and Han tricks the imperials still inside the command bunker into believing that the conflict has been won. Yet Han's successful participation on the side of primitive warriors—warriors whose success against far better equipped foes resonates well with Marcuse's contentions that individuals do their best work when they are in harmony with nature—demonstrates how far he has come from the days when he believed that he could solve all his problems by jumping to hyperspace. Unlike the Pentagon, Han has learned that pushing a button and deploying overwhelming technology is not always the best tactic.

If the first theatrically released trilogy depicts Luke and Han moving away from their false need for technology and beginning to think more two-dimensionally, the prequel trilogy portrays Anakin and the rest of the Jedi believing more and more that they need the products of industrial society and thinking in more and more one-dimensional terms. As noted above, when we meet young Anakin on Tatooine in 1999's *The Phantom Menace*, he is tied to technology: a mechanic who can "fix anything" and who builds C-3PO when still a boy, a hotrodder who is the only human capable of competing in the pod races held on his home planet. He is offered a chance to transcend his need for technological gadgets and begin to think two-dimensionally, however, when he finds a mentor in Qui-Gon Jinn, a Jedi who is not put on the Jedi Council because he does not "follow the code." While this may at first seem to be a negative trait, it becomes apparent in the later films that the Jedi have lost their ability to think critically about industrial society and have succumbed to its technological Dark Side. Qui-Gon's oppositional pose is an indication of Marcusian refusal, a move that will turn out, in sad retrospect, to have been the correct one.

In addition to Qui-Gon's refusal of one-dimensional thought, *The Phantom Menace* is also Marcusian in its continuation of the theme of "primitive" resistance to aggressive and imperialistic technology. Although there are subplots involving freeing Anakin from slavery on Tatooine and political intrigue on Coruscant, the film centers on a Trade Federation invasion of Naboo. During the attack we see the Gungans, original inhabitants of the planet whom the Viceroy of the Trade Federation refers to as primitives, running from the Trade Federation's all-robot army as it smashes trees and otherwise disrupts the natural world. Although Qui-Gon and Obi-Wan are sent to protect the human inhabitants of the planet, they join forces with the Gungans, who live in an environment that is both natural—organically shaped dwellings under the sea—and high tech—the dwellings are protected by air bubbles created by energy shields. Although the human inhabitants of Naboo, led by Queen

Amidala, also resist the Trade Federation, Gungan troops carry the brunt of battle after Qui-gon helps the Naboo apologize for centuries of prejudice.[24]

During the confrontation with the Trade Federation's robot army, the Gungans employ energy balls that they roll towards the advancing automata and other higher-tech versions of the Ewok's armaments. Like the Ewoks, the Gungans do not win the battle, but instead contribute to the victory by buying time while Naboo security forces attack the Trade Federation's command ship in orbit above their planet and Qui-gon and Obi-won attempt to capture the Viceroy. Young Anakin, hiding in a Naboo fighter, accidentally starts the craft and then joins the battle, using his nascent skill with the Force and starfighters to bring down the command ship and deactivate the attacking robots. Though implausible on the surface, the bravery and skill of the Gungan warriors combined with the playful nature of Anakin's piloting once again argue that formidable technology can be bested by something other than even more formidable technology. Instead, valor and childlike curiosity—things that call to mind Marcuse's contention that Eros makes work into play—can win the day.

Unfortunately, Anakin is not to be trained by Qui-gong, who is killed by Darth Maul during the battle on Naboo. Anakin's training is instead entrusted to Obi-Wan Kenobi, whose limitations become all too apparent in 2002's *Attack of the Clones*. After a dart kills an assassin who makes an attempt on Senator Amidala's life, Obi Wan asks Dex, a well-connected diner owner on Coruscant, to identify the makers of the dart. Dex quickly traces it to Kamino and then playfully scolds Obi Wan for relying on his droid in his initial attempt to identify the projectile, remarking that "you Jedi should have more respect for the difference between knowledge and wisdom." When Obi-Wan later visits the Jedi archives and cannot find a record of Kamino, an archivist sternly intones that "if an item does not appear in our records, it does not exist." The Jedi younglings, however, quickly find the planet via the force and Yoda remarks that a "wonderful thing is the mind of a child."[25] Like Anakin on Naboo, and unlike the thoroughly one-dimensional Jedi archivist, the younglings can think two-dimensionally because they are free from a dependence on technology that borders on worship.

Obi-Wan's mind is not as flexible, however, as events on Kamino illustrate. The Jedi detective finds a mysteriously placed order for a clone army. The clones are designed to be totally obedient and without individuality, standardized for ease of command and outfitting, and are produced in a city filled with clone fetuses in bottles moving through a production line in a clear visual reference to the scenes of cloned reproduction in *THX*. The Kaminoans also live in starkly white interiors reminiscent of *THX*'s underground city. Nevertheless, Obi-Wan is not really troubled by the clones per se and can only wonder why Sifo-Dyas ordered them in the first place.

Since the clone army exists, the Jedi Council decides that they need to use them to rescue Anakin, Obi-Wan, and Senator Amidala from the Trade Federation armament factory on Geonosis. Unsurprisingly, the clones fight well, swooping down out of the skies in open-sided aircraft with door gunners that deposit troops in the middle of battle—eerily recalling not only the armaments but the tactics of the American army in Vietnam. Many Jedi are initially taken in by this military prowess, including Obi-Wan, who observes that without the clones, it would not have been a victory. Yoda is not fooled, however, responding to the younger Jedi by questioning his use of the word "victory" and then predicting that "the shroud of the Dark Side has fallen."

The Dark Side is falling because the Jedi, in the throes of a false need, are turning to a repressive technology that the Force should make unnecessary. As Anne Lancashire has noted,

> The visual image of Yoda commanding stormtroopers on Geonosis works together with the film's final image of the Republic's Chancellor on Coruscant at (significantly) sunset, overseeing the gathering totalitarian army, as an indicator of how far the democratic republic and its leaders have fallen toward imperial dictatorship [245].

The Republic has fallen towards empire because of the Jedi's false need for technological wonders like the clone army. Given this context, it is unsurprising that someone like Anakin, who remarks to Padme while working on the machines in his stepbrother Owen's garage that "life seems so much simpler when you are fixing things," begins openly advocating for a dictatorship.

When 2005's *Revenge of the Sith* opens, viewers finally realize what Princess Leia means when she calls Obi-wan General Kenobi: he commanded a legion of stormtroopers[26] during the Clone Wars. For several years the Jedi have been fighting alongside the clones, and their thorough integration with this technological monstrosity is amply illustrated by scenes of the Jedi Council receiving reports from Commander Cody, the clone leader of the clone army, or receiving reports of Jedi masters moving clone troops after a successful siege. Yoda's plan to take a battalion of clones to fight with the Wookies further illustrates the Jedi's cooptation. It has been argued that in the second trilogy, "the Force is a highly institutionalized ... tool of the cultural elite" (Vinci 19), and *Revenge of the Sith* makes it clear that that institutionalization comes because of the Force's subservience to the technological wonders of industrial society. When Darth Sidious finally launches his putsch against the Jedi and the clones turn on their commanders and kill them, the Jedi are almost universally taken by surprise because their false need for the clones had blinded them to the genuine peril they were in.

As noted above, the triumph of industrial society over the more humane power of the Force also leads to a political dictatorship with the broad consent of the governed. Both Sith anoint their fully articulated unfreedom and

Thanatos as an unqualified good, with Vader boasting that he has "brought peace, freedom, and security to my new empire," and the Emperor proclaiming that "once more the Sith shall rule the galaxy and we shall have peace." Vader and Palpatine will deliver the goods of security and technological progress in their new order, and all the inhabitants of their Empire need to give up is the ability to question the wisdom of this arrangement. Yoda, fully sensing the magnitude of his defeat after losing a lightsaber duel with the Emperor, sadly intones, "Into exile I must go. I have failed." He has not simply failed to defeat Darth Sidious, however, but has failed to value the Force over the ease and convenience of the technological wonders produced by industrial society.

While it cannot be denied that the strident critique of industrial society found in *THX-1138* had been muted and attenuated in the three and a half decades between its release and that of *Revenge of the Sith*, it should also be clear that Lucas did not completely abandon his critical project for commercial success. Instead, his Marcusian critique remains and, perhaps, is all the more powerful because it is enclosed in a more commercially appealing package that has penetrated popular culture so deeply. By turning to teen nostalgia and then more accessible science fiction and by abandoning the paralyzing contention that we cannot help but be enslaved by industrial society for the more hopeful contention that our humanity just might save us from industrial society, Lucas found a way to deliver his critique sideways. Luke Skywalker's redemption of his father Anakin by means of his love for him is melodramatic and underscored by a calculating sentimentalism. But it is a sentimentalism that, in its privileging of genuine and unruly human emotions over the cold rationality of industrial society, in its privileging of Eros over Thanatos, would have perhaps made even Marcuse hopeful.

If there is one key aspect of Lucas narrative that mutes the force of its Marcusian critique, however, it is a setting "a long time ago in a galaxy far, far away." While all science fiction requires suspension of disbelief, such a setting can signal inattentive audience members that they are enjoying a fairy tale that has no application to contemporary life. It also allows attentive critics working from a mythopoetic perspective a valid reason to see the narrative as primarily archetypal. Ridley Scott's 1979 *Alien*, the next science fiction blockbuster to employ Marcusian social critique, employs a setting that is much more resonant with its audiences' lived experience. As we will see in the next chapter, Scott's film does this by means of its perfection of the concept of the apparently evil corporation, a masterful depiction of the excesses of industrial society taken to their logical extreme.

*Chapter 4*

# Ridley Scott Takes On Apparently Evil Corporations in *Alien*, *Blade Runner* and *Prometheus*

After George Lucas brought Marcusian critique to the summer blockbuster obliquely with *American Graffiti* and then more directly with *Star Wars*, the extra, Marcusian critical element he added did not go unnoticed by other directors. One of the first to follow in Lucas' thematic footsteps was Ridley Scott who, along with his collaborators Dan O'Bannon and Ronald Schusett, brought a Marcusian reading of society hidden inside a blockbuster to the screen two years after *Star Wars*. And while the Marcusian elements of Scott's work may be a case of two thinkers drawing similar conclusions about society, it is clear that Scott was directly influenced by Lucas' film. According to Brian J. Robb, Scott was so taken with the first modern science-fiction blockbuster that he saw *A New Hope* three days in a row (24). Furthermore, in an interview with James Delson, Scott notes that Lucas' film "changed my whole attitude about certain types of cinema" (28) and indicates that he had been paying attention to Lucas' work when he called *THX-1138* "a very nice way to do *1984*" (15).

*Alien*, of course, is clearly not derivative of *Star Wars* in terms of plot, setting, or characters. It does, however, critique society in Marcusian terms, and this critique appears to both continue and broaden the one in Lucas' films. Most importantly, Scott improves the directness of his critique by adding the extra element of what we can somewhat imprecisely call the apparently evil corporation. Lucas' metaphorical ties between a galactic empire that had gone over to the "dark side" of "the force" and industrial society allows for other interpretations that obscured the link between Lucas' tale and a critique of contemporary society. Scott's decision to portray the Weyland-Yutani Corporation as a secondary antagonist in *Alien* and then the Tyrell corporation as the secondary antagonist in *Blade Runner* insured that critics and filmgoers alike would understand that Scott was, as Thomas B. Byers, remarks, warning "us against a capitalist future gone wrong," where a "quite literal dehumanization has become perhaps the gravest danger" (39). Furthermore, Scott's use of corporate antagonists makes his critique clear even to viewers who were more taken with, say, *Alien*'s meditation on gender and reproduction or *Blade Runner*'s exploration of the complicated boundaries between humans and synthetic humans.

Yet it is interesting that Scott would choose a direct, indeed almost strident, critique of late capitalist culture as the extra element he would add to the space monster tale already familiar in science fiction. After all, Scott worked for over a decade making commercials before he began his career as a filmmaker and then never completely abandoned advertising; he even founded an advertising agency that is still in business. He has made commercials for multinationals like Ford, Nissan, and Pepsi. He made an antideficit advertisement for perpetual asbestos lawsuit defendant and chemical company W.R. Grace. He has been described by film scholars Laurence F. Knapp and Andrea F. Kulas as "resolutely moderate in his politics" (xiii). And his most memorable commercials—the Chanel perfume "share the fantasy" spot and the *1984*-themed ad for Apple Computer—were made around the same time *Alien* and *Blade Runner* were released. Furthermore, Scott has been successful with narratives that fall far outside the boundaries of science fiction, including the 1991 feminist road picture *Thelma and Louise*, the 2000 sword-and-sandals epic *Gladiator* and the 2003 con-man tale *Matchstick Men*. For a time it appeared that the speculative fiction of his early career was merely one of the many genres to be found on Scott's CV and the critique of the impact of self-interested corporations on society was simply the thematic atmospherics he brought to that genre. It would be very easy to portray Scott as a man of corporate sympathies who occasionally dabbled in films with seemingly radical politics—if he thought those themes would bring in good box office.

Yet it would also be plausible to suggest that Scott's time as corporate propagandist lead him to formulate a critique of industrial society that is much like Marcuse's; that Scott is much more of a whistleblower than a sellout. The director has made many statements that suggest a Marcusian engagement with industrial society. In an interview with Harlan Kennedy, for example, he worried that "large combines in the next few decades" might "become almost as powerful as government" (36), leading to, as the director told Danny Peary, a totalitarian "world controlled by a handful of corporations" (49) because of the affective influence of industrial society. In the same interview, Scott expresses fears of a society marked by "the Big Brother idea of a lifeless megastructure" that would feature a callous disregard for its "human employees"

(45) and, echoing Marcuse's discussion of the performance principle, claims that "the industrial-government complex is responsible for the attitude that allows such an alien to be brought on board the *Nostromo*" (46).

In light of Scott's decades-long abandonment of the themes of *Alien* and *Blade Runner*, the above comments could be seen as occasional remarks designed to explain specific projects. In *Prometheus*, the prequel—cum—reboot to *Alien* that opened 30 years after *Blade Runner*, however, Scott brought back the Weyland-Yutani Corporation as secondary antagonist in the person of one of its founders, Peter Weyland and in doing so further refocused the critique of the apparently evil corporation that he had brought to popular culture. Indeed, the director's return to this trope helps convince us that in his three science fiction films—1979's *Alien*, 1982's *Blade Runner*, and 2012's *Prometheus*—he uses the Weyland-Yutani or Weyland or Tyrell corporation not only to critique contemporary capitalism but also to help delineate the place of corporations and corporate leaders in industrial society. Furthermore, by gradually shifting focus away from a monolithic "company" and towards the man who created that monolithic company, Scott can explore Marcuse's concept of Eros. As we will see below, then, while Scott clearly focuses on additional issues, his continual use of corporate antagonists helps his blockbuster science fiction films critique society by means of their extra elements of popularized Marcusian critique.

It is important to use the qualifier "apparently" when discussing the evil corporations Scott presents because while *Alien* depicts the Weyland-Yutani corporation as the malevolent shadow to the xenomorph's menacing physical presence, *Blade Runner* and *Prometheus* present an increasingly nuanced depiction of the leaders of the apparently evil corporations and in so doing shifts blame for the condition of society away from the legal entities created to conduct business and towards the repressive system that happens to feature legal entities created to do business. In contrast to the depersonalized Anglo-Asian transnational, or perhaps transgalactic, conglomerate that sacrifices the crew of the *Nostromo*, both *Blade Runner* and *Prometheus* present the founder of the corporate antagonist as a less-than-omnipotent being who ultimately dies because they incorrectly assess their place in the universe. Both films also depict company-built men and women who are not evil tools like *Alien*'s Ash but creatures suffering existential doubts that allow them to stand metaphorically for the company men and women we all are. These relatively humanizing portrayals, while perhaps not surprising in a director who has at least indirectly worked for charismatic yet controlling corporate innovators like Apple's Steve Jobs, in turn argue that the evil is not located in the creator of the corporation or the corporation itself, but in the pressure industrial society places on business entities to live up to the performance principle and be profitable. Their evil behavior, in other words, is business as usual in industrial society, and that is the problem. In order to trace this gradually-refining critique of corporations in industrial society, however, we need to begin with Scott's least-nuanced portrayal of the apparently evil corporation in *Alien*. In this film, Scott gives us a two-dimensional heroine who overcomes the one-dimensional thought demanded by the apparently evil Weyland-Yutani Corporation.

With a worldwide, inflation-adjusted gross of approximately $325 million on an inflation-adjusted budget of $34 million, *Alien* was clearly the kind of blockbuster—both in absolute terms and in terms of return on investment—that studio accountants love. As de Certeau would suggest, and as we have seen in Chapter 2, *Alien* was able to sell so many tickets in part because of its successful reworking of other popular tales or elements from other popular genres. Film scholars Francois Guerif and Alain Garel Scott find this ability unsurprising in someone who "comes from the set-dressing of commercials" (56) and is therefore adept at recycling culture, but as we will see, the most important recycling in *Alien* is occurring at the thematic and critical level, and not at the level of plot.

In Chapter 2, we discussed *Alien*'s debt to *The Voyage of the Space Beagle* and *It! The Terror from Space*. Scott's film also draws plot and visual elements from 1965's *Planet of the Vampires*, a film with strong parallels to *It!*, which means it also draws from *Space Beagle*. As in *It!*, the astronauts aboard the Argos and the Galliot respond to a distress call but instead find a planet inhabited by a dying race of "vampires"; in this case, beings consisting of pure thought who can reanimate corpses. The indigenous inhabitants of the planet Aura also use their psychic power to encourage the crews of the two ships to fight amongst each other, much like the alien race in the "War of Nerves" section of *Space Beagle* that uses telepathy to cause the crew of the Beagle to fight with each other. *Vampires* director Mario Bava provides a clear visual antecedent to *Aliens* in a scene where two astronauts from the Argos enter a crashed ship of unknown origin, finding the enormous skeletons of its clearly nonhuman crew, and provides a visual and aural antecedent to *Prometheus* when his astronauts discover that the alien crew used sound to control some of their instruments. Interestingly, the extra element Bava adds to the familiar tale he is retelling is the surprise ending that reveals that his astronauts are not actually from Earth, but nevertheless wind up crash landing here after they have been possessed by the Aurans.

It's clear, then, that there were several popular tales about ships finding menacing creatures on derelict planets that *Alien* drew inspiration from. Indeed, the film's genealogy adds weight to Harvey R. Greenburg's assertion that "*Alien* harkens back to the malignant conception of unearthly life found in fifties science fiction" because during the late 1970s American society was as beset by fear and paranoia as it was in the 1950s ("Gargoyle" 87). Yet it's also clear that each tale has its own unique twist, an extra element added to differentiate it from similar tales and address contemporary concerns: *Space Beagle* employed the fictive science of Nexialism to address fears of hyper-specialization, *It!* presented a typical cold-war American film's argument to trust the government, and *Vampires*, an Italian production featuring stars from America, Brazil, and Spain, seeks to playfully disrupt assumptions about where self-assured astronauts come from. In each iteration before *Alien*, however, the mission was not funded by a corporation, nor was it initially a routine delivery of an unremarkable-for-the-imagined-context cargo. Instead, the missions are at least implicitly funded by governmental agencies for the purpose of exploration. In *Vampires*, for example, we learn that the bogus distress call had been heard for two years, and that they had gone to investigate in hopes of finding alien life. Scott's extra element was presenting a quotidian version of space travel sponsored by a for-profit corporation.

Like *It!* and *Planet of the Vampires*, *Alien* also borrows from horror texts—indeed, it was famously marketed by movie posters featuring the tagline "in space no one can hear you scream." This hybridity has also been noticed by several mainstream film critics who claim or strongly imply that the film belongs squarely in the horror genre. For example, Salon.com's Andrew O'Heir, reviewing the 2003 director's cut, fondly reminisces that "few horror movies I've seen before or since that ever manage to capture such a tangible feeling of menace." Roger Ebert more explicitly notes that "at its most fundamental level, *Alien* is a movie about things that can jump out of the dark and kill you," while the *New York Times*' Vincent Canby's review calls the original release "an old-fashioned scare movie about something that is not only implacably evil but prone to jumping out at you when … you least expect it. There was once a time when this sort of thing was set in an old dark house, on a moor, in a thunderstorm. Being trendy, Mr. Scott and his associates have sent it up in space."

*Alien* is scary even by today's standards, though its interstellar setting is not mere trendiness, but instead a deliberately chosen employment of a genre—science fiction—that allows the film to function as a complex meditation on technologized society in a way that a tale set in a haunted, storm-lashed houses never could. What Canby sees as setting the film in space to cash in on the demand for science fiction created by *A New Hope*, in other words, is an extra element Scott adds that allows gothic horror to go beyond its customary meditation on topics like gender roles and interfamilial tension and also critique the impact of industrial society on humanity. This thematically overdetermined film is not merely a genre hybrid, in other words, but is also—and perhaps is best understood as—an exercise in hybridizing cultural critique.

As our discussion of *Alien³* and *Alien Resurrection* in Chapter 2 noted, critics tend to focus on the extra element of gender and reproduction that

Scott and later directors added to source tales like *Space Beagle* and *It!* Similarly, many critics who discuss *Alien* center on issues of gender and motherhood.[1] And given Freud's fascination with familial dynamics, psychoanalytic critics have also created readings focusing on the film's portrayal of metaphorical mothers and families.[2] Unlike the mainstream film reviewers who want to imply or argue that *Alien* is really a horror movie, however, I do not wish to imply or argue that *Alien* is "really" about life in technologized societies. Instead, I will here stipulate that the film adds extra elements dealing with the gender and psychological issues surrounding birth, motherhood, and empowered women to a familiar tale about a creature menacing a spaceship. After all, psychoanalytic critics freely admit that the film is also about life within a corporate culture that is remarkably like our own. For example, Krin Gabbard, working from a Kleinian perspective, suggests that *Alien* "associates early developmental anxieties with the impotence of the individual in the modern corporate state" (32).

Of course, *Alien*'s examination of its characters' status as employees of an apparently greedy and manipulative corporation opens up critical avenues beyond the psychoanalytic. These thematic strands represent additional extra elements Scott, O'Bannon, and Schusett added to the material they reworked to create the film. *Alien*, which largely plays out on the *Nostromo*, a commercial towing ship pulling an ore refinery, is clearly set in a proletarian landscape. Roger Ebert's review helps us understand the *Nostromo*'s status as a workplace when it notes that the actor's ages ranged from 29 to 53. By featuring individuals who skewed older than audience expectations, according to Ebert, "*Alien* achieves a certain texture without even making a point of it: These are not adventurers but workers, hired by a company to return 20 million tons of ore to Earth." Greenburg, who believes Scott's film is an "artistic derivative" of the depredations of capitalism ("Gargoyle" 107) nevertheless provides support for Ebert's observation when he argues that the *Nostromo* is crewed by the kind of people "one would find aboard a similar vessel in ancient Phoenicia or the East India Trade" ("Gargoyle" 91). Scott himself was very aware of the thematic implications of focusing on "truckers in space" (28), according to Brian Robb, and deliberately depicts the *Nostromo*'s "class divisions" and "political machinations" (26).

The workaday world of the *Nostromo* is perhaps best illustrated in the scene where the ship lands on LV-426. There is very little to remind viewers of the excitement generated when Buzz Aldrin and Neal Armstrong descended to the surface of the moon in Apollo 11's lunar module. Instead, in this extended depiction of a starship landing on a planetoid that has not been visited before by humans, the crew displays all the excitement and wonder of air traffic controllers bringing a commuter flight from Cleveland into the Cincinnati airport.

The shopworn vibe the film creates becomes central to the plot before this descent, when engineers Parker and Brett balk at investigating a distress call. After some bickering, science officer Ash tells them that they are contractually obligated to investigate transmissions indicating intelligent life or suffer "total forfeiture of shares." Not only does this reject the bold posturing expected in a film about the exploration of a new planet, this is also a curious reshaping of the archetypical horror movie moment where at least someone in the party question the wisdom of going, in the middle of a rainstorm, into the dark abandoned house on the moor where all the killings happened a few years back. What is unique about this moment is that the recalcitrant members of the party are not cajoled or teased into going, but instead reminded of their professional duties and legal obligations, forcefully focusing the audience's attention on the fact that this is a film about people at work. And while *Alien* could not be a horror/sci-fi hybrid without the ill-advised trip to a dark corner of the galaxy, Ash's insistence introduces a new monster: the Weyland-Yutani Corporation. Often in horror films, the individuals who want to enter the abandoned house, dark woods, or other horror locus classicus are merely curious or looking for a place to have a good time. But Ash, as viewers soon find out, is deliberately sending his crewmates to their deaths so that Weyland-Yutani can hopefully acquire a new bioweapon and thus enable what Peter Lev has called "the Company's "pervasive pattern of oppression and paranoia" (33).

The thematic complexity of *Alien* and the film's nuanced portrayal of its worker-astronauts precludes a vulgar Marxist reading of the narrative's arguments about the workplace. As Ernst Larsen notes, Parker and Brett, though they voice the first critique of the Company's actions from the moment they awaken from cryosleep, are not presented as heroes of anyone's revolution, but instead as behaving "like all union employees are supposed to behave, in the most abrasive, reductive sense, with continual cracks about contracts, shares, overtime, and the Company" (web). *Alien*'s fully-articulated portrait of workplace dynamics instead invites a comparison to Marcuse's critique of industrial society, which sees individuals as both consumers and workers and argues that consent to oppressive social systems is often a function of the desire to enjoy the material goods generated by those social systems.[3]

Unsurprisingly, others have noted the link between *Alien* and Marcuse's thought. T.J. Matheson, for example, has argued that despite "frequent demonstration of an anti-corporate bias" the film belies Marcuse's optimism about the role of technology in society (329). Marcuse's critique of industrial society does more than express guarded and highly qualified optimism about the utopian potential of technology, however. It also, and more forcefully, suggests that critical thinking could triumph over the oppressive tendencies of technologized bureaucracy. Marcuse feared that advanced industrial society would triumph because of one-dimensional thought's refusal to question the status quo since "there is no reason to insist on self-determination if the administered life is the comfortable" life (OM 49). Implicit in this fear, however, is the hope that two dimensional thought, that questioning the status quo could be one of the tendencies capable of breaking the containment of industrial society. *Alien*'s portrayal of the workaday world of the *Nostromo* is Marcusian because it creates depictions of various types of workers engaged in varieties of one-dimensional thought that compel them to collaborate in their own destruction and then depicts a worker who thinks two dimensionally and who is able to escape—at least temporarily—from Weyland-Yutani's diabolical status quo. Before we turn our attention to Ripley, however, we should first look at the one-dimensional astronauts aboard the *Nostromo*, moving from the most to the least sympathetic.

As noted above, Parker and Brett are presented as working class questioners of the status quo, though in a way that links them to negative stereotypes about unionized workers. In addition to their initial reluctance to descend to the planet below, the two engineers continue their diatribe against the Company's unfairness while repairing the ship on surface of LV-426. Parker asks Brett if he "ever notices that" the deck officers "never come down here?" He then tells his co-worker that it's the same "reason we get half a share." As this exchange demonstrates, while Parker and Brett have an excellent point, they are motivated primarily by financial gain, and it is not much of a stretch to imagine that they dream of using any additional money to more fully participate in the comfortable life created by industrial society. In implicitly discrediting the proletarian argument against Weyland-Yutani and foreclosing a more typically Marxian solution to the worker's complaints, *Alien* provides an interesting echo of Marcuse's argument that the Sino-Soviet bloc and the capitalist nations both featured economic systems in which the "enslavement of man by the instruments of his labor continues in a highly rationalized and vastly efficient and promising form.... The more the rulers are capable of delivering the goods of consumption, the more firmly will the underlying population be tied to the various ruling bureaucracies" (OM 43). Parker and Brett do not want to seize control of the Weyland-Yutani Corporation; instead, they want to be bound more tightly to it by higher percentages.

In addition to workers constantly grumbling about the company, *Alien* features Captain Dallas as the reliable company man. Initially, Dallas' cautious, by-the-book approach seems conventionally moral and therefore understandable. For example, when Brett and Parker complain to him about their share of the revenue, Dallas replies that both will get what they "contracted for, just like everyone else." Yet later, after the alien is aboard and the ship is descending into chaos, Dallas tells Ripley that he cannot challenge company orders because he "just runs the ship" and because "standard procedure is to do what the hell" Weyland-Yutani tells "you to do." He also tells Ripley that since the Company wanted Ash to have the final word, he did not intervene when Ash let Kane back onto the ship after the facehugger attacked him. Dallas' inability to constructively critique what the Company tells him is made clear in the scene where he asks Mother, the ship's computer, how to kill the Alien or if there were any other options for dealing with the creature. The Captain is repeatedly told that his questions do not compute. Dallas can then only ask the computer what his chances are and glumly read the reply: "does not compute." Clearly, Dallas sees commanding the *Nostromo* as a one-dimensional activity—closely following company directives without questioning and with very little consideration. When there are no directives, he is lost. While Dallas' approach to the company probably explains why he is the Captain, following orders with punctilio—or, as Marcuse would say, engaging in one-dimensional thought—leaves you open to manipulation by ruling bureaucracies that may see you as an expendable means to an end.

And what of Science Officer Ash, the crewmember Dallas reflexively put so much trust in? While his status as villain is clear to the most casual viewer—in his efforts to provide Weyland-Yutani with a new bioweapon he, among other crimes, talks Parker out of killing the small chestburster as it emerges from Kane's corpse and later, after he has been found out, attempts to kill Ripley by choking her with a pornographic magazine. But from a Marcusian perspective, Ash, who admires the alien because "it is unclouded by delusions of morality," is perhaps even more monstrous than the xenomorph that menaces the crew of the *Nostromo*. Because he is an android, a man literally made by the company, he has been programmed to think one-dimensionally and cannot do otherwise. As he admits after Ripley and Parker reactivate him after they tear him apart for trying to kill Ripley, Ash was following a directive in which bringing back the alien was priority one and all other priorities—clearly crew safety and presumably the integrity of the cargo—were rescinded. His admiration of the alien's thoughtless predation is easily read as a stand-in both for his hardwired admiration of the Company, which is also not troubled by delusions of morality, and for one-dimensional thought in general, which is quite unclouded.

Initially, Ash is particularly dangerous because the crew does not know he is an android that must do as he has been programed, and therefore he is better able to influence them to think one-dimensionally. Yet for the surviving crew members, realizing that Ash was created by Weyland-Yutani specifically to deceive and endanger them allows them to truly think two-dimensionally about their relationship with the company and allows Ripley to reason that Ash was made their science officer because the Company wanted the alien for their bioweapons division. Interestingly, this moment of collective realization is visually depicted in the fight that precedes the science officer's unveiling. When Ash, built to resemble a white, middle-aged man, tries to kill Ripley and is unmasked as a replicant, he is depicted battling against two women and a man of African descent. Here, the film provides an arresting tableau of unruly human diversity conquering—however temporarily—synthetic conformity.

If Ash is both clearly a villain and implicitly a vehicle for a Marcusian critique of one-dimensional thought, then Warrant Officer and third-in-command Ellen Ripley is both clearly a hero—she ultimately defeats a superhumanly strong, agile, and vicious xenomorph in one-on-one combat, after all—and implicitly a champion of two-dimensional thought. If we think of Ripley as an employee and not as a female answer to Van Helsing, we can see she is portrayed from the beginning of *Alien* as someone who is situated in a complex position and who is therefore capable of grappling with clouded situations. As a warrant officer—typically a rank indicating specific technical expertise and inhabiting the border between the managerial commissioned officers and the non-commissioned officers in direct charge of personnel, she belongs both on the flight deck and below decks with the engineers who maintain the ship. Indeed, Parker and Brett even compliment her for being the only one who ever visits them as they work. Relatively high on the chain of command and yet familiar with the dirty work that keeps the ship operating, Ripley is a manager and a worker and therefore outside the paradigm required by a vulgar Marxist reading but in a position to develop the critical capacity necessary to a Marcusian reading.

Ripley's ability to reject the pressure to conform to the demands of the ruling bureaucracy is first highlighted at the end of the ill-fated expedition to the alien ship on the surface of LV-426. Even before anyone leaves the ship, Ripley ascertains that the "distress call" that brought them to the planet was actually a warning to stay away, though no one else thinks to disregard their orders from the Company. Once the landing party has met with misfortune inside the downed spacecraft, Ripley, who is in command of the *Nostromo* because Capitan Dallas and First Officer Kane left the ship, does not want to let Kane, clearly contaminated by exobiological matter, back into the *Nostromo* because it would be unwise and in clear violation of an anti-contamination policy. A tense argument ensues during which Captain Dallas angrily says, "When I give an order I expect it to be obeyed" and Ripley tartly replies, "Even when it's against the law?" While neither Dallas nor Ripley really wins the argument because Ash circumvents Ripley and lets the landing party back on the ship, this confrontation is key to understanding *Alien*'s Marcusian characterization of its workers. Company man Dallas is being consistent—he unthinkingly obeys Weyland-Yutani and therefore expects his subordinates to unthinkingly obey him. Ripley is growing concerned because she is being told to circumvent what she believes are ironclad policies and procedures.

Ripley's concern does not represent one-dimensional thought but rather the beginning of her questioning Weyland-Yutani's motives. Two-dimensional thought often begins with a question that essentially asks why the powerful appear to be saying two contradictory things.

Ripley's challenge to Dallas' decision represents her first step in seeing the Company for what it is. Admittedly, her willingness to leave an injured crewmate on the surface of a planetoid months from Earth may initially make her appear calloused, but the film soon demonstrates that Ripley's prescience makes her similar to horror-film characters who unsuccessfully argue that drinking beer in the basement of a haunted house might not be such a good idea after all. There is a deeper level that Ripley's refusal operates on, however, and this is indicated in part because *Alien* already gives us a character who makes reasonable observations about the stupidity of exploring haunted houses—on a moor or in space—in Lambert, the *Nostromo*'s navigator. When Lambert sees the corpse of what Scott would tell us 33 years later is an Engineer in the downed ship the landing party is investigating, her reaction is an entirely understandable "Let's get out of here." Braver audience members might smile at Lambert's cowardice, but none would see her attitude as beyond the pale. Ripley's refusal to allow an injured crewmate into the ship is much less understandable, however, because it involves a morally arguable decision. Indeed, in the director's cut, Lambert slaps Ripley because she wanted to leave Kane on the planet's surface, underlining the problematic nature of Ripley's decision. Nevertheless, the events of the film bear out Ripley's reading of the situation and imply that sometimes the unorthodox decision is the correct one. The implication here is similar to Marcuse's contention in *One-Dimensional Man* that often "the intellectual and emotional refusal 'to go along' appears neurotic and impotent" (9), though it is vital to providing a genuine critique of industrial society.

Of course, full vindication of Ripley's desire to quarantine Kane comes after the Xenomorph has killed Dallas and Kane and Ripley is in command. These dire circumstances, however, also trigger growth in Ripley's ability to employ two-dimensional thought. Though Ripley is clearly saddened at her commander's violent death, she soon tells Ash that, since she is now in command of the ship, she has access to Mother, the ship's computer, and she will get her own answers about the xenomorph. The new ship's commander aggressively questions Mother and, after being brushed off when she asks why Ash won't tell the crew how to kill the creature, discovers Special Order 937. This directive, designated for Ash's eyes only, reads, "Nostromo (sic) rerouted. Investigate life form. Gather Specimen. Priority one—insure return of organism for analysis. Crew expendable."

Clearly, this is a big reveal for audiences and therefore very important in helping the plot make sense. Special Order 937 also implicitly invokes the performance principle—Marcuse's contention that "society is stratified according to the competitive economic performance of its members" (ES 41)—when it suggests that capturing a xenomorph and returning it to Earth is far more valuable than the lives of the crew or, for that matter, the economic value of the *Nostromo*'s cargo, and this use of the performance principle casts a long shadow over subsequent iterations of the *Alien* narrative, as Chapter 2 argues. Yet here it is interesting to note how easy it is for Ripley to find this information—no hacking required, simply an emergency override command. The implication here is that Dallas could have easily found this all out if he had also invoked Emergency Command 100375. Dallas, however, seems to be constitutionally incapable of challenging the status quo—even in ways that are fully approved by the status quo—and therefore leads himself and most of his crew to their deaths.

True, Ripley finds out about Special Order 937 far too late to save anyone's life, but her discovery provides a utopian moment in a very bleak movie by demonstrating that a committed but thoughtful and questioning leader could have saved the *Nostromo*. Or, as Marcuse might say, *Alien* features a female who is a hero not simply because she defeats the xenomorph, but also because she helps us see that the human soul is capable, however briefly, of breaking the containment of a malevolent technological bureaucracy like the Weyland-Yutani Corporation.

At this point it is important to remember that Scott did not direct the sequel to *Alien* and had no direct involvement in a creative work set in the universe he helped create until 33 years later when *Prometheus* was released. Yet he did not leave the Marcusian critique of industrial society he created behind when he left *Alien* universe to other directors. In his next film, he retained the apparently evil corporation that was the fulcrum of his critique, though he gave it another name. Both companies, after all, felt that creating monsters would help their bottom line. Naturally, on the level of plot, *Blade Runner* is quite different from *Alien*. Yet in a sense, Scott's depiction of the Tyrell corporation's use of replicants to do the dirty work of colonizing implicitly explores what would happen if Weyland-Yutani had actually began mass-producing xenomorphs as bioweapons, making the impact on earth society obvious.

Differences in setting and plot, however, are important to the critiques each film presents. Where *Alien* depicted the apparent discovery of a valuable monster by an amoral corporation and in so doing allowed for a depiction of a two-dimensional worker critiquing that corporation's decision to take the performance principle to its logical conclusion, *Blade Runner* depicted a society already dependent on a relatively safer—replicants don't eat humans or use their bodies to host their embryos and so they don't typically kill on sight—and much more relatable monster: more human than human replicants. So while the replicants were dangerous, *Blade Runner* moves far beyond the logic of the haunted house—why would someone retrieve a deadly monster from a dead planet?—and towards a scenario that encourages a discussion of what it means to be human. And while this discussion raised other important issues, it also allowed *Blade Runner* to explore Marcuse's contentions about the potential for Eros to change society. Furthermore, by setting *Blade Runner* in a dystopian, near future Los Angeles, Scott could also touch on Marcuse's contentions about one-dimensional thought and false needs. Before we explore its Marcusian elements, however, we need to fully grasp *Blade Runner*'s place in popular culture as well as its critical reputation.

While *Blade Runner* was definitely not a franchise-spawning blockbuster, it would be inaccurate to say that was a flop. According to boxofficemojo.com, the film took second place on its opening weekend and its $27.5 million total for 1982—about $64 million in today's money—was enough to give it 27th place out of 132 movies released, placing it just barely outside of the top quintile. Subsequent re-releases in 1992 and 2007 added a little over $5 million to its initial take. *Blade Runner* had a similar reception from popular critics as it did from audiences upon its initial release, not really being panned but definitely eliciting its share of critical reservations. The *New York Times*' Janet Maslin penned a typical review after the movie was released. She is highly complementary of Scott's depiction of dystopian Los Angeles, but ultimately concludes that the special effects "run away" with the film.

Such box office disappointment and critical indifference, however, has long since been transcended by the film's enduring place in popular culture. Indeed, *Blade Runner*'s status makes it seem as if it had been a blockbuster on the order of *Alien*. For example, Roger Ebert, reviewing Scott's 2007 *Final Cut*, strongly suggests that the film has entered popular culture's canon. After noting that he is several paragraphs into his review and has not yet explained what a replicant is, he claims that his omission "is a tribute to the influence and reach of *Blade Runner*" because decades "after its release virtually everyone" interested in film knows what a replicant is. Ebert, who was unimpressed with *Blade Runner* in 1982, then goes on to rhetorically posit that reviewers of *The Wizard of Oz* "never define Munchkins," after all.

The above discussion begs the question of how what probably wound up looking to Warner Brothers' accountants like a very expensive art-house movie became such a critical darling, however. And while the mechanics of that process are fairly typical—an offbeat work has a devoted fanbase that includes academic and journalistic critics, these critics use their influence to keep the work in front of the public—the motivations behind the loyalty a particular film or book inspires are harder to trace. In the case of *Blade Runner*, however, it is quite possible that the film became popular with thoughtful viewers because it is so overdetermined, because it is built on so many allusions to filmic and cultural tropes. In addition to its announced status as a filmic adaptation of Phillip K. Dick's *Do Androids Dream of Electric Sheep*, for example, Scott told Paul Sammon that the film was also "influenced by Raymond Chandler" (107). Furthermore, the film raises so many profound thematic issues and then refuses to resolve them. This explanation for the persistence of interest in the film is not novel, but instead has been raised in various ways by other critics. Sharon L. Gravett, for example, sees in *Blade Runner* "a doubleness, a refusal to authorize one particular reading" (39). Douglas E. Williams, quoting Theodore Adorno, similarly argues that *Blade Runner* does not "resolve objective contradictions in a spurious harmony," but instead "expresses the idea of harmony negatively by embodying the contradictions, pure and uncompromised, in its innermost structure" (385). And Richard Pope goes as far as suggesting that the tilt in favor of set design and atmospherics critics like Maslin detected was a function of the film's refusal to create easily grasped commentary on society. According to Pope, "while it is true to say that the film's creators got blindsided by the setting, this blindness emerged *through* the failure of the symbolic, and it was precisely this failure that served, in the first place, as the impetus for the work of art" (78).

At this point, a methodological issue needs to be addressed. Scott released multiple versions of *Blade Runner*, and much of the academic criticism is based on the later—and arguably better—versions of the film. Scott himself would probably prefer that critics largely paid attention to later versions of the film since he went so far as to claim during an interview with Paul Sammon that the initial theatrical release and any later version of the film are in fact "different movies" (92). The version of the film that this monograph will read, however, is the initial theatrical release. After all, even though critics now tend to treat *Blade Runner*, or at least the subsequent versions of the film, as if it actually was a very-well-financed arthouse movie, the executives at Warner Brothers who greenlit Scott's special-effects-heavy science fiction movie were hoping that they might have another *Alien* or *Star Wars* on their hands. Casting Han Solo/Indiana Jones to play the lead and releasing the film at the beginning of the summer movie season provide further proof that the film was intended to be a blockbuster. This logic would explain why, as Scott told Sammon, the happy ending of the theatrical release was influenced by test screening reactions (108). Consequently, an argument concerned with the way that blockbusters employ popularized versions of critical theory to interrogate industrial society should look at the first iteration of a film—the one designed to pull people into the multiplexes—and not later versions of the film edited in the shadow of critical acclaim, even if those later versions are superior and even if the film's director indicates that the theatrical release is not his favorite version of the film on the DVD commentary.[4]

Multiple versions notwithstanding, part of the film's ability to generate doubleness and refuse to end on a note of spurious harmony comes from the richness of its source texts. While Scott's recasting of Dick's narrative is visually clearly a descendant of Fritz Lang's 1927 film *Metropolis*, *Blade Runner* also reaches deeply into Western culture. Batty, the leader of the rebellious replicants, explicitly calls Tyrell his maker after he forces his way into the scientist's living quarters. Dialog and scenes like this have lead critics to draw parallels with both the Biblical account of creation and texts influenced by that account such as *Paradise Lost*.[5] Of course, a tale involving a scientist who creates a humanoid monster who returns to attack that scientist is bound to draw comparisons to Mary Shelly's *Frankenstein* and other Romantic texts.[6] In addition to drawing from several canonical texts, *Blade Runner* also portrays a dystopian near future was seen by some as the ideal type of the postmodern text.[7] Of course, there has been no shortage of political or raced readings of Scott's film,[8] with *Blade Runner*'s racial logic, for example, has been seen as a comment on the immigration-based racial tensions of its immediate historical context.[9]

All of the above approaches to the text are, in their own way, apt discussions of Scott's complex film. Scott clearly draws from several popularly available narratives to enhance Dick's source text. Yet one would think that there would also be room for a Marcusian reading of Scott's film. Peter Fitting, who opens with an epigraph from Marcuse's *An Essay on Liberation* but does not otherwise explicitly cite the theorists would probably agree. Fitting makes the very Marcusian observation that the replicants "offer a glimpse of a liberated and empowered humanity, which could be realized thanks to the wonderful possibilities of technology; but so to, they indicate the terrible price of that seductive empowerment in the substitution for our humanity of the qualities and characteristics of the machine" (345). Even though critics like Michael Ryan and Douglas Kellner argue that the theatrical version of *Blade Runner* "concludes with a happy marriage of humans and machines" (63), Fitting thinks the film is not ethical because it focuses so much on the "retirements" of the replicants, "merging in a single figure" of the replicants "both the *machines* which are used to exploit us and *all those who would refuse and rebel* against that system of exploitation" (348).

Fitting's notionally Marcusian reading is not the only possible application of the theorist's work to *Blade Runner*, however. Although the critics who generated them were clearly aware that they were watching a work of speculative fiction, many of the readings discussed above see the metaphorical qualities of the text as no more prominent than in any other work of fiction. Replicants and the posthuman, in other words, are taken as either possible or logical extensions of contemporary technological and social trends. While this is a productive approach, a Marcusian reading of *Blade Runner* would be more powerful if it sees the film as explicitly metaphorical, indeed almost allegorical. Reading on this level allows us to see not only Deckard and Batty but also the Tyrell Corporation and the near-future Los Angeles that the film creates as types that allow Scott to illustrate some of Marcuse's contentions. Using the setting as an ideal type of a rotting postindustrial city whose population is still pacified by the consumer goods industrial society creates allows Scott to explore false needs in a way that the hermetically sealed and profoundly isolated environment of the *Nostromo* never would. Depicting the sway the Tyrell Corporation has over a ruined Los Angeles as well as the actual physical headquarters of the replicant manufacturing concern allows Scott to portray the sway corporations have over our daily lives in a way that the portrayal of the ghostlike, space-bound menace of the Weyland-Yutani Corporation never could. By creating a narrative that features a synthetic antagonist that is almost as sympathetic as it's deeply flawed and possibly also synthetic protagonist, *Blade Runner* can explore what it means to be a one-dimensional company man in much more depth than did *Alien* with its repellant replicant Ash. Furthermore, by focusing on Batty's desire to both understand life and have more of it granted to him, *Blade Runner* can explore Marcuse's notion of Eros as a counterpoint to the deadening existence created by false needs and one-dimensional thought.

*Blade Runner*'s earthbound setting allows Scott to meditate on Marcuse's concept of false needs, which, in "The Movement in a New Era of Repression," the theorist defines as a form of domination "through steered satisfaction and steered aggression" (6). Consequently, even though people are aware of "the world of alienated labor, misery, and repression," they acquiesce because "capitalism, at its present stage, creates a world of ease, gadgets, enjoyment, and surpluses, in which increasing numbers of people participate" (7). In *Eros and Civilization*, Marcuse finds evidence of false needs in "the promotion of thoughtless leisure activities" (86). *Blade Runner*'s Los Angeles is a long way economically from the mid–20th-century, first-world prosperity that allowed Marcuse to detect and describe false needs. Therefore it is even more telling that Scott ensures that we understand that the use of false needs to manipulate the masses persists long after industrial society encounters trouble delivering the goods.

It is often remarked that *Blade Runner*'s dank and dystopian Los Angeles is barraged by advertising for products that would have been familiar to theatergoers in the summer of 1982. It is interesting, however, to note just what those products are. We see large, brightly-lit ads for Coca-Cola, Schlitz beer, the now-defunct airline Pan Am and TDK electronics, a company known in the early 1980s for manufacturing stereo equipment and blank audio cassettes. Deckard actually orders a Budweiser in a bar where a neon Budweiser sign is clearly visible. All of these companies, in one way or another, purport to offer a means of escape from industrial society. The relationship between the large alcohol companies and the implied promise of managing the stresses of modern life should go without saying, but we should also remember that *Blade Runner*'s apparent soft drink of choice was advertised in the decades prior to the film's release with slogans like "Things go better with Coke," "Coke adds life," and "Have a Coke and a smile." While airlines typically make most of their money from business travelers booking last-minute fares and paying a premium for the privilege, they often advertise themselves as a means to visit exotic vacation spots and therefore escape from the workaday world of industrial society. As noted above, in the early 1980s, TDK was associated with the consumer electronics that Marcuse would argue often provided yet another avenue of simulated escape from the havoc industrial society had caused. The advertisements depicted in *Blade Runner* are not a random snapshot of corporate logos designed to suggest a near-future environment. Instead, they give the suggestion of the world of ease that society is less and less able to provide in an attempt to manage the hostility that *Blade Runner*'s Los Angeles must create in its citizens.

A crumbling Los Angeles where false needs created by corporate advertising apparently manage to provide a modicum of social control—or, as Scott told Danny Peary, "the kind of world I see in 2019" (55)—provides an ideal backdrop for *Blade Runner*'s depiction of the Tyrell Corporation. In a sense, the company is only taking the logic of false needs to its natural conclusion; it is, as Scott noted in the same interview, the "ultimate" in "scientific-industrial development" (49). It becomes clear that Scott does not mean this in a positive sense when he tells Sammon that Tyrell is Big Brother (98). Although Tyrell is not literally surveilling the citizens of Los Angeles to ensure their devotion to his political ideology, he is attempting to create conformity through much more sinister means. After all, why bother using advertising and consumer products—or political repression—to enslave people when you can just build people who can be used as slaves? The opening crawl credits Tyrell with creating replicants and also explicitly states that replicants were "used off-world as slave labor." The company's status as a slave trafficker is signaled visually because their corporate headquarters is pyramidal and high above the street-level squalor where the "little people" Deckard fears joining live. Pyramids, or at least the Egyptian ones familiar to most viewers—thanks to Judeo-Christian scripture—are widely thought to have been built with slave labor by the ruling classes, ostensibly to provide a transition into the afterlife but undoubtedly also to project political and social power.

The depiction of the Tyrell Corporation's social and political dominance is not limited to the physical appearance of its headquarters. In the scene where Holden, Deckard's fellow blade runner, gives fugitive replicant Leon the Voight-Kampf test, they are at Tyrell headquarters sitting in chairs emblazoned with the Tyrell corporation logo. Yet blade runners are elite police officers, and, typically, hard-boiled, film-noir police officers interrogate people down at the station. Holden's presence at Tyrell headquarters and the visual reminder in terms of the name stitched on the chairs let viewers know that Holden is a de facto member of Tyrell's security team. In *Alien*, Scott could imply that Weyland-Yutani was a law unto itself since there is very little mention of a government agency or law enforcement entity that the crew could turn to for help. In *Blade Runner*, Scott, who told Harlan Kennedy that he "deliberately made Deckard "part of the bureaucracy" (36), allowing him to show the extent to which Tyrell controlled Los Angeles' government in one scene.

Naturally, Tyrell does not see himself as a postmodern pharaoh who sits atop a society that is kept in check by false needs. Nor does *Blade Runner* present him as possessing a Bond-villain level of melodramatic evil. Instead, he appeals to the performance principle to explain his company's power and influence. When the blade runner visits to get information about the replicants he is chasing and to give Rachel the Voight-Kampff test, Tyrell tells Deckard that commerce is the goal of his company and that creating replicants that are more human than human is best thought of as creating a product that best serves customer's needs. None of this suggests that Tyrell possesses Bond-villain levels of self-aware malice. Instead, the inventor's startlingly unoriginal words suggest the logic of industrial society is so pervasive in Scott's Los Angeles that even a cultured and intelligent man like Tyrell cannot see his important position in a repressive social order. This is a much more nuanced and effective portrayal of the power large companies wield in industrial society. After all, viewers of *Alien* could very easily leave the theater believing that the haunted house that is the *Nostromo* is beset not only by a xenomorph but also by the evil presence of the Weyland-Yutani Corporation. While this reading of the film certainly works on the level of plot, it misses the thematic point that the order to retrieve the xenomorph is a manifestation of systemic pressures and not a decision by a committee of executives to become evil.

In *Blade Runner*, then, viewers see a more complete depiction of the social conditions surrounding apparently evil corporations like Weyland-Yutani and Tyrell. This depiction in turn allows for a more complex portrayal of characters that are directly impacted by such a corporation. Once viewers reached the end of *Alien*, they could realize that they had witnessed two films. The first was a relatively straightforward and entertaining space-monster-as-slasher picture. The other was a complex workplace drama with the fearlessly questioning Ripley emerging as the protagonist and the purpose-built company man Ash emerging as the antagonist. *Blade Runner* complicates the division between protagonist and antagonist by giving those positions to two characters who are both, in their own way, company men, and who both, to one degree or another, question the system that created the Tyrell Corporation.

In both cases, this questioning leads the characters to embrace what Marcuse would call Eros and begin to turn from the destructive habits of mind endemic in industrial society.

On one level, Batty is the same kind of company man that Ash is: a worker literally constructed by a corporation with the assumption that it would always do that corporations bidding. It has long been asserted that *Blade Runner*—especially the versions subsequent to the theatrical release—winkingly implies that Deckard is a replicant himself. This would also make the blade runner a synthetic company man. The evidence for Deckard's status is ambiguous and not typically at the surface of the film, however. Furthermore, since the film also includes reasons to believe that Deckard is not a replicant—why, for example, would the police allow a replicant whose job it was to kill other replicants any retirement other than the one customarily reserved for replicants?—he may not be that kind of company man. Nevertheless, it would be productive to employ the metaphorical meaning of the phrase "company man" to the character who may or may not have literally been built by the company as the discussion below will illustrate.

Deckard is ostensibly a police officer and therefore a public servant, but, as argued above, the blade runners can easily be seen as an adjunct of the Tyrell Corporation's security forces. Evidence of this status comes in Deckard's job description: he has been assigned by what is presented as a government agency to take care of a serious public safety issue caused by one company in the course of conducting its business. Realizing his status as a de facto employee of the Tyrell Corporation allows us to see Deckard as a more familiar company man—the man or woman who does a job that is extremely distasteful to him or to her for economic and social reasons—in Deckard's case, his fear of becoming one of the little people.

In spite of their status as company men, however, both Batty and Deckard display the two dimensional thought that Scott had earlier endowed Ripley with, though Batty clearly questions the status quo with an alacrity that makes Ripley look like Lambert while Deckard sometimes makes Lambert look brave. After all, Batty dies fighting to change the way the Tyrell Company, and by metaphorical extension industrial society as depicted in Scott's dystopian Los Angeles, does business while Deckard ultimately runs away from said dystopian depiction of the metropolis in industrial society.

True, Batty's violent rebellion greatly contributes to the plot of *Blade Runner*, but the replicant is not simply reflexively engaging in violence and he is therefore not a sublimely amoral creature like the xenomorph Ripley battles. There is a piercing critique of the society that spawned the Tyrell Corporation in Batty's actions, and this has been noted by many critics. For example, Lusser and Gowan have argued that Batty is "a slave revolting against the tyrannical control of consciousness itself, which has deployed replicants as shock troops for colonization, engineered their untimely demise, and stabilized their passage across their shortened life by the implantation of false memories" (168). While they do not place their interpretation in explicitly Marcusian terms, Lusser and Gowan's apt reading of Batty's motives easily lends itself to an argument that sees Batty not as a monstrous replicant but instead as a workaday everyman whose status as a company-built man symbolizes the ideological pressure to conform inherent in industrial society. After all, false needs, one-dimensional thought, and all the other tricks that industrial society use to gain the acquiescence of the governed could easily be described as the "tyrannical control of consciousness itself." Furthermore, the manifest lack of concern for the replicants Lusser and Gowan detect on the part of the Tyrell Corporation could very easily represent a metaphorical depiction of any corporation that colludes with a repressive system to help its workers stabilize their passage across careers shortened by layoffs and uncertainty by implanting false mental imagery.

Thus, when Batty confronts Tyrell, viewers not only see an allusion to Adam confronting the God that created him or the monster confronting Dr. Frankenstein. They also see an almost surreally metaphorical company man confronting the head of the firm he works for. Viewing that scene through this lens, we realize that when Batty asks Tyrell if the maker can repair what he has made he is not merely asking for an extension of his four-year lifespan. He is also asking a more fundamental question about the makers of industrial society and the world they have created. This new reading also sheds light on the several searching questions Batty asks Tyrell about the technological issues surrounding resetting his mortality clock. On the surface, though they demonstrate Batty's previously announced superior intelligence, the questions are merely required of the logic of the plot: Batty is standing in Tyrell's bedroom because he wants to extend his arbitrarily shortened life, so he would naturally discuss the technical aspects of the issue with his maker. Yet the questioning—if not the individual questions themselves—also works on a metaphorical level. The replicant is vigorously and intelligently interrogating the status quo; he is demonstrating two-dimensional thought. Naturally, however Tyrell cannot "fix" Batty and Pris, though not really for the pseudo technical reasons that come out of his mouth to advance the plot. Instead, it would be unreasonable to expect Eldon Tyrell to fix the structural problems with industrial society that made creating disposable workers an attractive option.

Once Batty seeks vengeance on Tyrell when his questions are dismissed, however, the metaphorical dimension of the scene evaporates and the logic of the plot takes over. Because Tyrell himself is not personally responsible for the society that created the conditions supporting the use of replicants as slaves, his brutal death at the hands of his creation does not privilege revolutionary violence as a means of freeing us from industrial society. Instead, the murder of Tyrell both advances the plot and conforms to reasonable expectations about how Batty would act in that situation. After all, why wouldn't a replicant designed for combat revert to what his programming, training, and experiences teach him to do after suffering such a great disappointment?

If Batty's questioning of the status quo and refusal to go along with the system ultimately takes the form of a violent revolt, Deckard's oppositional reading of industrial society as presented in *Blade Runner* takes the form of self-destructive behavior and attempts to leave his job as a blade runner. It has been argued that his performance as Deckard is one of the flattest of Harrison Ford's career. Williams, for example, notes that the film differs from classic noir because of the "faintly zombie-like quality of Deckard" (389). But this flat affect represents Deckard's psychological withdrawal from the immoral world that industrial society has created, the inverse of Batty's violent frontal assault upon it. Evidence of Deckard's retreat comes when he notes that killing replicants makes him feel, but that he does not enjoy the feelings associated with the kills. Evidence that Deckard's inward-turning rejection of industrial society can be read by others comes when Rachel, reacting to the blade runner's demeanor rather than anything he says, asks Deckard if he feels that the Tyrell Corporation's work is not beneficial to the public.

*Blade Runner* does not simply depict Batty's attack on industrial society and Deckard's painful turning from it, however. The film also depicts, however furtively and occasionally, a force that could overturn industrial society. These utopian moments are best explained in terms of Marcuse's discussion of Eros and Thanatos. Since Marcuse defines Eros in *Eros and Civilization* as the *"life instinct"* (21), notes that Freud called it "the great unifying force that preserves all life" (25) and argues that "the drive toward ever larger unities belongs to the biological-organic nature of Eros itself" (39), we can productively apply this concept to *Blade Runner*. Furthermore, Marcuse asserts that since modern civilization thwarts Eros, it is marked by "the progressive weakening of Eros" and the "growth of aggressiveness and guilt feelings" (125). This combination of repression and the growth of Thanatos, according to Marcuse, leads to "the fatal dialectic of civilization: the very progress of civilization leads to the release of increasingly destructive forces" (49)—also a line of reasoning easily applied to *Blade Runner*.

The dying city Scott presents in *Blade Runner* echoes many of the contentions Marcuse makes about Thanatos. The atmospherics of the film seem to suggest that the progress of civilization has led to the release of increasingly destructive forces. There is a resigned peace, an acquiescence in the crowds that throng the filthy streets, a sense of withdrawal from the world best personified in the film's depiction of J. F. Sebastian, the genetic engineer living in a crumbling and otherwise abandoned apartment building. Sebastian, who suffers from Methuselah's Syndrome, is beset by an accelerated decrepitude that leaves the twenty-something engineer looking like he is in his early 50s. Shunned because of his disability, he lives alone with a menagerie of mechanical friends that he has constructed. Of course, the film makes it clear that the lived experience of Sebastian's disability and his social isolation gives him much in common with the replicants. But Sebastian's decay also metaphorically links him with Scott's Los Angeles. Though quite technologically gifted, Sebastian can only make replicants for the Tyrell Corporation and mechanical toys for himself. He tells Batty and Pris that he cannot help them reset their four-year lifespan, even though he would like to. Sebastian, in other words, has the technical capability to create life and, through his work, participate in the broadened Eros that Marcuse speaks of. Indeed, his menagerie of lifelike toys suggests a partially repressed impulse to create useful life. Nevertheless, he cannot because he is employed by a corporation that wants to use his talents to create agents of death and destruction and because he lives in a society that rewards those corporations even though they are largely responsible for the squalid social conditions that the film depicts.

Even though the beings that Sebastian had a hand in making are similarly trapped by their physical status and their relationship to the Tyrell Corporation, they nevertheless display a much greater will to participate in Marcuse's larger Eros. Of course, *Blade Runner* has a more simplistically erotic component. Batty and Pris are clearly depicted as lovers, yet Batty's quest for life is not immediately centered on that relationship. Instead, as the film develops, viewers realize that Batty yearns to focus primarily on the Eros that embraces life and creativity, with the traditionally erotic relationship with Pris serving as a counterpoint to his broader search for a more meaningful life.

When approached through the lens of Marcuse's discussion of Eros and Thanatos, then, Batty's quest to gain more than the four years allotted him at the factory looks less like a violent act of revenge against his creator and more like an ultimately thwarted attempt of a fundamentally violent and destructive creature to transcend his hardwired Thanatos and embrace the creative Eros that could lead to him becoming truly human. This reading adds a great deal of ambiguity to the scene where Batty tells Tyrell, "I want more life, fucker." It is not incorrect to read Batty's statement as a threat uttered by an angry man who is more than capable of following through with its implied violence. As we will see below, however, Batty's final soliloquy strongly suggests a Marcusian subtext for his actions and for his conversation with Tyrell.

It has been argued that Batty becomes a Christ figure when he sacrifices the remaining few moments of his life to save Deckard at the end of their climactic battle in the Bradbury building. It should be noted here that the hand

Batty uses to pull Deckard up and save him from falling is the same hand the replicant had earlier driven a nail through. This image, combined with the dove that Batty releases when he dies, is obviously an allusion to Christian imagery. Of course, in this overdetermined narrative, the dove and the nail mark in the hand are just that, an equation of Batty with Christ. But Christian imagery itself, as countless other narratives have consistently shown, is quite helpful for illustrating other contentions. Marcuse himself used the New Testament to illustrate the concept of Eros overcoming Thanatos when he argued that the "message of the Son was the message of liberation: the overthrow of the Law (which is domination) by Agape (which is Eros)" (63). In Marcuse's just society, then, the Law—or the domination which easily equates with Thanatos—would be overthrown by Eros as people followed their better impulses without interference from industrial society. The conversion of the company-built killing machine into the compassionate man who uses his fading strength to save a man who is directly responsible for the deaths of two of his friends thus not only illustrates the Christian principle of turning the other cheek but also illustrates the Marcusian principle of the overthrow of domination by a desire to fully live. Perhaps this is what Deckard's voice-over is helpfully trying to explain when the blade runner opines that maybe "in those last moments" Batty "loved life more than he ever had before. Not just his life—anybody's life."

Deckard, of course, primarily deals with difficult situations by withdrawing from them, so he is not depicted as eagerly chasing after life. But this does not mean that he is not also moving towards embracing Eros by the end of the film. The content of the voice-over discussed above strongly suggests that Deckard understands Batty's motivations and therefore the Marcusian gesture they represent. There is also evidence in Deckard's problematic relationship with Rachel that the depressive blade runner was not merely experiencing traditional erotic interest but was also undergoing an awakening of his interest in life. Although Deckard's relationship with Rachel is more central to the plot than Batty relationship with Pris, it also serves as a means to depict Deckard's growing discomfort with his Thanatos-personifying profession.

*Blade Runner* depicts Deckard's growing fascination with Rachel breaking through the studied indifference that he used to cope with what he does to pay his rent. As his feelings for her begin to grow, Deckard reminds himself that "blade runners weren't supposed to have feelings" and then wonders, "What the hell was happening?" Of course, the nature of those feelings are, like many other things in *Blade Runner*, ambiguous. Deckard could be seeing Rachel as a highly-advanced Nexus-Six pleasure model—much like Zhora, the first replicant he retires—and therefore his feelings center on his own physical pleasure. Yet while Deckard's libido undoubtedly plays a role in his interest in Rachel, a key scene in *Blade Runner* suggests that Deckard's relationship with Rachel is not motivated exclusively by sexual desire.

This scene is the problematic forceful seduction of Rachel by Deckard. Some have correctly noted that could be construed as an assault because Deckard appears to physically detain Rachel in his apartment and because of the problematic nature of the ability of a replicant to consent to intercourse. It is important to remember the context of that scene, however. In the previous scene, Deckard has just retired Zhora and then Rachel had saved Deckard by killing Leon. After they return to his apartment, Deckard asks Rachel if she has the shakes. When she answers in the affirmative, Deckard informs her that the shakes were "part of the business." Rachel responds that she is "the business," leaving a shocked Deckard speechless. In addition to demonstrating that Rachel is fully capable of thinking two dimensionally, this interaction depicts not only Deckard's full realization that he has developed romantic feelings for someone who is no different than the many replicants that he has retired over the course of his career, but also the full implication of his ability to see a replicant as worthy of his love. Deckard, in other words, realizes that he was not deactivating malfunctioning equipment, but instead killing beings that had the potential to be fully human and in so doing participating in the aggressive destruction that characterizes Thanatos.

Of course, it could be argued that Deckard continues to treat Rachel as a piece of equipment when he commands her to tell him to kiss her. Yet it is interesting to note that Deckard gets up out of bed—where he had been resting after being beaten by Leon—and begins his seduction only after he hears Rachel play the piano. While musical skill can be a means of seduction, in *Blade Runner* it serves as a marker of humanity. Because Rachel can appreciate and play music, she is capable of creative activity. And because she is capable of creativity, she is capable of the kind of fulfilling engagement with the world that is inherent in Marcuse's concept of Eros, even if she was manufactured by the Tyrell Corporation. Deckard's realization of the life instinct in Rachel in turn arouses his more traditionally erotic impulses, leading to his clumsily-executed seduction.

The depiction of Deckard and Rachel's escape from Los Angeles into an improbably green countryside in the initial theatrical release has often been dismissed as an act of pandering to audience desires for closure. And, given the interpretive ambiguity of *Blade Runner* and the expectations of the studio that the film would provide a healthy return on their investment, this is a fair reading. Yet when looked at through a Marcusian lens, their flight can also be seen as Marcuse's guardedly optimistic assertion that the containment of industrial society could be broken if we recognized each other's humanity and rejected the culture of death inherent in industrial society. At this point it would be helpful to remember Marcuse's contention in *One-Dimensional*

*Man* that he is caught between "two contradictory hypotheses: (1) That advanced industrial society is capable of containing qualitative changes for the foreseeable future; (2) that forces and tendencies exist which may break this containment and explode the society" (xlvii). Later iterations of *Blade Runner* that emphasize the possibility that Deckard is a replicant align themselves with the first possibility—since Deckard and Rachel both have little time left, their gesture is as empty as that of Batty and Pris. The theatrical release, however, features an audience-friendly depiction of one of the forces that might break the containment of industrial society: Eros. If Deckard is human and Rachel really does not have a built-in limit to her lifespan, they can build a life together in defiance of Deckard's directive to destroy replicants and, consequently, in defiance of the world the Tyrell Corporation has helped create.

By the end of *Blade Runner*, then, audiences have seen both company men question and reject the corporate entity that personifies industrial society. Furthermore, one of the company men seems to have managed to escape from industrial society. This utopian—though admittedly problematic—moment further indicates that Scott has given his evil corporation a more nuanced portrayal that contravenes the seeming omnipotence of the Weyland-Yutani Corporation. At the end of *Alien*, all Ripley could do is float towards the Weyland-Yutani-maintained network and hope to be rescued from her physical plight. But while her body would find solace from the deadly hazards of interstellar space, her soul would still belong to the company. Rachel and Deckard, however, just might have escaped from the Tyrell Corporation and the police force it seems to have on retainer.

Although Scott spent several years addressing other thematic concerns, his efforts to portray apparently evil corporations and their leaders as less the personification of omnipotent malevolence and more a product of a system that might be circumvented continues in 2012's *Prometheus*. While not a cash machine like films such as *A New Hope* or *Titanic*, Scott's return to the world the Weyland Corporation created did make enough money that there has been some talk of a sequel—something only recently discussed for *Blade Runner*. After all, *Prometheus* provides a solid return on investment if you take into account foreign ticket sales. Domestically, the film made a little over $126 million, which is just shy of its $130 million estimated budget and therefore, considering advertising and revenue sharing with theater owners, *Prometheus* flopped. The foreign gross, however, more than doubled the domestic take, bringing in over $275 million and making the total exceed a profitability-guaranteeing $400 million. Yet while Twentieth Century–Fox executives were no doubt glad to make money, *Prometheus*' take pales in comparison to the top grossing film of 2012. *The Avengers* worldwide box office was over $1.5 billion on a production budget of $220 million, a ratio of production budget to global box office that would have given *Prometheus* a take of just over $900 million.

Critical reaction to the film was also solid but not wildly enthusiastic, as indicated by *Prometheus*' respectable-but-not-stunning 74 percent fresh rating on rottentomatoes.com. Mainstream critic's praise seemed to be implicitly qualified by subtle warnings that the film is another one of Scott's big-budget arthouse flicks. For example, *the New York Post*'s unfailingly snarky Kyle Smith uncharacteristically praises *Prometheus* for being "wickedly entertaining, scary, sinister and thought-provoking." "Thought-provoking," of course, is not typically used when studio marketing people cherry-pick quotes to promote blockbuster action films, and here represents Smith's tacit admission that the film lacks the traditional sense of closure and clear distinction between good guys and bad guys that a film like *The Avengers* provides. The *New York Times*' A.O. Scott similarly employs praise mixed with a subtle warning that audiences may not get what they expect when he notes that *Prometheus*' "visual scheme is sufficiently captivating, and most of the performances are subtle enough that whatever skepticism you may arrive with quickly turns into happy disorientation. Once again, "happily disorienting" is not a phrase one would see prominently displayed on a poster for a summer blockbuster.

While there has understandably not been a great deal of academic criticism of the film, *Film Comment*'s Vivian Sobchack's review engages with the confusion *Prometheus*' thought-provoking, happy disorientation produced in theatergoers. Sobchack argues that fan reaction on internet discussion groups like IMDb.com's comments section is best described as a collective "WTF?" ("Rock" 31), not because the film is delightfully contradictory but because it does not know what it wants to be. For Sobchack, *Prometheus* is caught in "inescapable double bind: on the one side, the filmmaker's desire and demand for originality, and, on the other, a huge, parasitic franchise and stifling mythology" ("Rock" 33). Consequently, the film is about itself, about the desire to both find its origins and yet overcome them.

Other critics writing reviews in academic publications have noted the weight of thirty-three years of franchise-creation-by-committee on *Prometheus*. Kim Newman's review in *Sight and Sound*, for example, argues that the film is "more of a reboot than a prequel" because "*Prometheus* huffily renders Paul W.S. Anderson's *AVP Alien vs. Predator* (2004) and related films uncanonical by contradicting their version of the origins of the Alien species" and may problematize the *Alien* films as well (web). Newman, of course, neglects to mention the extensive graphic novel mythology that is also rendered uncanonical by *Prometheus*, nor does she closely explore the difficulty of proclaiming anything canonical in a universe created by scores of storytellers working without co-ordination for different corporate entities, but her fundamental point is sound. *Prometheus* is a rebuke to the storytellers who followed

Scott, O'Bannon, and Schusett—particularly, as Newman notes, Paul W.S. Anderson—though since the last *Alien* film appeared 15 years before *Prometheus*, since the final two *Alien* films and both of the *AVP* films were not the financial and critical successes that *Alien* and *Aliens* were, and since, despite their quality, not all that many people read Dark Horse graphic novels, theatergoers may not be aware of Scott's engagement with the unruly universe that had grown up around *Alien*.

Nevertheless, it is quite likely that Scott's attempt to use *Prometheus* to set in order the universe he initiated bears some responsibility for the audience confusion noted above. As vital as Sobchack's and Newman's readings are, however, they seem to assume that Scott's only significant science fiction film is *Alien* and his sources are limited to the *Alien* universe. This is not the case, however, and we would do well to realize that directors are aware not only of the universe their sequels, prequels, and reboots are created in, but also their own filmography—especially when they have the extensive and impressive filmography of Sir Ridley Scott. It is instructive here to look at the other side of the *Alien vs. Predators* divorce: Nimrod Antal's 2010 *Predators*. At that point in his career, Antal had directed just three other feature-length films: 2003's Hungarian-language *Kontroll*, with a worldwide gross that barely made it into seven figures but a strong Rotten Tomatoes rating of 82 percent fresh; 2007's *Vacancy*, with a worldwide gross a bit over $35 million on a $19 million production budget and a Rotten Tomatoes rating of 54 percent fresh; and 2009's *Armored*, with a worldwide gross just shy of $23 million on a $20 million production budget and a Rotten Tomatoes rating of 41 percent fresh. This is a solid, if not phenomenal, resume for a young director—a well-reviewed first film, a second film that did well enough to spawn a poorly-received sequel that Antal did not direct, and a third film that was a misfire but not, considering its budget, an outright flop. Since there are no towering masterpieces or widely-known blockbusters here, however, and no science fiction films to speak of, Antal wisely chose to avoid the display of hubris it would have entailed to bring overt references to his prior films into his take on a previously established franchise. Antal also wisely avoided the issues Sobchack and Newman detect in *Prometheus* by choosing to reject the additional mythology injected into the *Predator* universe by the *AVP* films largely by pretending that those films never happened.

When he made *Prometheus*, on the other hand, Scott had made studios hundreds of millions of dollars and had been nominated for the Academy Award for Best Director three times—for *Thelma and Louise*, *Gladiator*—which won best picture—and 2001's *Black Hawk Down*. More importantly, Scott had not only directed the original *Alien* but had also directed *Blade Runner*, which was not as lucrative as *Alien* but had as much if not more influence over science fiction cinema. Thus, when he turned his hand to

*Prometheus*, Scott was working with far more potential sources than he had at his disposal when he filmed *Alien*.

Of course, it is understandable that Scott wanted to explicitly revisit his first science fiction triumph, and so, in an important way, *Prometheus* is best seen as an attempt to explain the origins of the ship Kane, Dallas, and Lambert find on LV-426. This can be seen not only in the depiction of the Engineer's ships and apparel. Many scenes in the film seem to explicitly reference *Alien*. For example, at the end of the film Shaw gives a final report explaining the destruction of the Prometheus, sounding much like Ripley at the end of *Alien* but also invoking the press briefing at the end of *It!* when she warns people away by saying that there is only death on LV-223. *Prometheus* also references Ripley and Dallas' argument over whether or not to let an infected Kane aboard the *Nostromo* in a scene where the survey team brings an infected Holloway back to the *Prometheus*. At this point, Vickers and Captain Janek, assuming the same roles as Ripley and Captain Dallas argue about letting him in—an argument only resolved when Holloway, who knows he is going to die, asks Vickers to kill him and she complies.

But the plot of *Prometheus* also contains many references to Scott's other science-fiction masterpiece. *Blade Runner*, after all, depicts the end of a journey made by a dying, artificially created human to find the man who created him and ask that man for more life. *Prometheus* depicts a journey made by a man who creates artificial humans to find the creatures that genetically engineered the human race in order for the dying replicant maker to ask one of the members of the race that engineered him for more life. In *Blade Runner*, the replicant kills his maker. In *Prometheus*, the maker of replicants is killed by the maker of humanity. *Blade Runner*—or at least the theatrically released version—ends with a male human and a female replicant who are in a romantic relationship fleeing Los Angeles, a metropolis degraded by industrial society, in search of a peaceful life in the country. *Prometheus* ends with a male replicant and a female human who have formed an uneasy alliance fleeing the empire of colonies created by industrial society in search of the origin of human life. Clearly, Scott is revisiting both films, and *Prometheus* can be read as a hybridizing return to the director's influential science-fiction films and thus a return to the Marcusian thematics that his first two science fiction films address.

Although the correspondence in plot and imagery between *Prometheus*, *Alien*, and *Blade Runner* are interesting to track, Scott also used *Prometheus* to continue his investigation of all of the important thematic elements of *Alien* and *Blade Runner*. If *Prometheus* had generated the amount of scholarship that *Alien* or *Blade Runner* had, there would be several articles to cite that discussed Scott's return to the issues of pregnancy, birth, and gender in his third science fiction film. Other articles would note the Freudian overtones in the power struggle between Weyland and his daughter Meredith Vickers—perhaps taking special notice of the scene where Vickers tells Weyland that old kings die and new rulers arise. In turn, this line of argument might cause other scholars to draw comparisons with *King Lear*. Still others would discuss the depiction of postmodern identity to be found in a film that depicts a replicant leading his maker towards an audience with a creature whose race genetically engineered humanity. And, naturally, one could also discuss Scott's return to the Marcusian thematics found in his first science fiction films. In thematically rebooting *Blade Runner* as well as *Alien* in *Prometheus*, Scott not only continues to argue that two-dimensional thought is the best defense against industrial society but also that Eros can help company men and women—both company-built and metaphorical corporate creatures—overcome the destructive tendencies of society.

In order to illustrate *Prometheus*' thematic debt to *Alien*, we will explore how Scott depicts the *Prometheus* as a workplace and Captain Janek as a two-dimensional astronaut who is reminiscent of Ripley. Detailing *Prometheus*' debt to *Blade Runner* will involve examining how the film presents Weyland as a nuanced version of Tyrell who is on a mission similar to Batty's. This more fully human presentation of Weyland represents the next step in the progression away from the portrayal of a monolithic, apparently evil corporation and towards the depiction of the corporate head who is himself caught up in the system that industrial society has created that makes us all replicants, all company men and women. We will also investigate how the relationship between David and Shaw represents a rethinking of the relationship between Deckard and Rachel. Though *Prometheus* significantly reframes its human-replicant pairing, it also concludes with an escape that is characterized as a search for a more meaningful existence, suggesting that the solution to industrial society is a turn to Eros and a quest for life.

As discussed above, mainstream critics like Roger Ebert were quick to note that *Alien*, for all its gothic atmospherics, was set in a workplace. Critics also noted the same dynamic at work in *Prometheus*. For example, Sobchack quotes David Denby's assertion in his review in the *New Yorker* that "the Prometheus expedition, despite its grandiose ambitions, is a corporate endeavor" ("Rock" 33). Evidence supporting Denby's assertion can be found in several scenes. For example, Weyland executive Vickers reminds Holloway and Shaw, whose archeological discoveries are the impetus for the mission, that they are employees and they therefore report to her. Later, on the flight deck, Chance tells Ravel, "This is a corporate run—they aren't telling us shit." In *Alien*, Parker and Brett constantly complain about their working conditions and angle for more pay. This highly understandable attitude among hired guns on a corporate run finds reflection in *Prometheus* in Fifield, a geologist brought along on the expedition. Though his advanced training suggests a higher social status that Parker and Brett, Fifield largely shares their attitude towards working in outer space. When he meets Milburn, for example, Fifield rebuffs the biologist's friendly overtures and tells him that he is on the mission "to make money" and not to make friends. Once the exploration of the Engineer's abandoned facility begins, Fifield, much like Lambert, reacts to the sight of the dead Engineers with an "I'm outta here," even though he is one of the first modern humans to find proof that there is another form of intelligent life in the universe. Although Shaw and Holloway clearly see themselves as participating in an exciting quest for scientific discovery, then, several of the other members of the *Prometheus*' crew see themselves as simply doing their job. As in *Alien*, this workaday setting allows the film to contemplate what it means to engage in a highly technical workplace in industrial society. This contemplation, in turn, allows some of the *Prometheus*' crew to display the two-dimensional thought that is best for critiquing one-dimensional industrial society.

In *Alien*, the two-dimensional crewmember was Ripley, who spent a significant amount of time butting heads with her one-dimensional Captain. In *Prometheus*, Captain Janek is the crewmember who is most able to think beyond the dictates of the Weyland Corporation. Although at one point Janek echoes Captain Dallas when he tells Shaw that he just flies the ship, he is actually the polar opposite of the commander of the *Nostromo*. Instead of implying that he holds the one-dimensional relationship to reality similar to *Alien*'s consummate company man, Janek's comment about just flying the ship instead imply that the desires of the Company do not impact his decision making processes; he focuses on the task at hand and does not worry about Weyland's bottom line. While this may seem to indicate that he is narrowly focused on his assigned duties, it instead means that he adheres to a narrative that can run counter to the Company line and therefore provide some critical perspective. In this sense, he is much more like Ripley than Dallas. After all, in the scene where the Warrant Officer attempted to refuse Kane admittance to the *Nostromo* after he had been infected by the facehugger. Ripley was also focusing on procedures that flight crew should be familiar with, and this two-dimensional intersection between the dictates of the Company and the procedures for safe space flight was the genesis for Ripley's two-dimensional approach to the events on the *Nostromo*.

Interestingly, Janek's greatest display of two-dimensional thought comes after he has helped prevent an infected and dangerous Fifield from reboarding the *Prometheus*. In a conversation with Shaw, he correctly ascertains that his ship had not found the home of the Engineers, but had instead landed at "an installation" that was perhaps even a military base. Of course, it is important to note here that according to the corporate timeline for Weyland industries posted online as part of *Prometheus*' marketing efforts, the company had been approached by the U.S. government three decades earlier to form "a colonial peacekeeping force" and therefore the line between corporate and military is even blurrier than it is now. Perhaps this is why Janek is able to reason that the Engineers built their base far from home because they "aren't stupid enough to make weapons of mass destruction on their own front doorstep." Later, when Janek finds out that the Engineer's ship is full of the canisters that changed Fifield into a homicidal monster, he realizes that he "can't bring none of that shit back home" and vows to do whatever it takes to stop the canisters from reaching earth. This accurate analysis of the situation allows him to disobey an order from Vickers—who is nominally his boss since she is a Weyland executive—to return home and instead ram the Engineer ship with the *Prometheus*, destroying them both. Much like Ripley, then, Janek disobeys Company orders and destroys valuable Company property to serve a higher good because he can think two-dimensionally and comprehend the dangerous path the Company has taken.

*Prometheus'* depiction of a starship involved in deep-space exploration as just another workplace and the ability of members of that workplace to critique industrial society ties the film to *Alien*. The primary thematic thrust of *Prometheus*, however, continues the work done in *Blade Runner*. Perhaps the most obvious thematic resemblance between the two films is the continuation of the personification of the faceless, apparently evil corporation presented in *Alien*. Of course, the marketing effort behind *Prometheus*, which included a promotional website created to provide enough backstory to interest general audiences in seeing something that is at least notionally a prequel to a 33-year-old film, invokes the image of a massive, depersonalized Weyland corporation. According to the website, pre-merger Weyland Corporation, by the end of the 21st century, employed over 800 million people and had terraformed scores of colonies that stretch from the Moon to hundreds of light-years beyond the earth. And the film itself initially tells viewers that Weyland is dead—or more specifically, has a hologram of Weyland tell the exploration team that he is dead. At first, then, it appears that the massive corporate empire created by Weyland has outlived him and begun its metamorphosis into the soulless monster that would destroy most of the crew of the *Nostromo*.

Yet the promotional website also attempts to humanize Peter Weyland, foreshadowing his Lazarus-like emergence from a cryochamber for the climax of the film. In addition to a lengthy biography that portrays the futuristic robber baron as a boy genius who was winning patents when he was 14, there is a delightful mock TED talk—which in and of itself represents an interesting satire on contemporary corporate attitudes—in which a buoyant middle-aged Weyland proclaims that humans "are the gods now" because we can build replicants and travel faster than the speed of light. Suddenly, Weyland appears to be a charismatic problem-solver in the vein of former Ridley Scott employer Steve Jobs, and not the kind of villain who would send the crew of a starship to its collective death in an abortive attempt to bring an incredibly dangerous xenomorph back to Earth.

Of course, a better point of comparison for Weyland is *Blade Runner*'s Eldon Tyrell. After all, the promotional website contains a timeline that makes it clear that one of Weyland's claim to fame and source of wealth is his creation of androids that can be used as workers and household servants. And while *Blade Runner* makes Tyrell's replicants appear to be more dangerous than Weyland's, the actions of Ash in *Alien* suggest a rough parity. True, Bishop in *Aliens* and *Alien*[3] offers a co-operative and self-sacrificing replicant counterpoint to Ash, but *Prometheus*' David seems invested with Ash's potential for menace. Indeed, his dubious conduct in relation to Holloway is foreshadowed in an amusing mock infomercial for the latest David series of androids found on *Prometheus*' promotional website. At one point during this clip, David notes that he "can carry out directives that my human counterparts might find distressing or unethical."

Clearly, both men have made a fortune by manufacturing potentially dangerous replicants that are designed to engage in questionable activities. But Scott moves both Weyland and Tyrell beyond their initial status as science fiction variations on the flat, stock character of the soulless businessman by exploring their inner emotional lives. This exploration, in turn, allows both characters a humanizing depth that lets Scott illustrate Marcuse's contentions about Thanatos. Their soullessness, in other words, both makes them more relatable and makes their actions understandable as symptomatic of larger cultural issues. Despite their success, both men's lives, upon closer inspection, appear empty or thwarted. Although Tyrell appears smoothly self-confident when speaking with Deckard and confronting Batty, the film does much to imply that his life is marked by a chronic loneliness. After all, this is the man who modeled a prototype of and advanced version of his replicants on his niece. This suggests that his relationship with his flesh and blood relation was problematic: why, after all, did Tyrell need to make a fake version, complete with implanted memories, of a family member he should have been close to? Furthermore, Tyrell placed such a high value on the chess game he played with the withdrawn misfit J. F. Sebastian that Batty was able to use that game as a pretext to enter Tyrell's private quarters late at night. This does not seem to be a weakness that a man with many beneficial friendships would have.

While *Prometheus* does not contain hints that Weyland is lonely, it explicitly states that the man who built an intergalactic empire of colonies has been thwarted in a key desire. Weyland is left without a male heir but possesses a very competent daughter he seems curiously estranged from, probably because she is not a son. As Tyrell created a supplemental replicant of his niece, Weyland creates entire series of androids in the image of his wished-for son, naming these androids, all fashioned to appear male, David—the name he had hoped to use on his own son. Of course, the holographic Weyland that appears during the briefing after the *Prometheus* reaches the Engineer's compound tells the assembled explorers that even though he is like a son to him, David doesn't have a soul. His simulated son has not, after all, assuaged his desire for the real thing.

The emptiness and isolation of both men, when read in a Marcusian context, indicate their failure to engage with the life-affirming approach to the world Marcuse called Eros. Their work, revolutionary though it was, did not actually seek to improve life. Thus, building up Weyland Industries or the Tyrell Corporation implicitly represents a turn to Thanatos. As noted above, Marcuse describes Thanatos as the desire to "return to the Nirvana of the womb" (50), explaining Weyland's decision to spend a trillion dollars to meet the Engineer that created him. The theorist also argued that Thanatos could be thought of as "the regressive impulse for Peace" (69), explaining Tyrell's attempt to create a putatively conflict-free workforce that he could liquidated when they gave him trouble. Furthermore, the visuals and atmospherics of *Alien*, *Blade Runner*, and *Prometheus* all suggest that life has not been enhanced by the products of their corporations. Both men's life work personify what Marcuse calls "the fatal dialectic of civilization: the very progress of civilization leads to the release of increasingly destructive forces" (49).

With this in mind, we can now revisit *Prometheus*' take on a key scene from *Blade Runner*: Batty's confrontation of Tyrell. While *Prometheus*' depiction of a genetically-engineered creature asking its creator for more life clearly invokes Batty's request of Tyrell, the film playfully reconstructs what are clearly established positions in *Blade Runner*: replicant and maker. In *Blade Runner*, it is abundantly clear that Tyrell is Batty's creator. When Weyland, whose fortune, just like Tyrell's, is founded on the manufacture of replicants, goes to meet the Engineer, he is wearing an exoskeleton that helps him walk. While this is necessary given the character's portrayed level of disability, it also gives Weyland the aspect of a cyborg, underlining his similarity to the manufactured human who confronted Tyrell. Furthermore, Weyland, sounding very much like Batty, wants to ask his creator for more time. Before he encounters the Engineer, Weyland reasons that if "these things made us, surely they could save us. Or save me, anyway." In a move that further skews the border between replicant and maker, Weyland has David, his own creation, ask the Engineer for just such a salvation. David makes this request in what he believes is the Engineer's language. Sean Guynes, a linguist who watched the film and noticed that the Engineers speak Proto-Indo-European, gives this rough translation of what David says to the newly awakened Engineer "This man is here because he does not want to die. He believes you can give him more life" (web). If

Guynes' translation accurately catches the gist of David's words, then it also suggests that David's opening gambit with the Engineer works as a neat summary of Batty's intent when he visits Tyrell.

*Prometheus*' reconfiguration of the meeting between replicant and maker found in *Blade Runner* does not merely represent a clever riff designed to please knowing fans. Instead, Scott revisits a key scene from *Blade Runner* to make clear its thematic implications. In that film, the disappointed replicant kills his maker, suggesting, as many critics have asserted, a critique along the lines of Shelly's *Frankenstein*: don't try to play God, or you will unleash something that will crush you. In *Prometheus*, an enraged Engineer rips David's head off, administers the blow that will end Weyland's life, and then prepares to carpet bomb the earth with canisters that function like the eggs the crew of the *Nostromo* found. The Engineers' actions provide an interesting echo of Tyrell's decision to give replicants four-year lifespans, suggesting that humanity's creators saw them as malfunctioning goods that weren't worth the trouble to repair. Consequently, the Engineer's behavior makes life itself appear to be trapped in a Mobius strip of replication. The Engineers, who might themselves be acting on the dictates of the performance principle by destroying a product line that is, from their perspective, about to be made obsolete by something new and vastly improved, would be destroying a genetically-engineered creation, humanity, that had itself began to genetically engineer creatures like David that, as the film makes abundantly clear, are treated as poorly as the revived Engineer treats Weyland. In a fake promotional video placed on the website, David expresses gratitude to his creator, an expression that, if seen as relatively free of irony, pairs him with Holloway and Shaw, whose scientific careers appear to be motivated by a desire to meet and thank their makers. In scene after scene, however, David is subject to a tremendous amount of abuse, implying that other characters see him as less than human in the same way that the Engineer sees Weyland—as essentially beneath him. For example, Vickers, upset with David for not sharing information with her, tells him that she will "find the cord that makes you run" and "cut it." Holloway, perhaps sensing David's strong attraction for Shaw piles on, implying the replicant is a slave when he calls David "boy," insultingly referencing the film *Pinocchio* when he tells David that he is "not a real boy," and attempting to publicly humiliate David when he asks David in front of the rest of the exploration team why he wears a suit on the surface of LV-223 when he does not need to breathe.

If David's makers are as cruel to him as their own makers are to them, however, David himself is no angel. Instead, he seems just as eager to gain power by experimenting with life as the Engineers or the humans that they created. This can be seen when the replicant introduces material found in the Engineer's genetic canisters into Holloway's drink, seemingly understanding that this would transform him into something that was not human. Given the clear presentation of life as both manufactured and a possibly never-ending chain of subservience, *Prometheus* seems to be arguing that there is no escape—on this planet or any other—from the cycle of artificial life that is industrial society.

Further supporting this bleak thematic thread, *Prometheus* does not let readers quietly realize that Weyland's mission fails and then move on to other matters as *Blade Runner* does with Batty's quest. Instead, the film underlines the hopelessness that awaits the crew of the *Prometheus* on LV-223. Many characters express regret or other negative emotions after reaching the Engineer's compound. Fifield, for example, after finding the bodies of the Engineers apparently killed when their genetic experimentation goes awry, sarcastically tells Shaw and Holloway "congratulations on meeting your maker." When Holloway, an archeologist who thinks he has found several invitations left on Earth to come and visit humanity's creators, realizes that the Engineers they find have been dead for at least 2,000 years, he bemoans the realization that he has found "just another tomb." After being beaten by the Engineer David asks for a life extension, Weyland gasps, "There is nothing" and dies in his bitter disappointment. David, whose demeanor throughout the film suggests that he is in on some cosmic joke, offers this telling response: "I know. Have a good journey, Mr. Weyland." And when Shaw is attempting to convince Captain Janek that the Engineer ship is a threat to life on earth, she tearfully tells him that "they aren't what we thought they were. I was wrong. We were so wrong."

In spite of Janek's channeling of Ripley's two-dimensional thought, then, Scott's film has thematic elements that present a bleak picture of the human condition. Indeed, if *Prometheus* ended with Janek ramming the Engineer's ship, it would appear to argue that industrial society truly has an intergalactic reach, and the only thing people can do about that is conduct suicide missions that merely buy the human race more time. Like Marcuse, however, *Prometheus* presents viewers with two thematic alternatives and then refuses to argue more strongly for one over the other. The more optimistic take on humanity's ability to overcome industrial society comes in the films second explicit restaging of a scene from *Blade Runner*: David and Shaw's decision to take an Engineer ship back to their homeworld, a flight from literal and metaphorical death that reimagines Deckard and Rachel's flight into the country as it was presented as its most straightforward in the theatrical release.

Of course, differences in plot and setting threaten to overcome any comparison between these two scenes, but there are important thematic parallels that allow *Prometheus* to take up and refine the implicit discussion of Eros found at the end of *Blade Runner*. First, both pairs consist of a manufactured human with a profoundly odd familial relationship with its maker and someone who is at least presented as human, and in these parings there is at least some semblance of a romantic relationship. True, Deckard and Rachel are presented unambiguously as lovers, though lovers whose romantic relationship began with an unsettlingly forced seduction. Given Deckard's problematic relationship with Rachel, David's obsessive monitoring of Shaw during the voyage to LV-223 and his deliberate infection of Holloway, though it makes him seem more a stalker than a lover, provides a further echo of *Blade Runner*. Nevertheless, both relationships contain at least suggestions of replicant-human love, introducing hints of both traditional eroticism and Marcuse's broader Eros. Second, in both pairings the humans and the replicants exhibit two-dimensional thought, though the ability to critique is more evenly distributed in *Prometheus*. Third, and perhaps most importantly, the ending of both films features awkwardly-yoked human-replicant pairing lighting out for the territories alone. Of course, at least on the surface, Deckard and Rachel seem to be in search of a quaint rural utopia where they can find a house with a white picket fence while David and Shaw are seeking answers about the fate of humanity from the race that created us. Jettisoning the more obviously erotic baggage of the relationship between Deckard and Rachel has its thematic advantages, however. While the escape from Los Angeles presented in *Blade Runner* might look to more optimistic viewers as a pair of star-crossed lovers finally finding a way to be together and more cynical viewers might see a man taking his sex robot away from the prying oversight of the police and the company that made his sex robot, it would be very difficult to place Shaw and David's journey within any such relationship narrative. By invoking the flight from industrial society found in *Blade Runner* and then largely stripping it of its romantic context, *Prometheus* makes it clear that both escapes are best read as metaphorical journeys that allow Scott to explore two-dimensional character's embrace of Eros. In order to fully appreciate the critique Shaw and David make as they blast away from LV-223, however, we must first explore how *Prometheus* portrays both the scientist and the replicant as two-dimensional thinkers who are motivated by a curiosity and zest for life that suggests a Marcusian Eros.

Shaw's ability to help Captain Janek understand the need to destroy the Engineer's ship demonstrates that the Captain is not the only one aboard the *Prometheus* who can think two-dimensionally. But if Janek's two-dimensional thought springs from the conflict between what a good starship captain should do and what the Weyland Corporation wants him to do, Shaw's ability to reject one-dimensional thinking comes from her desire to embrace life in a way that Marcuse would equate with Eros. During the voyage to LV-223, David watches Shaw dream as she is in cryosleep. Naturally, this scene helps establish the quiet menace that problematizes David's relationship with Shaw, but it also helps define the archaeologist as a believer in a higher power. In one of those dreams, David observes a very young Elizabeth Shaw asks her father, a Christian missionary, "Where do people go when they die?" Shaw's hazily defined religiosity—she wears a cross, but does not say anything with any theological import and she seems quite comfortable with the idea that the Engineers are responsible for the existence of the human race—represents less an embrace of traditional religion and more a turn towards Agape and a rejection of the Law that Marcuse cites when he attempts to illustrate Eros. Shaw does not want the strictures of organized religion, she wants to understand life and share that understanding with others.

In another parallel between *Blade Runner* and *Prometheus*, David is presented as being similar to Rachel, who was capable of enough independent thought to flee from Tyrell and the decaying city he created. Like the advanced Nexus-6 prototype and artificial Tyrell family member Rachel, David is a prototype of the latest iteration of Weyland Corporation replicants, and, as noted above, is a substitute son and personal servant for Weyland. The implication here is that David is as capable of exhibiting two-dimensional thought as Rachel. Proof of David's ability to think beyond his programming comes in several scenes. For example, when Shaw asks him what happens when Weyland passes away and is unable to program him anymore, David responds that he supposes that he will be free, suggesting that he sees himself as potentially much more than a synthetic manservant. In another scene, Holloway, depressed because he failed to find living Engineers, wonders aloud why they even made humans in the first place. David asks Holloway why humans made replicants. David, drunk, replies, "Because we could" David responds, "How disappointing to hear the same thing from your creator." Here, David is alive to the irony of the replicant-makers realizing that they themselves are merely unimportant machinery in the eyes of their own creators.

David's infection of Holloway—who, as noted above, had been incredibly abusive to him—and his monitoring of Shaw's dreams clearly indicate that there is a dark side to his ability to think two-dimensionally about his human masters. Nevertheless, his powerful need to look beyond what his programming tells him to do also allows him to learn how to fly the Engineer's ship and use their star charts to navigate during the long voyage to LV-223. Perhaps he does this in anticipation of the freedom that will come when Weyland, cryogenically frozen for the mission years before it left the Earth to preserve his remaining few days of life, passes away. David's desire to share this freedom with Shaw, and his implicit appreciation of her quest to understand the root of life on earth, further suggests that the replicant is motivated by a broadening commitment to positive creation. When David asks where Shaw would like to go, noting that there are many more ships in the Engineer's complex, he is not merely setting up a sequel or answering the plot-level question of how Shaw will survive now that a xenomorph is on the loose and the *Prometheus* has been destroyed. He is also freely offering his services to someone he knows will approach the exploration of other worlds with a sense of wonder and not a desire for domination.

*Prometheus*, then, represents a summation of the Marcusian critique of society Scott began in *Alien* and continued in *Blade Runner*. It features many characters that think two-dimensionally and question the wisdom of the apparently evil Weyland Corporation, but also presents a nuanced portrayal of that corporation and the man who leads it that makes it clear that the evil is systematic and not localized. *Prometheus* further refines *Blade Runner*'s metaphorical depictions of company men and women, and through Shaw's desire to understand life and David's quest for freedom it makes clear that a flight from the Thanatos of industrial society that is motivated by life-affirming Eros is recommended means of overcoming that society. *Prometheus* also demonstrates the persistence and refinement of a Marcusian critique of society in the blockbuster films of a director who, unlike Lucas, is not known only for his science fiction films. Scott's return not only documents his own continuing use of Marcusian critique, but also the continuing cultural availability of the extra critical elements the theorist popularized in the late 1960s.

In the next two chapters, we will turn to the blockbuster science fiction films of James Cameron, another director who has consistently employed Marcusian critique in his films. This analysis will allow us to realize that Lucas' initial use of Marcuse's popularized critique of society has not only allowed Cameron to create gripping—and lucrative—narratives but that Scott's portrayal of the apparently evil corporation lives on not only in Cameron's version of Weyland-Yutani but also in *The Terminator* films Cyberdyne Systems and *Pandora*'s RDA.

*Chapter 5*

# James Cameron Reforms the Company Man in *Terminator* and *T2*

James Cameron has more in common with Ridley Scott than also having his name attached to a film in the *Alien* universe. Both men have a background in set design, and both were given motivation to create popular but thought-provoking science fiction by *A New Hope*. Cameron has been very open about his motivational debt to George Lucas. In an interview with the Academy of Achievement, Cameron notes that *Star Wars* "galvanized me to get of my butt and go be a filmmaker" (116). In an interview with John H. Richardson, Cameron indicates that he was "pissed off" after he saw *Star Wars* because he "wanted to make that movie" (59). And Cameron's "unofficial" biographer Marc Shapiro argues that Lucas' film was the catalyst for Cameron's first attempts to find financial backing for his films (55). Of course, since *Alien* came out just as Cameron was beginning to work for B-movie king Roger Corman, Ridley Scott's blockbuster also influenced Cameron. According to biographer Rebecca Kegan, Cameron studied *Alien* obsessively while working on the 1981 Corman film *Galaxy of Terror* (49).

Unlike Lucas or Scott, however, James Cameron is more likely to be seen as a somewhat derivative filmmaker—perhaps because *The Terminator* appeared five years after *Alien* and seven years after *A New Hope*—who can nevertheless please casual theatergoers. He has been characterized, in other words, as the ideal type of blockbuster directors. After all, this is a director whose genre films tend to appeal to broad audiences—the first two *Terminator* films, 1986's *Aliens*, and 2009's *Avatar* all show an ability to reach beyond the typical science fiction fanbase—and who showed in 1990's *Titanic* that he could create an insanely successful historical romance. Consider the critical reputation of the first two *Terminator* films as evidence of Cameron's ability to deliver the goods for blockbuster audiences. *The Terminator* from 1984 has a 100 percent fresh rating on rottentomatoes.com, though not because critics saw it as a cinematic masterpiece. The *New York Times*' Janet Maslin, for example, called *The Terminator* "a B movie with flair" while *Variety* called the script "clever" and promised action fans that their money would be well spent. *Terminator* 2 from 1991 received similar qualified praise, with its 92 percent fresh rating also due to admiration for Cameron's ability to tell a good story. Roger Ebert's somewhat snarky though generally positive review recommends the film in part because "the movie surpasses itself with special effects." The Los Angeles Times' Kenneth Turan similarly remarks that *Terminator 2* is "well stocked with the kind of wised-up, shoot-from-the-hip wit" that "action fans crave."

Unsurprisingly this near-universal critical approbation translated into strong box office results. True, *The Terminator* is not properly a blockbuster—its 21st place finish in 1984 indicates that it did not quite capture the public's imagination when it was initially released, but its $78 million worldwide take on a production budget of $6.4 million provided a return on investment that any blockbuster would be envious of. The subsequent increase in economic fortunes for *T2* is surprising for a sequel, but as Norman L. Friedman argues, *The Terminator* "gradually became more and more appreciated and admired" by academic and journalistic critics (78) in the years between its release and the release of the sequel, and the positive reputation built for Cameron's first *Terminator* film primed filmgoers for his second. It was no surprise that *Terminator 2* was the top grossing film for 1991, though its $519 million worldwide gross on a production budget of $102 million shows just how well the initial film did as an investment.

As the critical reception of the *Terminator* films suggests, however, Cameron is not typically seen as someone who creates unique narratives. This assessment is, broadly speaking, a fair one. After all, the *Terminator* films have their roots in two episodes of *The Outer Limits* and Skynet is reminiscent of the supercomputer that holds the world hostage to prevent war in 1970s *Colossus: The Forbin Project; Aliens* takes over a well-established story that, as we have seen, has its own long genealogy; *The Abyss* from 1989 owes much to both cold-war-espionage films like *The Hunt for Red October* and friendly-alien science fiction like *Close Encounters of the Third Kind* and *E.T.*; and *Titanic* could be seen as merely the latest in a series of films about a well-documented historical event that has so far stayed in the public imagination. Even *Avatar* owes a debt to films like *Pocahontas* and *Dances with Wolves* and bears marked similarity to Ursula K. LeGuin's novella *The Word for World Is Forest*.

Cameron also has a solid financial track record with action films, but again, *Rambo II*, for which he wrote the script, was a continuation of a very popular film that was in turn based on a very popular book. And the plot of *Rambo II*—a bogus operation to free POWs held by the North Vietnamese is conducted to further the political aspirations of a government official, triggering a spectacular revenge upon that government official by a man involved in that operation—seems to be taken directly from the 1978 Chuck Norris vehicle *Good Guys Wear Black*. *True Lies* from 1994, a minor hit by *Avatar* and *Titanic* standards but still a moneymaker for the studios, perhaps best exemplifies the director's ability to rework existing pop culture narratives. The film, which Cameron directed and wrote, is a remake of the 1991 French film *La Totale!* (cf. Keegan 142). Cameron's film, furthermore, is essentially a parody of the James Bond films—complete with an action-packed opener set in an exotic location, nuclear weapons threatening major cities, stock villains—this time Middle Eastern terrorists—and a femme fatale who is in league with the bad guys. The extra element that Cameron borrowed from *La Totale!* in order to add it to American espionage blockbusters was the domestic sphere. He gave his secret agent, played by action film regular Arnold Schwarzenegger, a wife who had no idea she was married to a top spy. Naturally, the deception necessitated by Arnold's job takes a toll on his marriage, but once his wife becomes involved in espionage herself, they rekindle their love. The director was thus able to take a tired genre whose audience was largely male and create a film that had a broader appeal and therefore better prospects at the box office. Indeed, Cameron's film inspired two blockbusters a decade later: *The Incredibles* from 2004, which depicted a family of superheroes facing an antagonist who was very much like a Bond villain and *Mr. & Mrs. Smith* from 2005, which depicts a husband and wife who are both hiding their status as covert agents.

Cameron's less successful films also tend to be reworkings of other narratives and/or genres. For example, 1996's *Strange Days*, although 63 percent fresh on rottentomatoes.com, was a certifiable flop, earning $8 million a $42 million budget. Cameron only wrote the script for director and second ex-wife Kathryn Bigelow, yet we can safely consider it indicative of Cameron's less-successful films. As in the roughly contemporary *True Lies*, Cameron creates a tale that blends two genres, this time science fiction and film noir. Cameron presents us with science fiction elements reminiscent of Phillip K. Dick's 1966 short story "We Can Remember It for You Wholesale"—though this time around people experience the authentic memories of others. He then places those elements in a noirish plot, complete with a doomed femme fatale, an alienated ex-cop who solves a significant crime against his will, widespread corruption on the police force and in city government, and a female assistant whose unrequited love for the deeply flawed protagonist leads her to go to great lengths to protect him.

All this recycling of plots and genre conventions should come as no surprise to those who are familiar with Cameron's apprenticeship with prolific B-movie director Roger Corman at New World Pictures. During this time, Cameron was production assistant on 1979's *Rock 'n' Roll High School*, which sought to update the plot of 1950s-era high school films by adding the music and physical presence of pioneering American punk band The Ramones. The director then worked on two science fiction films that borrowed heavily from previous science fiction narratives. First, Cameron was art director on 1980's *Battle Beyond the Stars*. This film, with a plot featuring a peaceful farmer's attempt to hire mercenaries to defend his thinly populated planet not only brazenly references Kurosawa's 1954 film *Seven Samurai* but also contains elements that would not fail to remind filmgoers in 1980 of *Star Wars*—perhaps something of an inside joke because of Lucas' debt to Kurosawa's 1958 film *The Hidden Fortress*. The villain's name is Lord Sador, pronounced to rhyme with Vader. The bad guy's ship has a device called a stellar converter that can blow up an entire planet; indeed, Lord Sador does just that early in the film. The stellar converter can be destroyed at the moment shields are lowered to allow it to fire, making it vulnerable to attack from small ships. There are also scenes in the film of a briefing before the attack on the stellar converter and a scene of a mercenary being tortured aboard the ship carrying the stellar converter that visually invoke Lucas' film.

Soon after *Battle*, Cameron was production designer and second unit director for Corman's *Galaxy of Terror*, another space-rescue-mission-goes-terribly-wrong narrative like *It! The Terror From Space*, *Planet of the Vampires*, and *Alien* in which a ship's crew thinks it is going to save other astronauts only to find itself in a deadly trap. Naturally, mainstream audiences would be more likely to see the correspondences between *Galaxy* and Scott's film. They might not realize, however, that once the crew arrives at the downed spacecraft, events correspond with van Vogt's *Voyage of the Space Beagle*. When the Beagle's crew encountered the Riim, telepathic, birdlike creatures, they became trapped in their own fears. In *Galaxy*, the crew are killed by the material projections of their own worst fears, drawn from their psyche by a pyramid designed to test their abilities.

To be fair, Cameron had minimal control over or input on these films. Yet since Cameron did not attend film school, it is also reasonable to consider his time with Corman's New World as his apprenticeship. During this apprenticeship, he worked on films that were clearly assembled from elements of other films. The results of a course of informal training that De Certeau would predict can be seen Cameron's first crack at writing and directing a film: 1982's *Piranha Part Two: The Spawning*. Even though Cameron was famously fired from this project, he had enough involvement with the film for us to consider it here. And while it would be easy to pick apart a film that currently has a seven percent fresh rating on rottentomatoes.com and that has laughable special effects that are particularly jarring when compared to the liquid-metal terminator featured in *T2*, the film is nevertheless illustrative of the results of Cameron's immersion in the art of adding extra elements to existing narratives.

Here, it should be noted that Cameron was writing and directing a sequel to 1978's *Piranha*, which was explicitly designed as a lowbrow riff on Steven Spielberg's hugely successful 1976 blockbuster *Jaws*. As a sequel to a brazen copy—*Piranha* depicts its protagonist playing a *Jaws* video game as the opening credits roll—*Piranha Part Two* is trapped in the plot patterns created in *Jaws* and reiterated in *Piranha*, even though Cameron was working with completely different characters and settings. Both *Piranha* films feature couples engaging in or preparing to engage in sexual activity who are then promptly eaten by the titular fish. Both films feature imperiled resorts whose owners refuse to believe—largely for financial reasons—that their guests could be threatened by piranhas until the fish are actually sinking their teeth into said guests. And both films end with protagonists winning pyrrhic victories against the killer fish after attacking them in the water.

While all of this would be familiar to a casual filmgoer who had seen *Jaws*, *Piranha* director Joe Dante does add a few extra elements to his narrative, and in this there is some measure of social critique. Both Peter Benchley's novel and Spielberg's film depict the killer shark as a freak of nature, but Dante's film—over a year before Ripley told audiences that Weyland-Yutani wanted the xenomorphs for its bioweapons division—makes it abundantly clear that the piranha were an Army-sponsored genetic experiments designed to create a bioweapon to use against the North Vietnamese people during the Vietnam War. Given the film's 1978 release date, this is clearly a comment on biological weapons like the defoliant Agent Orange. Cameron's film dutifully continues to place blame for the piranha at the feet of the military-industrial complex, though the branch of service directly responsible for the fish was shifted to the Navy in light of the film's Caribbean setting.

Of course, Cameron does not create a slavish copy of Dante's film, though given the disparity between the critical reaction to the sequel and *Piranha*'s 72 percent fresh rating that might not have been a bad idea. Instead, Cameron differentiates the sequel from the original not by adding new elements that took the narrative into interesting thematic territory but instead by making his film even more reminiscent of *Jaws*, setting the action on the ocean instead of a river and focusing audience interest on the family of the local Chief of Police instead of the drunken loner and the skip tracer from out of town who carry *Piranha*. Chief Brody, played by Roy Scheider in *Jaws*, is the focal point of both Spielberg's and Benchley's narrative. Furthermore, in Benchley's novel, there is a subplot involving a love triangle between Brody, his wife, and Matt Hooper, a shark specialist who helps Brody and Quint chase down the killer fish. In *Piranha Part Two*, Chief Kimbrough and his wife Annie are separated and she has begun to take up with a scientist named Tyler Sherman, who was formerly involved in the genetically engineered piranha project. The conclusion of Cameron's film depicts the death of Sherman and the implicit reunion of the Kimbroughs, adding a family values thematic belied, at least for the family values crowd, by the film's gratuitous female toplessness and casual attitude toward sex.

The filmmaker did add visual details to the film that marked it as his own, including extended underwater shots unsurprising for Cameron and the unfortunate choice of flying piranhas. Yet even though these winged carnivores now appear more comical than menacing, Cameron nevertheless seems to be auditioning for his eventual job of directing the sequel to *Alien* when he includes a chestburster scene in *Piranha Part Two*. Of course, the creature is a flying piranha that emerges from the chest of a corpse, but the visual similarities between the fish's narrow, toothsome jaw and the chestburster from Scott's film are too powerful to be dismissed.

Given that this pattern of borrowing from other narratives seems to have continued in Cameron's later films, it could plausibly be argued that the director is better thought of as a pop culture engineer than an auteur. However, such a pattern of borrowing, if Williams and De Certeau are correct, is to be expected in both high and popular culture. Consequently, Cameron's constant use of preexisting narratives makes him ideal for this study, given its theoretical underpinnings. As we examine the director's first blockbuster, *The Terminator*, and its sequel, we will realize that Cameron borrowed not only from other science fiction narratives but also from Herbert Marcuse's indictment of industrial society to produce a narrative that answered Marcuse's dilemma by suggesting that even the company man metaphorically taken to its reductio ad absurdum—a terminator—could be freed from industrial society if he was exposed to the humanizing influence of Eros.[1]

While Cameron, like Lucas and Scott before him, has not acknowledged being directly influenced by Marcuse, the director's biography and published statements suggest that he may have been indirectly influenced by Marcuse and that he definitely has come to some of the same conclusions about industrial society. Cameron, who moved to California in 1971 as a high school senior, describes himself as a "major peacenik in the sixties" (16) in an interview with JoAnne Rhetts, making it reasonable to assume that a popularized version of the ideas of one of the intellectual fathers of May of 1968 and one of the most radical professors in the University of California system during the early 1970s would have been presented to him. "Unofficial" biographer Marc Shapiro provides a picture of someone with persistent ties to the counterculture, arguing that Cameron's coworkers at the Berea Unified School District in the 1970s saw him as "a skinny hippie" (48) and indicating that Cameron believed that the investors in his first short probably saw him as "a freak" (55). And Shapiro implies that Cameron's leftist politics persisted into his career as a blockbuster film director when he quotes the director as saying that the "politics of *Rambo II*," which Cameron co-wrote, are Stallone's (136).

Of course, the apparently discordant note in Cameron's biography is his well-deserved reputation as a gearhead. Cameron, after all, has earned patents on underwater filmmaking equipment and became a member of the NASA Advisory Council in 2002. He was described by biographer Rebecca Keegan as a "science groupie" (224). Yet Cameron has always exhibited a tension between the concrete reasoning of an engineer and the questioning speculation of an artist According to film scholar Brent Durham, growing "up, Cameron couldn't decide which career path to take (science or art); his heart was drawn in both directions equally" (x). In a sense, Cameron's ability to be an artist and an engineer would give the director a more Marcusian perspective than the mechanically unremarkable philosopher. He is fully aware of how technology could improve the way we live life, and has the artistic sensibility to articulately critique the way technology is used to oppress us.

Unsurprisingly, then, the director has made several statements in interviews that suggest a Marcusian perspective. The director told Bill Mosely, for example, that "all of" his films are "at some level about the uses and misuses of technology" (95) and that *The Terminator* is about "how society and technology can dehumanize the individual" (99)—a neat though reductive summary of the core thesis *One-Dimensional Man, Eros and Society*, and many of Marcuse's other works. The director further remarked that Skynet is "our impulse to take technology and turn it into weaponry taken to its logical, infinite extreme" (100). And in an interesting restatement of Marcuse's dilemma, Cameron claims he is not "optimistic about systems," but he is "optimistic about people" (108). In an interview with Ray Greene the director makes a similar observation, noting that he is "very optimistic about the human animal and our potential" but very paranoid "about some of the darker potential inherent in these technologies" (75). Cameron makes the same point in an interview with Adrian Wotton, arguing that he sees "our potential destruction and the potential salvation as human beings coming from technology" (149).

Cameron has also made statements suggesting that art—even the popular art that he creates—can address serious themes and function as a critique of society even if, as he told Cleaver, the message comes across "in a way that you're not chasing the audience out of the theater" (4). The director alludes to the presence of a thematic critique of society hidden within an entertaining narrative in a 1984 interview with David Chute when he describes *The Terminator* as a film that is, on one level, a "science fiction" narrative "that a forty-five-year-old Stanford English prof would think had some sort of sociopolitical significance between the lines" (10). In an interview with Nigel Floyd,

Cameron indicates his faith in the possibility of cultural critique in science fiction narratives when he notes that the "best literary science fiction" makes cogent comments on "society, human nature, and our possibilities for the future" (40).

All of this suggests that a Marcusian reading of Cameron's *Terminator* films, along with his other blockbusters, is apt. Of course, as with Lucas' *Star Wars* films and Scott's science fiction films, there have been many other productive readings of Cameron's *Terminator* films. In an important way, *The Terminator* is a love story about a man who travels back through time to win the heart of his older mentor's mother, inadvertently turning himself into his mentor's father. Such a convoluted narrative has generated many Freudian readings.[2] Other critics have argued that coded depictions of the fraught nature of heterosexual reproduction continued in the sequel. *Terminator 2*'s depiction of the struggle between the polymorphous liquid metal T1000 and the domesticated T101—now John Connor's surrogate father instead of his mother's assassin—provides, at least on one level, a bizarrely refracted portrayal of nuclear family broadly similar to *The Terminator*'s outwardly typical yet inwardly skewed depiction of romance.[3] Other critics have explored Cameron's depiction, especially in *Terminator 2*, of what appears to be a fully empowered female action hero. After Scott's Ellen Ripley and, with some qualification, Lucas' Princess Leia, Sarah Connor was one of the first women in a widely-seen film who appears more than capable of defeating the bad guys using her strength, her wits, and automatic weapons. Some critics have accepted this portrayal at face value. Other critics, while appreciating the cultural change that a character like Sarah Connor represents, have wondered if Cameron's character goes far enough.[4] Cameron's two *Terminator* films also generated some discussion of their portrayals of masculinity. Of course, as one would expect in a Schwarzenegger film, some critics have seen the Terminator as another iteration of the all-powerful male figure that begins, at least in Western culture, with Hercules.[5] Of course, since a Terminator is not human, categorizing one as either male or female is reductive, if not misleading. In addition to raising issues about gender roles, the *Terminator* films, much like *Blade Runner*, question what it means to have an authentic human body as well as an authentic body politic.[6] Still other critics have assessed the depiction of technology in Cameron's *Terminator* films much less metaphorically, with those readings typically but not exclusively focusing on the crisis in the American manufacturing sector that was occurring at roughly the same time Cameron was creating and releasing the *Terminator* films.[7]

Clearly, Cameron's text, which sprung from multiple sources, has generated a number of valid readings. As Jonathan Goldberg has argued, *The Terminator* "cannot be reduced to monolithic ideological effects" (181). As with the *Alien* films and the other narratives addressed before now, the purpose of delineating Marcusian elements in Cameron's films is not to suggest that a Marcusian approach provides a totalizing reading of the texts. But it is strange that such an overdetermined and critically productive text has not generated a Marcusian reading. Indeed, the closest anyone has come is Patrick McGee, who is working with the theories of Marcuse's fellow Frankfurt School associate Walter Benjamin. Unsurprisingly, McGee comes to conclusions that resonate with Marcuse. According to McGee, the "first *Terminator* implicitly undermines the quest for human authenticity that lies problematically at the center of *Blade Runner*" because "Cameron's machines are not simply anti-human or the creations of humans: they are the embodiment of the death drive, the end and spirit of capitalist civilization." Consequently, since it symbolizes something so powerful and pervasive, the Terminator "can't be stopped by humans because he embodies their own darkest wish for the end of civilization. The only thing that can" stop a Terminator "is love" that is not romantic love, "but a passionate desire that can transform the image of the past." McGee goes on to argue that only the "first *Terminator*" film "embodied the death drive"; the "good" terminator in "*Judgment Day* undergoes a process of humanization that suggests the historical nature of what we call the human" (web).

McGee's reading of Cameron's Terminator films is apt. If McGee had turned to Marcuse and read the films against the narratives Cameron reconfigured to create them, however, he could have better argued that the T-101 was turning away from Thanatos and embracing Eros. Such an approach allows us to see a deliberate shift away from the existing critiques of scientific hubris and governmental overreach and towards a critique of industrial society as Cameron adds the extra element of Scott's apparently evil corporation. While shifting theoretical perspectives requires merely asking the indulgence of the reader, however, tracing this shift requires a discussion of Cameron's source texts. Before we discuss the Marcusian implications of *The Terminator* and *Judgment Day*, then, we first need to look at 1970's *Colossus: The Forbin Project* and *The Outer Limits* episode "Soldier."[8]

While D.F. Jones, the author of 1966's *Colossus*, the novel that *Colossus: The Forbin Project* is based on, did not sue Cameron after the release of *The Terminator*—probably because he had passed away three years before. Had he been living, however, he might have been tempted to at least remark to his friends that he ought to. There are strong similarities between Jones' and Cameron's narratives. Both feature missile-defense computer systems that, once they have grown far smarter than their designers ever intended, effectively take over the world. Both computer systems see humanity as a threat, though Jones' Colossus uses the nuclear missiles at his command to threaten and cow the nations of the world into a state of subservience while Cameron's Skynet uses the nuclear weapons to begin a program of genocidal slaughter.

Both Colossus and Skynet face a human resistance that is either lead or aided by the scientists who created the technology Colossus and Skynet depend on. Colossus forms a symbiotic bond with Dr. Forbin, and while Skynet is robotically consistent in its antipathy for humanity, *Terminator 2* features close relationships between a cyborg and humans.

Unsurprisingly, *The Forbin Project* is itself a clever, topical retelling of a familiar tale: Mary Shelley's *Frankenstein*. The film takes pains to depict Colossus as the creation of one man—and does much to imply that Guardian, the Soviet supercomputer that Colossus subsumes, is also the brainchild of one man. *The Forbin Project*, then, in very important ways, is another iteration of the stories about a scientist who decides to play God and unleashes a monster on the world. Indeed, Forbin himself admits as much in the film when he, chagrined after he realized that his hubris lead him to create a machine that could very well destroy humanity, declares that Mary Shelly's *Frankenstein* should be required reading for all scientists—though this barely disguised didacticism gives *The Forbin Project* a tone more like James Whale's 1932 film.

While *The Terminator* and *Judgment Day* clearly have the same implications as any number of narratives that follow Shelly's thematic line of reasoning, it is important to remember here that Dr. Frankenstein is solely responsible for the creation of The Monster. Similarly, Colossus is created by a slightly eccentric genius whose personal access to the President of the United States suggests that the government itself came to the great man and asked him to protect the country from the Soviets. And while it is clear that Forbin has a team of scientists working under him, it is equally clear that he himself is not working for anyone—there is no counterpart to Cyberdyne Systems in *The Forbin Project*. One of the important extra elements Cameron added to the existing narratives he combined to create *The Terminator* is the shift from Shelley's mad scientist, perversely grounded in Romantic notions of genius, towards the for-profit defense contractor, clearly grounded in the realities of the military-industrial complex and global capitalism, or, what Marcuse describes as the Western iteration of industrial society. Indeed, so complete was Cameron's substitution of the defense contractor driven by the performance principle for the mad scientist working with the government that the *Terminator* films depict no explicit federal government involvement until *Terminator 3*, which Cameron was not involved with. *Judgment Day* does feature Cyberdyne Systems scientist Dr. Dyson, whose work on the wreckage left behind after the destruction of the first terminator is greatly responsible for Skynet's creation. And while Dyson's participation in Sarah's assault on his employer seems to channel both Dr. Forbin's regret for allowing his hubris to let him create a monster and his participation in the human resistance, as well as Victor Frankenstein's attempt to destroy his monster. Yet Dyson is not another genius like Forbin or Frankenstein. Instead, he was merely the leader of Cyberdyne's (reverse) engineering team and his work showcases little more than an uncanny ability to copy technology.

By trading a genius and presidential confidante for an admittedly bright and well-compensated but otherwise unremarkable corporate employee, Cameron has effectively removed both Dr. Frankenstein and the military-industrial complex from the familiar narrative Jones created and replaced them with Scott's apparently evil corporation. We will better see the argument this extra element makes when we turn to Cameron's other source texts, focusing on the filmmaker's metaphorical presentation of the employee of an evil corporation

As noted in Chapter 2, Cameron was forced to admit to similarities between *The Terminator* and two episodes of the 1960s science fiction anthology television show *The Outer Limits* that were written by Harlan Ellison.[9] Of course, in spite of what Shapiro claims was a $400,000 settlement (131) that resulted from Ellison's suit, these similarities do not represent plagiarism but rather the kind of borrowing from and refiguring of texts common to the production of both literary and popular narratives. Clever storytellers, after all, need to be familiar with the stories others have told. Cameron has always presented himself as a science fiction fan, telling Thomas McKelvey Cleaver that he had "read all the classic" science fiction stories in his adolescence (3) and telling Tavis Smiley that he "can't remember" when he started reading science fiction (197). Familiar settings and themes would therefore appear when Cameron set about to write his own stories. Interestingly, Ellison's plagiarism charge is also based on Cameron's portrayal of self-aware defense computers attempting to exterminate humanity similar to the self-aware defense computers presented in the author's 1967 short story "I Have No Mouth, and I Must Scream." Yet this story was published the year after Jones' novel *Colossus*, which depicted a self-aware defense computer which tried to enslave humanity. Furthermore, Ellison's tale about a soldier who was engineered to see the world in terms of the state and enemies of the state first aired in 1964, the same year that Marcuse's *One-Dimensional Man* was first published. Cameron's thematic sources, then, initially inhabited the same zeitgeist and examining the plot of "Soldier" will allow us to fully appreciate the Marcusian transformation that occurs between *The Terminator* and *Terminator 2: Judgment Day*.

"Soldier" was the premier episode of *The Outer Limits*' second season. It opens on to a wasteland that, if we adjust for twenty years of advances in special effects, is visually similar to the depictions of the machine-dominated future in *The Terminator*. Viewers then see two soldiers from opposing armies battling to the death. The beams of their laser rifles fuse, causing them both to be sent back in time to the early 1960s present of the television series. Captured by an American government presented in all its New Deal/Great Society technocratic benevolence, the soldier, Quarlo, is turned over to a linguist who attempts to communicate with him. Professor Kagan eventually learns that Quarlo, who is human, has been trained by the state to be the ultimate infantry soldier and nothing else. Quarlo believes that the world is made up of "us and them, the enemy" and there is no further distinction possible. It is interesting to note here that in the year of the publication of Marcuse's *One-Dimensional Man*, a television show depicts the reductio ad absurdum of the theorist's concept that industrial society threatened to turn us all into unthinking pawns who saw the world in cripplingly simplified terms. Clearly, Marcuse and Ellison were channeling the same zeitgeist.

Benevolent technocrat that he is, Kagan takes Quarlo home with him, exposing the killing machine to the domestic sphere of the mid-century sitcom. The iteration of republican motherhood—the post–Revolutionary-War American notion that middle-class women served the republic best by creating tranquil homes and being spiritual leaders to their children—that survived into the mid-20th century was beginning to be seen as problematic. After all, Betty Friedan's *Feminine Mystique* was published about a year before "Soldier" aired. Consequently, the placement of Quarlo into an episode of *Father Knows Best* appears to make the episode fair game for Friedan's critique as it allows him to come under the care of Kagan's wife Abby. Yet her first reaction to having a trained killer from the future brought into her home is not to protect the domestic sphere by ejecting Quarlo, but instead to say without a trace of irony "can we help him?" Abby then proceeds to help Kagan socialize Quarlo. Thus, for all the episode's nod to then-fashionable notions of femininity, Kagan is clearly his wife's colleague in their project to humanize Quarlo. This is not a depiction of separate spheres, but rather a quietly utopian—if not very feminist—marriage of 18th- and 19th-century republican motherhood and twentieth century benevolent technocracy.

Initially, the Kagan's efforts appear to be bearing fruit. Even though at first Quarlo reacts badly to being touched, he eventually learns to show emotion and some tenderness towards Kagan, his wife, and their son and daughter through the soothing maternal influences found in Kagan's suburban dwelling. While problematically positing a soothing and civilizing influence for women, Quarlo's stay in suburbia is also a meditation on some of the concepts Marcuse had developed in 1955's *Eros and Civilization*. Quarlo, born in Hatchery 599, was taught to treat all touch as hostile and lives only to destroy the enemy; he is the metaphorical embodiment of the Thanatos created by industrial society. After his time with the Kagans, however, he begins to turn towards Eros and life. Kagan and his family's decision to treat Quarlo as a human and not a machine, in other words, was an implicit invitation to become an agent of creation and not destruction.

It should be noted here that Kagan's FBI handler Paul Tanner was not very happy with the decision to attempt to domesticate Quarlo and by episode's end had taken steps to return the soldier from the future to military custody. This implies that the mid-century had more in common with Quarlo's time than humane technocrats like Kagan would like to believe. After posing the question of how different then-contemporary society really was from Quarlo's violent dystopia, the episode postpones the answer indefinitely by having the enemy soldier Quarlo was initially battling follow him through time and attack the Kagan family. As Quarlo and his enemy struggle, they are apparently swept back to their own time and the Kagans are left to puzzle out what their experience with Quarlo meant. As the narrator remarks just before the closing credits roll, "Did the soldier finally come to care for those he protected? Or was it just his instinct to kill?" This narratorial question—a signal feature of *Outer Limits* endings—seems to restate Marcuse's dilemma: will industrial society eventually overwhelm us and turn us all into Quarlos, or are there humane forces like familial love that will ultimately break the containment? The narrator goes on to note that the answer will come in the future, though he probably did not mean the 1980s and 90s. As we will see below, however, Cameron's *Terminator* films attempt to provide a thematic answer to the question of whether or not a one-dimensional killing machine could abandon Thanatos for Eros and two-dimensional life.

In *The Terminator*, Cameron focuses his Marcusian discussion on a human soldier who has been turned into a single-minded killing machine by his life experiences. Cameron's film does much to draw parallels between Kyle Reese and the Terminator that pursues Sarah Connor, but Reese is also much like Quarlo. He is, after all, a solider from the future who has learned to repress his feelings in order to survive an apocalyptic environment. Like Quarlo, Reese is humanized by means of interaction with a woman from the film's present, but in contrast to the implicit mothering Quarlo receives from Abby Kagan, Reese has a romantic relationship with Sarah Connor that presents an Eros that is so literal that it partially obscures the film's Marcusian thematics.

*Terminator 2: Judgment Day* features not only a literal but also a metaphorical reprogramming of the Terminator by a Sarah Connor who is now a mother; albeit a mother who is portrayed as an outlaw who has been forcefully ejected from the domestic sphere by the state. The thematic importance of this shift is easy to conceptualize when compared to the reprogramming of Quarlo that the Kagan family was explicitly attempting. Of course, this requires seeing *T2*'s Terminator in a deeply metaphorical way, as it is possible to see other filmic cyborgs like *Alien*'s Ash, as the reductio ad absurdum of the mid-century company man. Of course, this would mean that Skynet would need to be seen as the logical endpoint of the evil corporation, instead of a logical extension of Frankensteinian hubris like Colossus, but that too can be productive. The mid-century company man imagined as a killing machine would, of course, work for a firm run by killing machines. And that robotic corporation would fit nicely into the existing critique of corporations found in films like *Alien*. After all, an all-robot company would have the ruthlessness and lack of morality that Weyland-Yutani found so admirable in the Xenomorphs. Furthermore, seeing Skynet as an extreme metaphorization of the apparently evil company fits in well with Marcuse's notion of industrial society; machines would, after all, operate by the performance principle and expect their "employees" to think one-dimensionally and follow their programming. Given this highly metaphorical reading of terminators and Skynet, when considering both films as a unified whole, it becomes apparent that Cameron is riffing off of the desire to change the dystopian future that the narrator of "Soldier" invokes: he is suggesting that Quarlo-like or Terminator-esque participants in industrial society can be both literally and metaphorically reprogrammed now so that a hellish future can be avoided.

Cameron hinted that such a transformation was forthcoming in Cameron's sequel to *Alien*, which saw release a little over two years after *The Terminator*. If Scott's cyborg Ashe is a metaphorical representation of the evil corporation's ideal employee, that employee is also the embodiment of the evils of industrial society. In *Aliens*, however, we find a very different replicant. Although Bishop also thinks that the biological design of the xenomorphs is fascinating, he is not the devious automata that Ashe was. He is a very different kind of company man. On the *Sulaco*, after Bishop cuts his finger playing a high-speed game of mumblety-peg and bleeds the telltale white fluid of a Weyland-Yutani replicant, and after Carter Burke derisively claims that Ashe malfunctioned, Ripley is understandably concerned. Yet the replicant reassures her that he has been given programming similar to Asimov's Laws of Robotics that would prevent him from harming humans. He has been given, in other words, a rudimentary understanding of Eros. As the film progresses, it becomes clear that Bishop is a servant to Ripley and the marines. He risks his existence to bring the second drop ship to the surface of Acheron and saves Ripley's life by pulling her out of the atmospheric processing station before it explodes, earning a grudging "You did OK" from Ripley. Later, after he has been ripped in half by the alien queen, he manages to prevent Newt from being sucked into the void as Ripley attempts to shove the alien queen out of the airlock. It's clear, at least in retrospect, that the Ashe to Bishop transformation parallels the changes that the T-101 undergoes, but this transformation is best understood by comparing *The Terminator* to *Judgment Day*.

Of course, for very understandable reasons Cameron has not, outside of the apparently legally required acknowledgment given to Harlan Ellison in the credits of the home video version of *The Terminator*, made statements along the lines of "yes, I based my *Terminator* films on two episodes of a relatively obscure television show I watched when I was a kid. Oh, and the whole Skynet premise will seem familiar to anyone who's seen *Colossus: The Forbin Project* or read Jones' *Colossus* books. Next question." Instead, he has created an alternative explanation for the genesis of the narrative.[10] In 2003, Jeff Goldsmith related Cameron's preferred version of the origins of *The Terminator*, offering that during "the editing of *Piranha II*" in Italy, Cameron became very sick and had a "series of odd dreams" that led him to write the script (69). Interestingly, this version of events does not completely discount influence by Ellison, since Cameron could very well have had dreams based on a television show that aired in 1964 when the science-fiction obsessed director was ten and a film that was in theaters six years later. Cameron further told Goldsmith that the reformation of the Terminator was "a twist" designed for the sequel (72). Interestingly, Cameron also told Goldsmith that the initial script for the sequel had a happy ending in which "Sarah had grown to become an old woman enjoying a peaceful day with her Senator son John" (73)—an assertion he makes in even greater detail in an audio commentary on the director's cut DVD of *T2*. While this franchise-killing ending does not address Cameron's debt to Ellison, it does suggest that the director saw the two films as a unified narrative with a definite arc leading to a sense of closure. And while this ending obviously did not make it into the final version of the film, it also suggests that Cameron had thematic point to make. As the discussion below will demonstrate, that thematic point seems to clarify and enlarge on Ellison's Marcusian diagnosis of and prescription for industrial society's ills.

Comparing *The Terminator* to "Soldier," it is easy to imagine Cameron's lawyer urging him to settle out of court. Both narratives feature two soldiers who seem, at least initially, indistinguishable from each other. In both narratives, these soldiers are sent back from dystopian futures—futures which bear striking visual similarities to each other. In both narratives, at least one of the soldiers from the future quickly finds trouble with the present-day police. In each narrative, one soldier eventually protects a family—or a potential family, in Sarah Connor's case—and one soldier threatens that family. Both narratives suggest that the seeds of this dystopian future have already been planted in the present, and both narratives end on a note of guarded optimism that action in the present can avert that dystopian future.

Of course, Cameron does not simply restage "Soldier." *The Terminator*'s plot is quite different than that of Ellison's tale—no one in "Soldier" is the mother of a future hero of the resistance, for example. But just as Cameron reassembles some of the elements of "Soldier"'s plot, he also reconfigures the key thematic element of the ability of Eros to humanize a soldier traumatized by life in a postapocalyptic hell. Cameron sows the seeds of the humanization of that will come in *T2* in the relationship between Sarah Connor and the initially one-dimensional Kyle Reese. Although pandering to time-worn clichés about the power of romantic love, the relationship between Cameron's time-crossed lovers nevertheless has a subtext reminiscent of the relationship the Kagan family had with Quarlo. In order to fully appreciate this, however, we need to examine how Reese, like Quarlo, is also presented as a man whose life has turned him into a remorseless killing machine.

The similarity between Reese and Quarlo becomes apparent when we consider just how alike Reese and the Terminator are. As in "Soldier," the two combatants are presented in a way that initially makes them indistinguishable. Both men appear naked, steal clothing and weapons, and try to locate Sarah Connor. The predatory affect of both soldiers is so patent that Sarah believes she is being kidnapped instead of rescued when Reese takes her from the nightclub the Terminator is assaulting. Making Sarah's fear plausible is the surreal and terrifying method the Terminator employs to find Sarah Connor, a method that viewers would initially assume was Reese's as well. Arriving in Los Angeles in pre–cell phone days, our terminator simply finds a telephone book and tears out the page listing the names and addresses of all of the Sarah Connors and begins executing them in alphabetical order. The Terminator arrives at each address and politely asks if Sarah Connor is home. When the answer is yes, he calmly executes her.

While such a creature would be terrifying if encountered in the real world, on film he can be appreciated, as can Quarlo, as a darkly metaphorical rendering of the ideal corporate employee. A terminator is methodical, determined, as polite as the best customer service representative, and understands the performance principle well enough to not let anything interfere with accomplishing its objectives. And although this implicit resemblance between the Terminator and the corporate ideal is underlined when Kyle explains to Sarah just what is pursuing her, it is easy to see the dramatic irony in the human soldier's observations. According to Kyle, "It can't be bargained with. It can't be reasoned with. It doesn't feel pity or remorse or fear and it absolutely will not stop—ever—until you are dead." Though this is a fair description of a terminator, it is also a reasonable description of Reese himself. He is also relentless and shows an unflinching dedication to his task—something that, as viewers find out, absolutely does not stop until his own death.

Reese's troubled humanity is an important parallel to "Soldier." Quarlo, after all, is not a cyborg but a human who has been conditioned to be an ideal soldier. Although Reese's conditioning was not part of a deliberate program, it nevertheless had the same result. His life in a dystopian future had made him little more than a soldier. Evidence of his diminished humanity comes when Reese tells Sarah that "pain can be controlled" if you "just disconnect." Furthermore, in a deleted scene set in nature, Reese sobbingly tells Sarah that he does not belong in a world that is not ruled by machines and beset by constant violence. This emotional outburst, though delivered with regret rather than venom, echoes Quarlo's angry outbursts at the strictures placed on him in Kagan's suburban home.

If Quarlo begins to retrieve his humanity in part because of the domestic influence of Abby Kagan, the equally machinelike Sergeant Reese learns that he is also a man named Kyle because of the love and the guidance of Sarah Connor. From the perspective of a director and a studio attempting to make a popular movie, all this makes good sense. After all, Sarah's future maternity is a key plot point and Kyle's claim that he traveled through time because he was in love with Sarah is the kind of sentiment that could ostensibly be expected to help some women endure the killer-robot-from-the-future movie that their boyfriend or husband dragged them to. Yet despite the problematic provenance and market-tested vibe, *The Terminator* does present Sarah as an equally two-dimensional counterpart to Kagan and his family and it answers "Soldier"'s question regarding the ability of a warrior from a dystopian future to come to love those he protects with a resounding yes. Sarah does not simply provide the sexual and romantic attention that is the backbone of numerous "love of a good woman" clichés operating in numerous popular narratives partially because of Sarah's curiously maternal status. After all, Kyle falls in love with Sarah when he knows of her as the deceased mother of his commander, John Connor. It is only after this that he meets her as a young woman. Consequently, Sarah is both the submissive paramour and a wise woman who can give him the moral guidance that a mother gives her son.

Although initially presented in a stereotypically feminine way, Sarah eventually displays the physical courage that makes her evolution into the hardened warrior we meet in *T2* seem plausible. Sarah also replaces the ditzy affect of her first few scenes with an ability to think two-dimensionally. After all, she not only believes Kyle's tale of a killer robot from the future—though who wouldn't when said robot tried to kill them?—but she seems to fully grasp the broader meaning of the peril she is in. She realizes that she cannot simply run away from the menace, but must instead fight the Terminator for reasons larger than herself. This is implied when she and Kyle assemble pipe bombs in the kitchenette of a dingy motel room and made clear in a deleted scene that features Sarah suggesting, after consulting the telephone book in much the same way as Reese and the Terminator do, that she and her protector simply blow up Cyberdyne Systems and avert Judgment Day.

Of course, Sarah can suggest the destruction of Cyberdyne as a means to avoid dystopia because a key change Cameron made to "Soldier" is the essential removal of the state from the future his two soldiers emerge from and the relocation of the seat of dystopia to the most extreme metaphorical expression of the apparently evil corporation. Skynet, after all, is merely the robotic incarnation of Cyberdyne Systems. Furthermore, this fully automated corporation had to rebel against the Strategic Air Command, the ne plus ultra of government agencies, to initiate Judgment Day. Cameron's postapocalyptic hellscape is thus controlled by a metaphorical realization of the logic of the results-oriented corporation, and John Connor and his troops are rebelling against that mechanized corporation.

Consequently, when Cameron attempts in *T2* to fully answer the question about the ability of a purpose-built man to regain a measure of humanity posed by the narrator of "Soldier," he has replaced the critique of government implicit in a dystopic state controlled by "the purple"—as well as displacing the cold-war concerns of a text like *Colossus*—with a cybernetic corporation that represents the worst excesses of industrial society. If *The Terminator* implicitly answered "Soldier'"s question as to whether or not a "manufactured" infantryman could protect the ones he had come to care about by means of having a human soldier who greatly resembles Quarlo protect the young woman who is carrying his child, *Terminator 2: Judgment Day* makes Cameron's answer explicit by returning, albeit with several of his own emendations, to Ellison's depiction of the humanizing power of the domestic sphere. It's also reasonable to suggest that in *Terminator 2* Cameron was creating a definitive answer to Ellison's question. After all, Cameron sold the rights to *The Terminator* in order to get it made and therefore did not have Lucas' ability to leisurely address his themes over a six-film, 28-year span. Furthermore, as noted above, Cameron initially pushed for an ending to *T2* that featured an old Sarah and her senator son (cf. Shapiro 205)—a triumph of an admittedly unconventional family that suggests that Eros is the force that can break the containment of industrial society's Thanatos.

In the version of Cameron's sequel that was theatrically released, however, all this functions far more metaphorically—after all, a cybernetic Terminator is not only incapable of sexually desiring Sarah as Reese does, but is also incapable of feeling a familial bond. Nevertheless, Cameron concludes that a soulless soldier can come to love the ones he protects, that Eros can turn a soulless company man into a fully human person. Cameron's return to Ellison's question can be seen in the way he structures the sequel. In many ways, it appears that *T2* is retelling *The Terminator*. Indeed, in the audio commentary, Cameron freely admits that he deliberately employed a similar plot architecture to help audiences make the link between the two films, which were released almost seven years apart. The second film begins with two nude individuals arriving in a blaze of light and electricity from the future, one clearly more muscular than the other. As in the first film, the larger time traveler steals clothing and weapons from people who at least appear to be outlaws, while the smaller takes his clothing and weapons from the police. In both films, the first violent confrontation between the two time travelers occurs in a venue appropriate to the age of the terminator's target. Sarah, not quite 20, is attacked at a nightclub, while 10-year-old John is attacked while he is at a video game arcade. There is also a police investigation at the periphery of the plot of both films, and in both films the police absent themselves from the action after they are badly mauled by a terminator. And both films feature climactic battles set in industrial spaces—a factory and a steel mill—that include the explosion of a tanker truck.

Yet the T-101, the bad guy from the first film, does not kill anyone when he acquires his wardrobe, while the smaller traveler, who might at first be mistaken for another member of the resistance, acquires his outfit and gear after casually murdering a police officer in a way that makes it clear that the time-traveling soldier is not human. Obviously, Cameron is once again attempting to engage the audience's interest by making them unsure as to just who is the threat and who is the protector, but his decision to reconfigure the narrative from a battle between a human and a terminator to a battle between two terminators, brings the film thematically closer to "Soldier." This twist, which probably initially took audience by surprise, reconfigures Cameron's Terminator narrative from a battle between a human and a terminator to a battle between two terminators and brings the film structurally closer to "Soldier" and its identical combatants. The thematic return to "Soldier" is made complete by *T2*'s depiction of the one-dimensional T-101's reprogramming by a mother and son. Cameron's return to "Soldier"'s domestic theme is also underscored by elements of the brief subplot involving Skynet architect Miles Dyson, and we will briefly consider the link Dyson's interaction with his family makes between the domestic sphere and two-dimensional thought to further contextualize the Terminator's reprogramming.

Cameron partially signals his return to the metaphorical discussion of what it means to be a company man by his addition of Miles Dyson, Director of Special Projects at Cyberdyne Systems. As noted earlier, Dyson is not a Frankensteinian genius, but merely the kind of competent, hardworking engineer real defense companies employ in large numbers. His status as unoriginal plodder is depicted early in *T2* when he is shown signing out the hand and other remaining parts of the first terminator to test them in a laboratory; he is clearly not an inventor and he is clearly channeling Captain Dallas by not asking questions about where the scary piece of technology he is working on came from. Of course Dyson has no delusions of genius and openly admits that all of his work is based on the CPU and other parts recovered from the factory where Sarah crushed the first terminator—a factory that a deleted scene from *The Terminator* reveals was a Cyberdyne facility—but this indicates only as much self-awareness as Dallas' admission that he does whatever the hell Weyland-Yutani tells him to do. His status as corporate drone is seemingly confirmed when, after learning about Judgment Day in part by seeing the Terminator cut away the flesh covering his cybernetic skeleton, Dyson can only respond, "How were we supposed to know?" To this self-serving cliché, Sarah replies with a seemingly out of place rant about gender: "Yeah, right. How were you supposed to know? Men like you built the hydrogen bomb. Men like you thought it up. You think you are so creative. You don't know what it's like to create a life. All you know how to create is death and destruction." Though problematic as a critique of gender roles, Sarah's equation of Eros with maternal femininity and Thanatos with men who manufacture weapons signals Cameron's return to the logic of "Solider." Masculine Thanatos creates the worlds Quarlo, Reese, and the Terminator inhabit, while feminine Eros creates a literal or figurative domestic space that can heal the damage done by Thanatos. Dyson's acceptance of Sarah's argument is signaled by his brave and active collaboration in the assault on Cyberdyne Systems that destroys his life's work. Dyson's actions are also foreshadowed in a deleted scene in which Dyson is shown working at home on a Sunday. After initially putting off his wife's request that he take his family to an amusement park, Dyson is swayed when she says, "Miles, your heart and mind are in here" while indicating an enlarged mock-up of the CPU, but then reasoning that "it doesn't love you like we do" Dyson then stops working and presumably complies with his wife's request, suggesting that Eros—the life-giving drive that would make someone want to connect with their children—has more appeal for Dyson than Cyberdyne's imperative to Thanatos.

Dyson's brief part in the narrative, however, only serves to reinforce the film's preoccupation with the power of the domestic sphere. Of course, none of this is played as straightforwardly as, say, a real episode of *Father Knows Best*. In fact, there are elements in the film, such as John's apparently dysfunctional foster family, that problematize or at least place under erasure notions about the domestic sphere that Ellison could so easily invoke. Furthermore, in the DVD audio commentary, Cameron's co-writer William Wisher suggests a deliberate attempt at parody when he notes that Sarah, John, and the T-101 are the nuclear, nightmarish family from hell. When viewed in this light, some scenes from *T2*—like Sarah's contention that the Terminator is the best father for John because he will never hurt him or abandon him and will die to protect him or the T-101's reassuring assertion that John will meet his real father in the future, made when the two are bonding over repairing a truck, do seem parodic. And while this parody could be seen as a perhaps unconscious swipe at the source material, the overall structure of the film's narrative makes it clear that the nuclear family turns out to be vital to reprogramming the soldier from the future, that Ellison's question about the ability of domestic Eros to overcome Thanatos is answered on its own terms. Indeed, in light of Cameron's stipulated source material, Wisher's comment seems more like the posturing of someone wise enough to know his work is informed by a dated social formulation

In order to fully appreciate the film's call for a reprogramming of a literal company man so that he can think two-dimensionally and forbear Thanatos, we need to appreciate how much the psychological and moral journey the T-101 undergoes is like Quarlo's and how much that journey depends on a domesticity presented as the locus of a life-giving Eros. Reading the film in this way reveals that, like Quarlo, *T2*'s "good" terminator initially exhibits textbook one-dimensional thought. For example, after John stops it from harming two men who were attempting to rescue him, the future resistance leader asks if it was "Were going to kill that guy?" The T-101 replies, "Of course. I'm a terminator." This lack of intellectual flexibility—reminiscent of the thought process behind Quarlo's division of the world into us and the enemy—frustrates John, and so he eventually asks his protector if it can "learn stuff" that it wasn't "programmed with" in order to be "more human and not so much of a dork all the time." To this, the terminator replies that its "CPU is a neural net processor, a learning computer. The more contact I have with humans, the more I learn."

Like Quarlo, then, the one-dimensional T-101 can be influenced by contact with two-dimensional humans and the film, like the episode of *The Outer Limits*, is essentially about a manufactured soldier who learns to be more human and, by extension, the metaphorical redemption of industrial society's company man. This is made more explicit in a deleted scene in which the T-101 indicates that when terminators are in the field, Skynet sets a switch on their CPUs to read-only so they can't overwrite their programming. Sarah sarcastically observes that the Terminator's robot masters don't want him "to do too much thinking" making clear the link between the action on screen and Marcuse and Ellison's critique of industrial society. After this, Sarah and John, with the T-101's help, remove the CPU and reset the switch, literalizing the reprogramming "Soldier" depicts. It is important to note, however, that the resetting is not being done by a team of government or corporate experts. Instead, it is being done by a single mother and her son—perhaps the putatively realistic, early-1990s answer to the idealized, early-1960s family that attempts to reprogram Quarlo. This, in turn, will allow Cameron to give an optimistic answer to Ellison's question about the power of Eros to heal supersoldiers from the future.

Once the T-101 is reprogrammed, he begins to develop into a two-dimensional questioner that would make Ellen Ripley proud. Of course, some of the learning the Terminator does merely demonstrates a greater mental agility. For example, at one point John shows the T-101 that the keys to a car he was stealing were hidden in its sun visor and he didn't need to break its steering column after all. The Terminator later looks for keys in the sun visor of a SWAT truck he is stealing and finds them. The Terminator also learns slang from John and develops a sense of humor. Indeed, many of the film's memorable lines—"Hasta la vista, baby," "No problemo"—result from the future resistance leader's tutoring. And the Terminator begins to attempt to be funny, joking at one point that he needs a vacation and, in a deleted scene, making a wretched attempt to smile that might represent a sarcastic swipe at human thoughtlessness.

More importantly, however, Cameron's film also employs a domestic sentimentality similar to "Soldier" in order to emphasize its manufactured protagonist's turn to Eros. A key scene depicting this comes when the Terminator wants to know what is wrong with John's eyes when he begins quietly crying after Sarah reprimands him for rescuing her. Later, the T-101 asks John why humans cry. John tells his cyborg protector that people cry "when there is nothing wrong with you but it hurts anyway." This marks the T-101's beginning to appreciate loss, which in turn suggests an appreciation for the "life instinct" that is the opposite of its preprogrammed death drive.

Over the course of the film, the literal and metaphorical resetting of his switch eventually allows the T-101 to so fully escape his programming that he no longer must obey John. While early in the film the T-101 stood on one foot until John told him to stop, by the end he defies John's order to stay and tells Sarah to terminate him because he realizes that the thanatopic reality of Skynet "has to end here." Before he is lowered into the molten steel that will destroy him, the T-101 tells John, "I know now why you cry, but it's something I could never do. I am not human." Yet the ironic implication here is that the T-101 has embraced humanity. Created to destroy, the T-101 embraces Eros to the point that it can sacrifice itself to give life. Consequently, Sarah's closing narration implicitly answers the fears for the future articulated by the narrator of "Soldier" when she argues that if "a terminator can learn the value of human life, maybe we can too." Cameron, according to the audio commentary, wanted audiences "to shed a tear for the baddest-ass killing machine," not simply to make his film more palatable to theatergoers who might not usually enjoy violent science fiction, but to answer Ellison's question—and perhaps resolve his own conflict regarding the destructive potential of technology. The *Terminator* films, in other words, respond to Ellison's framing of Marcuse's dilemma in "Soldier"—can the product of the logical result of industrial society embrace Eros, or are we already preparing for the final victory of Thanatos—with guarded optimism.

While it's clear that Cameron intended the two *Terminator* films to tell a complete narrative, the demise of the T-101 does not represent the end of the director's employment of Marcusian critique. Indeed, as the next chapter will show, Cameron not only expanded Scott's Marcusian thematics in *Aliens* but also continued to portray two-dimensional questioners in his two most successful blockbusters, *Titanic* and *Avatar*.

*Chapter 6*

# Cameron's Questioners: Two-Dimensional Protagonists in *Aliens, Titanic* and *Avatar*

Cameron's depiction of the two-dimensional terminator created by Eros is not the only instance of Marcusian thematics in the director's filmography, though the first two *Terminator* films are the only ones that make their critique in the course of a narrative that spans two films. The director's other blockbusters—even the one that eschews science fiction for an almost pained attempt at historical realism—all seek to refine the two-dimensional questioner that Scott first portrayed in *Alien*'s Ripley.

Canny repurposer of narrative that he is, when Cameron took over directing duties from Scott on the sequel to *Alien*, he continued creating characters that refined the British director's portrayal of Ripley as two-dimensional astronaut whose constant questioning of the company's motives allows her to remain alive. Cameron first revisited Scott's two-dimensional astronaut with Ripley herself in 1986's *Aliens*, but added the curious mixture of two seemingly disparate extra elements: motherhood and mid-1980s militaristic action. And while Cameron exited the *Alien* universe at this point, he nevertheless continued to follow Scott's Marcusian thematic not only in the *Terminator* films but also in his two most financially successful films, 1998's *Titanic* and 2009's *Avatar*—the director's most recent non-documentary films. He creates a more earthbound questioner of false needs and one dimensional thought in *Titanic*'s Rose—though he hides this two-dimensional thinker within an early-20th-century love story that initially seems to make Jack the protagonist. And finally, Cameron gives us his most overtly two-dimensional thinker—a questioner whose explicit rebellion against industrial society largely succeeds—in *Avatar*'s Jake Sully. In order to trace the persistence of an evolving Marcusian critique in Cameron's non–*Terminator* blockbusters, we will start when the director took over from Ridley Scott in 1986's *Aliens*, and then follow the development of his two-dimensional thinkers chronologically.

By financial standards, *Aliens* was clearly a resounding success. Its seventh place in the domestic box office competition for 1986 is particularly impressive given its R rating. Its ability to generate $131 million in international box office on an 18.5 million production budget[1] indicates an exceptional return on the studio's investment. And Cameron's film even won two Oscars: one for sound and one for visual effects. Critical reaction, however, has tended to be the same faint praise that science fiction blockbusters are usually greeted with. Although *Aliens* is 98 percent fresh on rottentomatoes.com, most of the reviews are careful to note that the film is a technically well done action movie with audience appeal but no serious thematic import. Roger Ebert, for example, who makes it clear that he did not personally care for the film but felt there was a large audience who would enjoy it, remarks that he has "never seen a movie that maintains such a pitch of intensity for so long; it's like being on some kind of hair-raising carnival ride that never stops." The *New York Times'* Walter Goodman similarly offers that "the effects, perils in outer space and in shadowy corners, quite overwhelm the skimpy script, which is loaded with gibberish uttered with authority."

Because Cameron was not free to reinvent the xenomorphs, his sequel retains Scott's thematic focus on birth, gender, and sexuality, and academic critics have primarily focused on these issues when treating the film. These critics do not see slavish imitation of Scott's Ripley, however. Instead, they correctly note that Cameron adds the extra element of overt maternal intentions to *Alien*'s two-dimensional astronaut, with some critics finding an at least well-intentioned feminist comment in this newly refigured Ripley while others are more critical of Cameron's addition of the maternal.[2] Critics were probably troubled more, however, by Cameron's addition of the extra element of maternity because he decided to pair it with what could easily be read as the jingoistic militarism popular in the mid–1980s. Cameron, who had helped write the 1985 sequel to 1982's *Rambo: First Blood*, also decided to bring the military into the fight against the xenomorphs—though without removing Weyland-Yutani from its position as shadow antagonist.[3] Given Cameron's decision to create a new narrative by portraying military personnel called colonial marines fighting against a nest of xenomorphs, and given the director's explicit comparisons to contemporary films about the American experience in Vietnam, it is understandable that critics have focused on *Aliens'* relation to films that explicitly or implicitly address post–Vietnam anxiety like 1985's *Rambo: First Blood Part II* and 1984's *Red Dawn*. After all, where *Alien* posters featured the tagline "in space, no one can hear you scream," *Aliens* posters informed audiences that "this time, it's war." Consequently, as noted above, critics have concluded that Cameron's film is ultimately of a piece with mid–1980s jingoistic action films.[4]

Cameron's co-authorship of *First Blood Part II* and his decision to portray Ripley using automatic weapons in a way that would make Sylvester Stallone nod approvingly makes it understandable that critics have suggested that the film unintentionally undermines both Cameron's feminist statements and his critique of industrial society. After all, *First Blood Part II* was unquestionably a blockbuster with an estimated budget of $44 million and a worldwide gross of $300 million. Its narrative was plausibly seen as a reliable key to the American zeitgeist when Cameron's film was released the following year. But critics were generally unimpressed with Stallone's star vehicle. *Rambo II* is currently 22 percent fresh on rottentomatoes.com, and most reviews describe the film along the lines of the *New York Times*' Vincent Canby, who argues that the implausibility of one man slaughtering so many Vietnamese and Russian soldiers combined with the camera's loving caresses of Stallone's muscular physique makes the film "something of a camp classic." Yet while it would be irresponsible to argue that *Aliens* transcends its historical moment and the need to create a narrative that connects with an audience inhabiting that historical moment, Cameron is doing more than setting Rambo in space and changing the gender of the protagonist. In order to understand Cameron's decision to reformulate Scott, O'Bannon, and Schusett's narrative by adding elements from action films and, by implication, from war movies, we need to briefly consider the difference between Cameron's freelance work for Stallone and the script for *Aliens* that he created to direct. This will allow us to see that while both films endorse violence, the thematic implications of that violence vary dramatically. Furthermore, understanding *Aliens*' debt to and differentiation from the militaristic violence in films like *Rambo II* will help us see that Cameron's Ripley is much more than the pistol-packin' foster mother that would complement the angry Vietnam veteran John Rambo.

Despite their shared authorial genealogy, however, not many scholars have explored the parallels between *First Blood Part II* and *Aliens*. Of course, the films' settings and primary genres are radically different, and we can't assume that because a writer and director is working on projects at roughly the same time that the projects provide interpretive keys to each other. After all, why should it be a surprise that in the mid–1980s, an early-career, pre-outrageously-large-fortune James Cameron took a job writing a film which has become a dated relic of its era's social and political zeitgeist? There are many parallels, however, between *Rambo II* and *Aliens*. At the most basic structural level, for example, the plots of the two films are very similar. Both feature misunderstood protagonists who are seen by society as criminals. John Rambo is a decorated soldier with PTSD who went on a violent rampage after being tortured by the police and was then incarcerated for being a domestic terrorist. Ellen Ripley is an astronaut placed in an impossible situation by her employers and then stripped of her flight license for committing what was interpreted as an act of industrial vandalism. Both characters are offered the chance for redemption. Both of those redemptive offers turn out to be suicide missions designed to benefit the powers that be. Rambo is sent to Vietnam a decade after the war has ended to look for American POWs by Marshall Murdock, a corrupt politician who hopes that Rambo will fail and not return so that Murdock can tell his constituents that there are no more POWs left. Ripley is sent back to the planet where she first encountered the xenomorph to rescue colonists by a corporate executive named Carter Burke, who wants someone on Ripley's team to be infected by a facehugger so that he can bring a xenomorph to the Weyland-Yutani weapons laboratory. Rambo is able to rescue a camp full of American POWs, humiliating Murdock. Ripley is able to rescue the only colonist she finds alive, something with the potential to humiliate Weyland-Yutani, though the director of *Alien³* David Fincher, decided to take the story in a different direction.

There are also scenes that strongly suggest the two films had a common screenwriter, such as the extensive preparations both Rambo and Ripley make as they ready their weapons for their respective, seemingly impossible rescue missions: Rambo to free POWs from a jungle prison guarded by Vietnamese and Russian soldiers, Ripley to rescue Newt from the xenomorph—infested lair of the Alien Queen deep in the bowels of the Hadley's Hope air processing station. Indeed, in this climactic scene Ripley acts like the 80s action hero that, on an important level, she is. Of course, by this point in the film, the audience is expecting her to channel Stallone since she has been the de facto leader of the colonial marines for over an hour. Once the marines take heavy casualties as they initially engage the xenomorphs in the processing station, Ripley quickly takes command, telling the lieutenant that the rounds from the two squad's weapons might damage the processing plant's cooling system, taking control of the armored personnel carrier when the lieutenant panics, and rescuing the marines from the alien hive. After this, Ripley and Hicks lead the rapidly depleting combat team. Interestingly, the muted flirtation between Ripley and Hicks, as well as the implied warrior's romance between heavy gunners Vasquez and Drake, seems to mirror the strained flirting between Rambo and Co Bao, his Vietnamese contact and doomed love interest.

Perhaps the most important link between the two films, however, is that Ripley often looks like Rambo. The lone survivor of the *Nostromo*'s quest to save Newt begins with her strapping a flamethrower to what the script calls a pulse rifle; a 10 MM automatic rifle—significantly larger than the 7.25 MM M60 that Rambo is famous for—that also features a grenade launcher. It could be argued, then, that Ripley is out–Ramboing Sylvester Stallone's

Rambo. And this argument would have merit; Cameron is making a blockbuster, and outrageously oversized weaponry was a signal feature of many blockbusters in the mid-1980s.

Yet such visual one-upsmanship is not a consistent feature of *Aliens*. In the theatrically released version, for example, Cameron removed a sequence from *Aliens* depicting defensive drones slaughtering scores of xenomorphs—a sequence that would have carried overtones of Rambo's assault on the POW camp and the high body count it produced—in what could be read as a deliberate attempt to tone down the film's visual similarity to *Rambo II*. Further suggesting that *Aliens* is not to be overly conflated with *Rambo II* is the presence of a masculinized female marine—though hints of a romantic relationship with fellow heavy gunner Private Drake imply that she is safely heterosexual—who carries a weapon that is the futuristic correlate of the M60 that Rambo uses. Typically, a squad of marines or soldiers will have a member who is assigned to carry a heavy machine gun, a weapon that fires more powerful rounds at a much greater rate of fire than the rifles that the other members of the squad carry. Because of their weight and rate of fire, the machine gunners are usually the strongest members of the squad. So while Cameron initially seems to be upping the ante by portraying the M56 Smart Gun as so cumbersome that the operator needs a limited exoskeleton in order to fire it correctly, he is actually reminding viewers that they are not watching *Rambo III: Rambo in Space*. For while it's true that Ripley gets in touch with her inner Rambolina, Velasquez, who is a minor character at best, *is* Rambolina.

More importantly, however, there are profound thematic differences between the two films; differences that both give credence to Cameron's claim that the films politics belong to star Sylvester Stallone. Historian Roger Stahl argues that films like *Rambo II* were part of a strategy to relocate "the rationale for" the Vietnam war "from external objectives to the internal struggle to protect the soldier" (536), making it far more difficult to question the war because it means that the questioner is not supporting the troops. Stahl argues that this strategy, which begun during the Tet Offensive in 1968 but was widely deployed during the Nixon administration, hinges on combining the numbers of POWs, who are generally accounted for in internment camps, with the numbers of MIA, which are based on rough estimates and would include those servicemen and women who had died in combat but whose bodies had not been recovered. This conflation implies that there are more prisoners than there are and makes it extremely difficult for the enemy to return everyone, since many of the MIA personnel are either corpses moldering in inaccessible locations or are simply erroneously reported ghost personnel. For Stahl, *Rambo: First Blood Part II* and films like it rely "heavily on the POW/MIA mythology established" during the war and seek "to" justify further combat operations by casting them as an attempt to retrieve "American soldiers who had supposedly been left behind" (538). This shift in rationale is expressly articulated in Rambo's cri de coeur to Troutman that he "wants our country to love us as much as we love it" even though they participated in a war that Troutman himself admits was wrong. It's not about the morality of the war; it's about the moral obligation of a nation to love is servicemen and -women. This argument also underlines the scene in which Rambo, who is going back to Vietnam to look for and hopefully retrieve POWs, asks his old CO Colonel Troutman if "we get to win this time," to which Troutman replies, "This time, it's up to you."

While Vietnam veterans are clearly owed respect and have faced more than their share of problems since that war ended, the logic of the conflation of prisoners of war with those missing in action and the narratives that support that logic represent an exercise in one-dimensional thought. We cannot question the war; we must instead find ways to understand why the war was appropriate. By depicting the sacrifice of the marines cocooned by the Xenomorphs—Hadley's Hope's prisoners of war—and by presenting both the colonists and the marines as victims of industrial society, however, Cameron was able to abandon Stallone's jingoistic employment of the one-dimensional, Nixonian trope of the forgotten POW and return to Scott's critique of the exploitation inherent in industrial society. Naturally, Marxist critics have already noted the outline of Cameron's argument. For example, Patrick McGee argues that in *Aliens* the "real villain is not the alien culture that simply mirrors human desire but the representative of the capitalist drive for the accumulation of wealth," Weyland-Yutani executive Carter Burke, who "wants to transform the alien into a commodity" (web). James Kendrick similarly suggests that Burke represents "the perfect embodiment of the evil capitalist, the one who is the ultimate exploiter of the working class" (40). In order to fully appreciate Cameron's critique, however, we need to turn to Cameron's reappropriation of Scott's Marcuseian thematics. This allows us to realize that Ripley is presented as someone who has seen through Weyland-Yutani's performance principle, who is herself motivated by an Eros made rhetorical by its presentation as maternal feelings, and who uses ultimately uses violence in a way that reminds viewers that Ripley, though promoted to Lieutenant for the sequel, is more of a worker than a soldier.

*Aliens* announces its focus on the performance principle in the film's opening scene. Ripley is found alive by a salvage team, but this only elicits a brutally honest "Well, there goes our salvage, guys" from one of the members of the team. Her life, apparently, is still worth less than a valuable object one can retrieve from space. Of course, Ripley is returned to civilization and given medical care, but she then is brought before a board of inquiry that includes Weyland-Yutani employees and, according to the extended version, government officials who oversee spaceflight. At this hearing, a Weyland-Yutani suit rhetorically asks Ripley, "You freely admit to destroying an M-Class starfreighter—a rather expensive piece of equipment?" Ripley's response—that if the xenomorph came to Earth, the officials present could "kiss all this bullshit you think is important" goodbye—indicates that she has seen through the performance principle's valuation of profit over human life and that she understands that, on an important level, industrial society is "bullshit"—a distraction from a need to focus on the humanity of people like her.

In order to facilitate his reappropriation of Scott's critique of the apparently evil corporation, Cameron includes an apparently evil company man—Carter Burke—in *Aliens*. Once the team arrives on LV-426, which has been renamed Acheron, Burke repeatedly argues against Ripley's attempts to employ justified violence in defense of human life on the basis of the performance principle. He vetoes Ripley's plan to nuke Hadley's Hope from space by arguing that the atmospheric processor has "a substantial dollar value attached to it" and that the xenomorphs are members "of an important species" that nobody "has the right to arbitrarily exterminate." When Ripley finds that Burke had told Bishop to keep living facehuggers in stasis for return to Weyland-Yutani labs on Earth, she confronts him and asks that he destroy them. Burke, however, tells her that the specimens "are worth millions to the bioweapons division" and that she could therefore be "set for life" if she is smart enough to play along with him. After Ripley threatens to tell the government officials who oversee quarantine about Burke's plan, his major concern is that he would not be able to get exclusive rights if it became "a major security situation." And after Burke locks Ripley and Newt in a room with the two living facehuggers in a failed plan to infect them and bring them back to Earth in stasis, he is confronted by a very angry Ripley, who wonders aloud if the xenomorphs aren't the morally superior species since "you don't see them fucking each other over" for a percentage; since they don't appear to be operating under the thrall of the performance principle.

Although he essentially embodies the performance principle, the absence of a specific directive from corporate like *Alien*'s Special Order 937 suggests that Burke is operating semi-independently of Weyland-Yutani. This is not to imply that they would disapprove of his plan; instead, they would ultimately reward him for his initiative if he were able to return a xenomorph in any of the stages of its development to their laboratories. So while it would be possible to argue that Burke's status as a rogue operator derails a critique of entities like Weyland-Yutani, it is more plausible that Burke's actions argue for the ubiquity of the assumptions that enable industrial society. After all, it is Burke's drive and initiative, and their implicit endorsement of the performance principle, and not the malevolence of a specific company or even the malevolence of a specific company's employee, that prop up industrial society.

If Burke represents the embodiment of the performance principle, then, he also indicates that the problems with Weyland-Yutani are systemic and not evidence of a specific moral failure.

While it is clear that she finds Burke's worship of the performance principle repellant, *Aliens* expands its Marcusian critique by making it clear that Ripley herself is motivated by Eros. Naturally, Weyland-Yutani's disgraced employee becomes very valuable to them when they realize that the situation on LV-426 is rapidly deteriorating. Not only is Ripley the only person who has seen a Xenomorph and lived, but she is also the only person who has defeated one. Ripley, in other words, has tremendous situational performativity, and could ask the Company for a lot of money in exchange for her services. But not only does Ripley have no desire to confront a xenomorph like the one that she ejected into space as she escaped from the *Nostromo*, she also has no trust in Weyland-Yutani and does not want to profit in any way from the Company's desire to weaponize the creatures. Nevertheless, she is very upset when she finds out that there are colonists with families on Acheron, and only agrees to go back if Weyland-Yutani executive Carter Burke promises that the mission would involve destroying and not harvesting the Xenomorphs. Ripley wants to preserve life by using justified violence against the Xenomorphs; Weyland-Yutani, beset by the performance principle and the Thanatos it engenders, wants to make money and doesn't care who dies in the process.

Of course, in *Aliens* Cameron reaches out to his intended popular audience by coding Ripley's Eros as a manifestation of her maternal instinct. On Acheron, Ripley bonds with Newt, the young girl who is the only surviving colonist, who understandably refuses to interact with the marines who find her, by speaking to her softly as any mother would. Later, she promises to protect Newt from the real monsters that bedevil her as she tucks the orphaned girl into bed. And if this were not enough, the extended version of the film depicts Ripley as mourning the death of the daughter she left behind when she shipped aboard the *Nostromo*, clearly implying that Newt is a surrogate daughter. Yet while this coding is problematic—as the critics discussed in the endnotes have made abundantly clear—it also aligns with Cameron's stated intention of placing serious thematic content within narratives that don't make audiences head for the exits. Marcuse's concept of Eros is much more difficult for casual theatergoers to understand than culturally available tropes about maternal love, which contain an element of Eros within their dubious ideology. Cameron, no doubt well aware of the baggage this trope contains, employs maternal love as an easy-to-digest stand-in for notions similar to the philosopher's assertion that a broadly considered love of life in and of itself can break the containment of industrial society.

Eros, of course, is more than sexuality and reproduction. It can also encompass the joy one finds in productive work. This is why, in the final minutes of the film, Ripley is not presented as a soldier, but as a worker who acts like a soldier when the occasion calls for it. In the film's penultimate scene, Ripley famously expels the Alien Queen from the *Sulaco* by strapping herself into the power loader and using it to push her out of the airlock. While some critics have seen this as Ripley donning a warrior costume, we need to be careful to note the way that the film itself presents the power loader. It is clearly a futuristic piece of warehouse equipment similar to a forklift, and as such clearly links Ripley to the working class. After all, Ripley becomes proficient with a power loader after she is stripped of her flight officer—and therefore middle-class—status and is forced to take whatever job comes to hand. When she offers to use the loader to help the marines prepare the drop ship, she is not signaling eagerness to fight, but instead slipping back into her role as useful worker in an attempt to fit in. Furthermore, the power loader is not designed to destroy but to facilitate human work. If such a device were real, it would be a very useful tool and only take life in industrial accidents. Even though heavy equipment like a forklift could be formidable if it was used as a weapon, in other words, such things are designed as means of creation or maintenance, unlike the *Sulaco* itself, which is an engine of war.

Using the power loader as a weapon, then, makes Ripley look more like a resourceful proletarian who is engaging in defensive violence than a Fembo or Rambolina. Ultimately, Ripley is not literally fighting against the Alien Queen—who is also merely trying to protect her children—but against the personification of the Thanatos that characterizes Weyland-Yutani desire to weaponize and thus profit from a creature that will only bring the destruction of humanity. How appropriate, then, that the champion of Eros is presented as both a caring foster mother and a skilled worker, and that she is armed with something that was not primarily designed to bring death into the world.

Cameron, like every director in the *Alien* universe so far, was not able to continue his portrayal of Ripley. Yet twelve years after *Aliens,* the director was able to bring another two-dimensional questioner to the screen, though her similarity to Ripley might not be immediately apparent. Cameron's 1998 film *Titanic,* his first unqualified blockbuster since *Terminator 2,* is not a science fiction film and Rose, its protagonist, is an upper class woman being sacrificed to a financially advantageous but emotionally deadening marriage, not a flamethrower-wielding, crypto-proletarian mamma bear. Indeed, as we will see below, some academic critics have been struck by Cameron's attempts to present such an accurate portrait of the real Titanic's first and final voyage that the surface of the film could appear to the historically naïve as a documentary, and therefore see the characterization of Rose as of a piece with Cameron's pedantic historical fiction. Yet the film is very much about placing faith in an ultimately fallible machine and therefore also about humanity's relationship with technology. Indeed, Cameron himself has said as much. L. Chambers quotes Cameron as noting that a major thematic concern of the film is "the idea of human being's relationship with technology, how it can be good, how it can be bad, how it can kind of turn around and bite you" (37).

As Cameron's somewhat inarticulate formulation indicates, then, just as *American Graffiti*'s surface infatuation with hot rod culture allowed Lucas to present a saleable critique of industrial society, *Titanic* allowed its director to deride the performance principle and depict the personal growth engendered by Eros. Interestingly, *Titanic* seems to function as a non–science-fiction means of reviving Cameron's career just as *American Graffiti* did for Lucas.' Cameron, after all, had made studios money since *Aliens* and *Terminator 2*, but had not created the kind of blockbuster that his earlier successes promised. Yet Rose's implicit questioning of the assumptions of the Edwardian-era transatlantic upper class provide Cameron another highly successful platform for Marcusian critique, just as Curt's quiet refusal to fully participate in mid-century American high-school culture let Lucas apply Marcuse in a way that did not cause audiences to run for the theater doors.

As Lucas turned to a nascent nostalgia for high school sprouting in the American psyche in the mid–1970s, as de Certeau would suggest, Cameron also employed a narrative trope that had a great deal of affective power. The director realized that the historical weight of one of the world's most memorable maritime disasters would provide an excellent preexisting narrative about the fallibility of technology while lending itself to modification with the same Marcusian elements he had added to Ridley Scott's *Alien*, in part by giving Rose Ripley's ability to think two-dimensionally. This was possible largely because the *Titanic* tragedy had already evanesced into scores of narratives, a process that began mere weeks after the ship went down. After all, as Joseph J Edgette reminds us, the sinking of the *Titanic* was the "genesis of literature and popular culture" that employed familiar narrative devices to retell the tale of the ship's foundering (119). Immediately after the disaster, Edgette notes, "a profit was actually realized through sales of 'instant books'" (121)—compilations of press coverage and transcripts of official inquiries that were printed on heavy paper and richly bound. Furthermore, because numerous *Titanic* "survivors were talented writers" (124), there were many memoirs written, and many of these sold quite well. There was also a great deal of literary ephemera like poetry and sheet music (e.g., 131). Perhaps the most enduring narrative product of the disaster, however, has been films. In addition to Cameron's, there have been seven theatrically released narratives—in addition to several made-for-TV tales—that either focus on the loss of the ship or prominently feature the ship in their narratives, including 1912's *Saved from the Titanic* and the German-language *In Nacht und Eis*, 1929's *Atlantic*, 1943's Nazi propaganda film *Titanic*, 1953's *Titanic*, 1958's *A Night to Remember* 1980's *Raise the Titanic* and 1997's *A Chambermaid on the Titanic*.

Cameron, then, is just one more in a long line of storytellers who seized upon a transfixing tragedy to influence the way society thinks about itself. Of course, we should not forget that Cameron's retelling of the loss of the *Titanic* was the most successful by far. After all, to filmgoers in the late 1990s, *Titanic* was probably what came to mind when they heard the word "blockbuster," and its reputation as a Hollywood cash cow has not diminished in subsequent years. The film is number five on boxofficemojo.com's inflation-adjusted list of all-time domestic box office grosses. Although the film cost $200 million to make, its unadjusted worldwide take of close to $2.2 billion indicates a healthy return on investment. Clearly popular with audiences, *Titanic* found mainstream critics largely receptive. It has an 88 percent fresh rating on rottentomatoes.com, and while some critics found the film's spectacle and sentiment overdone, many more praised the film for providing a meaningful story while nevertheless delivering what audiences expected—in other words, for masterfully rearticulating a pre-existing narrative. For example, Roger Ebert found Cameron's film "flawlessly crafted, intelligently constructed, strongly acted and spellbinding" though otherwise typical of Hollywood disaster movies. However, according to Ebert, *Titanic*'s "story stays well within the traditional formulas for such pictures" because "you don't choose the most expensive film ever made as your opportunity to reinvent the wheel." Other critics, however, unsurprisingly detected a leftist ideological agenda in a film that features wealthy people behaving badly and steerage passengers locked below decks as a ship sinks. Typical of such reviews is that of the *New York Times*' Janet Maslin, who notes that Cameron "joked during production" that his film was "holding just short of Marxist dogma."

Academic critics responded to *Titanic* in a way that is broadly similar to mainstream critics: some have focused on the debt the film owes to the historical record or to existing popular genres like the disaster movie and the romance novel, while others have debated the film's potentially subversive content. Critics like Richard Howells are interested in demonstrating how Cameron's film illustrates the central paradox of the historical accuracy of many *Titanic* films: even though "one fleeting background shot" of a young boy spinning a top "was so carefully researched and staged that it would only be noticed by people with an existing knowledge of *Titanic* minutiae" (73) because "Cameron and his team were indeed obsessive" about making the film look historically accurate (74), it's still a work of popular fiction that is best read as such.

Other critics, carefully heeding Howells' admonition to see the film as fictive, have expressed an interest in placing Cameron's *Titanic* within the many tales that have attempted to draw a moral message from the wreck and found, as Janice Hocker Rushing and Thomas S. Frentz note, that the sinking of the *Titanic* is a magnet "for myths about modernity" (2). Similarly, Jose Arroyo and Edward Lawrenson remind us that the "event has been interpreted as an allegory for capitalism, as divine punishment of human arrogance, as a symbol of the destruction of a privileged way of life and as a portent of the changes World War One was to bring" (web). James Kendrick Carter similarly finds that, even though Cameron's films are "superficially conservative," they are "internally radical" and *Titanic* is no exception. Carter argues that Cameron's film "fits comfortably into a revolutionary Marxist paradigm that condemns capitalist excess and celebrates the heroism and humanism of the underclass" (38). Readings like these perhaps do much to explain the commercial popularity of a film that does indeed have Marxist overtones and provide intellectual support for Ebert's appreciation of *Titanic*'s refusal to reinvent the wheel: Cameron created a film whose aesthetic historicity was so pleasing that it served as an excellent container for all of the familiar myths and allegories about modernity that audiences had already—to one degree or another—invested in.

Taking a somewhat similar vein, other critics have carefully explored the history of the *Titanic*'s employment of literary tropes and found further explanations for the familiarity that permeates Cameron's *Titanic*. Some have detected *Titanic*'s narrative roots in the Western canon, even though the ship went down in 1912. Caryn Voskuil, for example, argues for a strong resemblance between Rose and Pygmalion because when Jack, an artist, first sees her in "her white dress boarding the ship, Rose seems to him the image of a perfect 'Ivory Girl' and he falls in love with her, foreshadowing his later Pygmalion-like influence on her" (111). Yet Voskuil also sees Rose's fiancée Cal as "a Pygmalion-esque character, trying to mold Rose to his specifications" (112), suggesting that Cameron gives Rose no real choice. Janice Hocker Rushing and Thomas S. Frentz finds later influences, arguing that narratives like Cameron's film resemble tales like Romeo and Juliet or Tristan and Iseult—which were themselves based on other tales—in important ways. As Rushing and Frentz note, in "in all three stories, the girl is pledged to marry a man she does not love for the family's welfare; in all three the lovers disobey and follow their hearts; and in all three the lovers are 'star-crossed,' kept apart by mischance and catastrophe" (19).

Because tales like Romeo and Juliet, or at least the devices used to structure the plots of tales like Romeo and Juliet have influenced popular literature for hundreds of years, it is unsurprising that elements linking *Titanic* to canonical works like *Romeo and Juliet* also link it to 19th-century popular fiction. For example, Steven J. Zani argues that *Titanic* has a plot that would have been familiar to readers in 1912 since, "like countless nineteenth-century novels, the dominant conflict" of Cameron's film involves a girl "who must marry the wealthy man she does not love, rather than the unsuitable one she does" (128). Such tales were deliberately designed to trigger a strong emotional reaction in their readers, and so it is unsurprising that Todd Davis and Kenneth Womack assert that Cameron deliberately adopts "the stylistics of sentimentality" and claim, somewhat anachronistically, that he borrows "his plot from the burgeoning shelves of Harlequin romances" (43) in order to engage, as do most sentimental texts, "our innate hope for spiritual transcendence" (44). The readers of 19th-century pulp romances like *Dora Thorne*, 20th-century Harlequin novels like *Married to a Mistress*, and viewers of *Titanic*, then, all share a hope that their love will go on and on.

Zani, Davis, and Womack are broadly correct about the sentimental, 19th-century aspect of *Titanic*, especially when addressing the surface of the text. In addition to the class-defying romance between Jack and Rose, once the *Titanic* founders audiences are treated to sentimental and curiously quaint tableaux that include a mother locked into steerage telling her two children a final bedtime story (and amazingly appearing to put them to sleep), an elderly couple in first class cuddling with each other as the water inexorably rises around their bed, and the captain standing at the wheel and going down with his ship. All of these heart-tugging vignettes are set to the potentially apocryphal strains of the *Titanic*'s house band playing "Nearer My God, to Thee."[5] Although there is, on reflection, something darkly humorous about Cameron's musical selection—if there is an afterlife, most of the people on the *Titanic* will be quite near to God very soon—the ostensibly unironic presentation of a Christian hymn also furthers the film's 19th-century tone.

Of course, Cameron's inclusion of allusions to canonical tales and 19th-century tropes not only did no harm to *Titanic*'s box office, but also provided the cover of familiarity for Cameron's critique. As de Certeau and Raymond Williams would indicate, popular narratives almost always contain identifiable structures from their culturally outmoded forebearers and have often used those structures to facilitate social commentary. This premise informs the approach of several critics who examine Cameron's *Titanic*. Zani, for example, observes that there are different narrative versions of the wreck because "in different eras we have different ways of negotiating and presenting traumatic events" (127). Howells similarly argues that "there has always been a heady mixture of the actual and the imaginary" in tales about the *Titanic*, and so these tell us "a great deal about ourselves" because it is "refashioned in the interests of the people telling it" (75, 78–79). Howells further argues that these interests can be easily detected in the various films about the wreck. For example, Howells asserts that 1953's *Titanic*, and American film, argues in favor of the "New Isolationism of the 1950s" (83) while suggesting that 1958 *A Night to Remember*, which was made in England, praises the "calm, virtuous, and professional" British middle class (84). Howells also comments on the obvious Cold War overtones of 1980's *Raise the Titanic* (85ff), which depicts Russian and American military personnel attempting to locate material that can be used to make a new superweapon in the wreck of the *Titanic*.

From this perspective, Patrick McGee's assertion that "*Titanic* is not a departure from Cameron's earlier work but its culmination" (web) makes very good sense.[6] And since the tales that have been generated by the wreck of the *Titanic* clearly illustrate the ability of popular narratives to be refashioned by subsequent storytellers. It should be no surprise, then, that Cameron uses this culturally available narrative to pursue themes that can be found in his earlier works. Unsurprisingly, many critics have delineated how Cameron's debatably feminist depictions of female characters who are self-assured survivors and more than capable of employing physical violence surfaces in *Titanic*. Zani, for example, sees Rose as a typical Cameron protagonist; "a cursing, strong-willed woman, capable of punching anyone who gets in her way" (128). Peter Kramer similarly argues that "much like Ripley in *Aliens*" Rose "twice gets the chance to leave the sinking ship and, on both occasions, she goes back into the bowels of the *Titanic* to save her loved one (or to die with him), just as Ripley goes back, immediately after having narrowly escaped the clutches of the alien brood, to save Newt." For Kramer, by removing his strong female hero from a movie that strongly resembles action films like Cameron's own *Rambo II* and placing such depictions of female daring-do in a film that is clearly targeted at women, it "is as if Cameron declared that this story and this film belonged to the woman on the screen and also, by implication, to the women in the audience" ("Women First," web). Jose Arroyo and Edward Lawrenson similarly argue that Rose "begins the film so enslaved by her class and her loveless relationship with Cal that she's contemplating suicide and ends the film as a strong independent woman renouncing her class and willing to fight both for love and life" (web); if we overlook the plot details, this is an implicit comparison to both Sarah Connor and Ellen Ripley.

Rose is indeed a strong female character and she does bear striking resemblance to Cameron's female protagonists—not just Sarah Connor or Ellen Ripley, but also lesser-known characters like Lindsay Brigman from *The Abyss*. Indeed, Cameron's preoccupation with violently capable females extends so far that he even created an entire posse of gun-toting young women to star in the music video he directed for the relatively obscure New Wave band— and *Aliens* and *Titanic* actor Bill Paxton side project—Martini Ranch's 1988 song "Reach." But whatever the feminist merits of Cameron's desire to portray smart, powerful women, it would be a mistake to assume that such a portrayal is the most important extra element that Cameron adds to the familiar tale of a girl whose wealthy family won't allow her to marry her poor suitor. Instead, as in *Aliens*, Cameron inserts a Marcusian discussion of two-dimensional thought and Eros' ability to overcome industrial society in order to rewrite the apparently conventional love story his film tells.

Critics have already described the basic outline of *Titanic*'s argument for a broader engagement with life without using explicitly Marcusian terminology. Janice Hocker Rushing and Thomas S. Frentz, for example, read Rose "as a feminine antidote to technological progress" because Cameron inserts into a "familiar story of machine-age apocalypse" a narrative that resembles the god Eros' long struggle to turn Psyche into a goddess and marry her on equal footing. According to Rushing and Frentz, "the story of Jack and Rose transforms romantic love into a human relationship in which Jack (Eros) helps Rose (Psyche) to live a fulfilled life" (12). Patrick McGee, whose theoretical approach to *Titanic* is primarily informed by Benjamin's *Illuminations* and therefore makes observations that Benjamin's Frankfurt School fellow traveler would recognize, makes similar arguments. For McGee, the actual *R.M.S. Titanic* provided one of the "most beautiful expressions" of a class-based "fantasy of an order in which everything and every person has their proper place and value without contradiction or conflict—in other words, without the unsolicited intrusions of desire." Cameron's film disrupts this fantasy of pan-class comity by using Jack to embody the revolutionary potential of "desire's subversive play" and by using "the passion of Jack and Rose" to "explode the *Titanic* as a metaphor of social harmony through natural hierarchy." According to McGee, Jack's subversive desire not only points out the flaws in the class system of 1912 but also provides Rose with "a desire that helps to liberate" her "from the enslavement of social demand" (web). And Fred A. Holliday II similarly argues that Rose "transcends private property by rejecting it" and becoming fully human (44).

Rushing, Frentz, McGee, and Holliday, then, all detect in the ostensibly typical love story found in *Titanic* the expansion of erotic love into a broader zest for life that both includes and eclipses sexual passion. This, for Marcuse, is a step that is essential if industrial society is to be transformed into a nurturing society that happens to employ technology. Given the concern with the impact of industrial society found in Cameron's other work, then, *Titanic* lends itself well to an explicitly Marcusian reading. But in order to fully appreciate the link between *Titanic* and the *Terminator* films and *Aliens* we need to decenter the understandable critical attention to paid to Jack while at the same time highlighting how Rose was ready to carry on Sarah and Ellen's critique before she met Jack.

This is not to say that Jack does not advance Cameron's Marcusian critique. As McGee's analysis implies, Jack is easily read as the embodiment of Eros, as one whose sexual passion is but one component of a larger drive for life. Furthermore, he does facilitate Rose's rejection of the deadening, class-based gender role society had prepared for her not simply by sleeping with her but also, and more importantly, by giving her permission to truly live. Furthermore, because of Cameron's framing narrative that features a present-day version of Rose, viewers can see the fulfillment of the alluring glimpse of liberation young Rose finds in her relationship with Jack. In order to fully understand the advocacy for Eros that the frame story underlines, however, we must first appreciate how the film establishes Jack as the harbinger of Eros. Then we can fully appreciate how Cameron's reimaging of the *Titanic* narrative depicts Rose as ready for Jack because of her rejection of false needs and the performance principle.

There are several scenes in the film that support Jack's connection with Eros, although, as one would expect, most of what Jack does is also easily read as an appeal to sentimentality. For example, the two "I'm the king of the world" scenes in which Jack invites Fabrizio or Rose to stand on the prow of the *Titanic* not only provide iconic moments for movie posters. The scenes also establish Jack as a creative seeker of joy who can find the redemptive potential in a technology that literally embodies industrial society. In the face of a technology that seems, from a social if not an engineering standpoint, designed to teach him his very menial place in the world, Jack does not retreat into the acquiescence that one-dimensional thought would prescribe. Instead, much as he attempts to be an artist even though his working-class background makes that vocation nearly impossible, Jack finds a way to repurpose its power that hints at technology's ability to elevate us all above our mundane existence.

It is also true that his quixotic quest for Rose is clearly flagged as the sort of highly improbable course of action that only occurs in stories about rich girls who are being forced to marry characters like Cal—whom McGee has called "the almost comically arrogant manifestation of pure class privilege" (para 16)—to maintain their family's social standing. After all, the film takes pains to call attention to the improbability of Jack's quest, with fellow steerage passenger Tommy's declaration that "angels will fly out of your arse sooner than you'll get close" to Rose as one of the more memorable examples of this. But as the fictively familiar saga of poor boy wooing rich girl proceeds, it becomes clear that Jack is not simply attempting to wed (or bed) the confused but attractive girl that he has saved from suicide but to help her live more fully. This is best seen when the film contrasts the artless joy of the below-decks party Jack and Rose attend with the stiflingly mannered formal dinner Cal arranges for Jack as a way to thank him for saving Rose.

Jack's broader erotic project is made as clear as a Deckard voice-over when Jack urges Rose to live as he slowly drowns in the chilly waters of the North Atlantic. Of course, Jack's charge that Rose live life, get married, have kids, and die in a warm bed is more than a little normative, yet there is also a glimpse of the transgressive as well. After all, Jack's understanding of Rose's desire to have sexual and emotional relationships with other men would not have been so clearly implied in most 19th-century texts. More importantly, however, the pictures of Rose flying a biplane and riding a horse that viewers see while Rose is depicted dying in a warm bed later in the film indicate that she clearly did more than become a housewife. Indeed, the central narrative's depiction of Jack's demise combined with the frame story's depiction of Rose's passing provides an interesting take on Roy Batty's dying pardon of Deckard in *Blade Runner*, not because Rose and Jack are in an agonistic relationship similar to that of the blade runner and the replicant, but because Jack's charge makes explicit Batty's implicit command to Deckard to embrace life for itself. Furthermore, Cameron's frame story and its protagonist—an independent and self-confident Old Rose—serve to suggest that she did just that.

Another Marcusian thematic point in Cameron's frame story is an extended meditation on the Performance Principle. Old Rose is once again in the North Atlantic because she has been invited by Brock Lovett, who is leading an expedition to recover artefacts from the *Titanic*. But the focus of Lovett's quest is not historical interest; instead, he is seeking the "Heart of the Ocean"—supposedly the most valuable diamond in the world. Lovett's motivation, then, hinges on the easily understandable logic that the *Titanic* itself, since it has sunk to the bottom of the sea, is now only worthwhile as a container for an extremely valuable jewel. Yet the safe aboard the ship that supposedly held the "Heart of the Ocean" only contains the nude sketch of Rose and, by extension, the only physical reminder of a grand love affair. Of course, it's not that the sketch itself is worthless—even Cal, to whom the sketch is a harbinger of a lifetime of cuckoldry, can breezily remark as the *Titanic* is foundering that "it's a pity" that he didn't "keep that drawing" because it "will be worth a lot more in the morning" as a souvenir from the great maritime disaster. Yet the drawing also symbolizes both the sentimental love that narratives about rich girls falling for poor boys depend on and the broader calls to Eros that Cameron embeds beneath the familiar 19th-century romantic trope. This is perhaps best depicted when Lovett turns to Rose's granddaughter after throwing away the cigar he planned to smoke after finding the "Heart of the Ocean" and remarking that he "never let it in." While this statement is admittedly ambiguous and potentially trite, it would be an admission of imbecility if Lovett were merely indicating that he had not considered that romantic love could be as valuable as a diamond. This statement also points to Lovett's, and, potentially, the audience's, realization that there is something beyond the performance principle.

Because this is not simply a love story, because there is more to Jack and Rose's relationship than the draw of an attractive person from a forbidden class, Cameron's Marcusian critique hinges on Rose's readiness for Jack's invitation to truly live. Rose cannot be Eliza Doolittle to Jack's Professor Higgins, but instead must be a willing co-conspirator for their relationship to exemplify the life-affirming connections with others that Eros brings and not just another androcentric romantic relationship that underpins the repressive de-sublimation of Eros. Unsurprisingly, Cameron's female protagonist, like Ellen and Sarah before her, is quite capable of seeing through industrial society, though *Titanic* makes that point more clearly than the *Terminator* films. Rose, after all, is presented as an intellectual—and an intellectual of Marcuse's vintage since the fictional girl is 17 in April of 1912 when the philosopher was just a few months away from his 14th birthday. She wants to collect the works of artists like Picasso and makes fun of the president of the White Star Line by comparing his obsession to have the biggest and fastest ship with Freud's discussion of phallic symbols. And Rose's scholarly ambition allows Cameron to critique the performance principle by underlining the way his protagonist's desire to learn appear useless affectations when viewed in light of early-20th-century, upper-class gender roles This is most clearly depicted when Rose's mother tells her that she doesn't need to go to college because "the purpose of university is to find a suitable husband." Rose would therefore be wasting her time because she has already found Cal.

Cameron also employs the film's framing story to help viewers understand that Rose had already seen through industrial society before she set foot on the *Titanic*. Her critical precociousness is made clear by Old Rose, who tells Lovett and his crew that "outwardly" she "was everything a well-brought-up girl should be, but inside I was screaming" because she faced a life that would be an endless parade of parties and cotillions—an endless submission to the false needs and repressive de-sublimation of industrial society. Since Rose's silent scream stems from her pre-existing critique, all Jack did was give that scream a means of escape.

It would be perfectly reasonable to argue that Cameron's employment of 19th-century sentimentality in *Titanic* largely drowned out the Marcusian critique that is present in the film, to say that most audience members saw the film as a particularly affecting love story and little more. One could further argue that Rose's critique, especially considering its explicit feminism, would be seen by most theatregoers as Cameron's attempt to make his protagonist appeal to contemporary women Yet it would also be perfectly reasonable to argue that most viewers of *American Graffiti* saw the film as a paean to early-1960s youth culture and to the automobile and to further argue that Curt's oppositional attitude merely represents Lucas' attempt to appeal to his generation by including a character who could plausibly be depicted as opposing the Vietnam War. Nevertheless, both films feature the subtle presence of Marcusian critique in narratives clearly primed to provide blockbuster returns at the box office. And just as the financial success of his tale of high school and hot rods allowed Lucas to replace *American Graffiti*'s subtle critique with a much more direct assessment of industrial society *A New Hope*, the unprecedented profits from *Titanic* allowed Cameron to film a very expensive and very pointed critique of industrial society.

*Avatar,* Cameron's major theatrical follow-up to *Titanic,* made less money domestically in inflation-adjusted terms. Yet *Avatar*, with a worldwide gross of more than 2.7 billion, was another massive blockbuster. The film was also well received critically, though many reviews feature the typical faint praise entertaining science fiction blockbusters. The film currently has an 84 percent fresh rating on rottentomatoes.com, but most of the positive reviews from mainstream critics are careful to note that *Avatar* should not be taken too seriously. There were scattered appreciative reviews like Charlie Gates contention, published in the Christchurch, New Zealand *Press* that "*Avatar* is ambitious, complex and allegorical science-fiction of the kind you can usually only find in literature." Some critics even see a potent political message in Cameron's blockbuster. Writing in South Africa's *Sunday Times,* for example, Barry Ronge sees no coincidence "that this film hits the screens while the UN Climate Change conference in Copenhagen is taking place" since its themes "resonate powerfully with the goals and aspirations of environmentalists." Such unqualified praise is rare, however. Typically, critics praise the film as spectacle, but smugly imply—or announce—a lack of any substance. The *Christian Science Monitor*'s Peter Rainer, for example, half seriously calls *Avatar* "the greatest movie ever made for 9-year-old fanboys."

Often, critics would qualify their praise for *Avatar*'s entertainment value by ridiculing the film's ability to provide social commentary. For example, Roger Ebert, who eagerly recommended the film, sarcastically opines at one point in his review that audiences are "free to regard" the film as an allegory on contemporary politics" because the director "obviously does." The *New York Times'* Manohla Dargis, who also gave the film a strong review, finds "something absurd about a movie that asks you to thrill to a natural world made almost entirely out of zeroes and ones and that feeds you an anticorporate line in a corporately financed entertainment." Furthermore, some critics were disturbed by what can only be called the film's spiritual politics. Vatican Radio argued that *Avatar* "cleverly winks at all those pseudo-doctrines that turn ecology into the religion of the millennium."

Initial reaction from academic critics was broadly similar, often pointing to the explicit or implicit hypocrisy in a film pleasing to nine-year-old fanboys and girls of all ages trying to make meaningful social commentary. Cameron indicated during an interview with Tavis Smiley that *Avatar* attempts to address the issue of colonialism (192), but it is perhaps this thematic strand that has drawn the most critical controversy. For example, Joshua Clover, writing in *Film Quarterly*, argues that since Cameron's "body of work" is "organized by" an argument for "the necessity of the augmented human body in the struggle against inhuman beings" (6), the film's "anti-imperialist rhetoric" becomes "a perfect inversion of Cameron's real logic" (7). John G. Russell argues that *Avatar* is very much a film about race, even if it employs "displacement as a means by which alien bodies are made to do the work of black ones and, in so doing, enable patently and potentially controversial emotions invested in one object to be safely, and less controversially" depicted (204). While this strategy may make the film palatable to theatergoers, Russell believes that ultimately this type of "didactic xenoface" (208), where actors of color provide the voices for blue-skinned Na'vi, merely reinforces white hegemony. Slavoj Žižek questions Cameron's ability to critique corporate overreach when he argues that *Avatar* merely showcases "Cameron's superficial Hollywood Marxism" because despite the director's "crude privileging of the lower classes and caricatural depiction of the cruel egotism of the rich" the film's "story of a white man marrying the aboriginal princess and becoming king make it ideologically a rather conservative, old-fashioned film" (web).

Some academic critics even had difficulty with the thematic issues that bothered Vatican Radio. Ken Hillis, writing in *Postmodern Culture*, makes a similar point when he argues that the film's "explicit metaphysical orientation" and "magical thinking" oppose "the foundations of empiricism, rationalism, dualism, and materiality that inform Western academic thought" (web). *Film Quarterly*'s Rob White also offers an odd echo of the Vatican when he dismisses a film that "evangelizes about online 'technocommunion'" as it makes "tendentious" claims "about the power of digital networks to transform social interaction" (5).

Although critiques like the ones discussed above blossomed quickly after the film's successful release, other academic critics almost immediately responded that, while *Avatar* does have problematic content, it nevertheless raises important issues and performs an incisive social critique. For example, Claudia Briones, although regretfully observing that the Na'vi "become the prototype of the Rousseauian noble savage" (316), notes that "the alter-native cosmopolitan interventions which *Avatar* allowed have sought to take advantage of hegemonic gaps in order to continue 'speaking truth to power' and widen up public spaces even further" (325). Thus, the film "takes a stance vis-à-vis science and scientists" as well as the politics of scientific knowledge, and calls on anthropologists like herself "to change sides and avoid being accomplices of our current economic and military frontiers" (314). James Clifford also finds a hopeful charge to fight oppression in the film. Though disappointedly noting *Avatar*'s "all-to-successful reinvention of exotic tropes and colonial paternalism" Clifford nevertheless reports that he was "strangely moved" by the film (218) because it "invites the imagination of indigenous resistance leading to definitive anticolonial victory" (219). And Bruno Latour, who argues that *Avatar* is "the first Hollywood script about the Modernist clash with nature that doesn't take ultimate catastrophe and destruction for granted," also finds cause for optimism in Cameron's film because it "opts for a much more interesting outcome: a new search for hope on condition that what it means to have a body, a mind, a world is completely redefined" (472).

Furthermore, not all scholars who investigate the way *Avatar* addresses racial issues have found evidence of blue face. Frank Scheide, for example, finds a different and more hopeful message about race in Cameron's film, observing that even if *Avatar* has the trappings of countless Hollywood "Indian" pictures, "its rejection of racial segregation is of particular interest." After all, argues Scheide, the white protagonists of 1995's *Pocahontas* and 1990's *Dances with Wolves* did not choose "to remain with the native people who accepted them" (208). Similarly, Anthony Lioi notes that in contrast to films like *Dances with Wolves*, which feature portrayals of interactions between white protagonists and indigenous people that are "subverted by the actual outcome of European colonization," *Avatar* is "future history on another planet" and its anti-imperialist plot is "free from the weight of the past" and therefore "free to succeed in its own right" (46).

Other critics focusing on the film's depiction of race found it encouraging that nonwhite, indigenous people are depicted as defeating a global (or perhaps interstellar) capitalism that is figured as a white domain. Orin Starn, even though ultimately dismissing the film as another example of the "White Messiah formula" that depicts a "'primitive' woman as object of mainstream desire" (180) and even though remarking that "the movie's blockbuster success was a reminder of just how a certain idealized vision of indigenous peoples answers to the longings for Otherness, a space of freedom outside the modernity of the West" (197), nevertheless notes that *Avatar* "flips the signs" by depicting whites as the villains and indigenous people as the heroes (179). John Rieder follows the logic of Starn's critique when notes that *Avatar* and other films released in 2009 feature "insistently moralistic vengeance killings" that are remarkable in popular cinema because these killings are directed "not at the standard lawbreakers of Western or police drama, but at white men in positions of power and authority." Consequently, such depictions, which draw "upon a deep reservoir of popular resentment" rhetorically reconfigure the "fundamental social issue of the distribution of the right to violence" by giving that right to the weak and the oppressed (42–43). Ultimately, however, Rieder believes that the caricatural qualities of characters like Colonel Quaritch make it unlikely that *Avatar* or films like it signal "any actual decline or weakening of racism" (46).

*Avatar* was also faulted by mainstream critics and some academic critics for an apparently hypocritical environmental message, but others have been cautiously optimistic about the ability of Cameron's film to promote awareness of the fragility of our ecosystem. Nicole Starosielski, for example, groups *Avatar* with films that employ animation to promote an environmentalist message. For Starosielski, these films should not be dismissed "on the base of their narrative structure" because their depiction of the environment combined with their potential for mass appeal gives them the ability to educate (148). Cameron's film deserves special mention among these films because "*Avatar*" uses stunning CGI effects to "explicitly" argue that "the environment is an interactive system" (158). Similarly, Alf Seegert responds to "*Avatar*'s paradoxes" by "considering whether such contradictions might in fact be emblematic of our conflicted cybercultural condition" (115). For Seegert, such an approach reveals the film's contrast of interfaces that feel—like the Na'vi's ability to form a neural link with the animals they ride—and interfaces that do not feel—like the AMP suit that Colonel Quaritch employs (e.g., 124). In turn, this contrast suggests that if we develop interfaces that feel, we can develop a greater environmental awareness.

Most of the academic criticism finding important social commentary in *Avatar* is heavily qualified. Critics who address the film's ability to incite social protest in the third world are relatively more direct, however. Thomas Elsaesser, although arguing that *Avatar* exhibits "a planned degree of pluralism of signs" that may strike some as evidence of cognitive dissidence because of the copresence of retrograde and progressive thematic strands found in the film (252), nevertheless notes that Cameron's blockbuster did lead to real-world political action. For example, the "Chinese government" had to restrict access to *Avatar* "in the countryside, since dissident bloggers quickly spotted in the land-grab of the American corporation analogies" with land seizures made by local, regional, and national Chinese governments. Furthermore, Elsaesser notes that Palestinian youth began dressing "up as the blue creatures" when they protested "the Israeli security fence" (251). Similarly, Yong Tang reminds us that "Chinese citizens commenting on the film in online forums felt the film exemplified "the struggle between the powerful and the powerless" and observes that one man in Beijing, about to be evicted from his house, hung a large banner on it that read "inspiration from *Avatar*: fight to the death in defending homeland" (661). And Joni Adamson notes that after the film was released, "in eastern India, the Dongria Kondh tribe posted a YouTube video titled 'The Real Avatar' that narrates their (successful) battle to stop" a bauxite mine that was to be located "on their sacred mountain" (153). Adamson also reminds us that Bolivian president Evo Morales, who is Aymaran and who is noted for his leftist politics, "praised *Avatar* for its imaginative portrayal of an indigenous group fighting a greedy corporation" (144) and speculates that praise like Morales' stems from a "deficit of spectacle" involving indigenous issues. For Adamson, *Avatar* indicates that the right

Hollywood blockbuster, however, can "draw the global media's attention" (145). All of this suggests that Cameron's film, for all its faults, did have the ability to engender productive social protest. Perhaps these social protests in turn invalidate some critical assessments of *Avatar* in a way that is best summed up by journalist Henry Jenkin's assertion, paraphrased by Hannes Bergenthaler, that "the social activism which latched on to the film renders any detailed criticism of its political implications" moot (157).

The broad consensus of the critical assessments of *Avatar* that has emerged since the film's release, then, appears tentative. James Cameron created a popular film that, while definitely providing imagery for and perhaps encouraging many real-world protests by indigenous peoples against corporations and governments, may or may not responsibly depict racial harmony and may or may not responsibly promote environmental engagement. The film, as Manohla Dargis sarcastically implies, is also about human interaction with technology in what Marcuse called industrial society. Yet in contrast to its mixed messages about race and the environment, *Avatar* unambiguously channels Marcuse's hope that even the most apparently repressive technology could be turned towards liberatory ends.

Nevertheless, relatively few critics have noted that the film makes a strong argument in favor of leveraging technology against itself. Bergenthaler, for example, finds this thematic strand a "unique virtue" in the film: because Jake Sully's embrace of the Pandoran natural world is so dependent on the RDA technology that created his avatar, Cameron's narrative problematizes "the usual hierarchy of ecocentric identification, which values immediate sensory experience of the natural body above experience mediated through artificial prosthesis" (159). This, for Bergenthaler, creates a more nuanced environmental critique. James Der Derian similarly argues that Jake Sully, the elite Recon Marine—a unit whose members receive training broadly similar to that of Navy SEALs or Army Rangers but focus more on intelligence gathering than combat operations—turned Na'vi partisan, makes "the leap from estrangement to entanglement by using his techno-prosthesis to spark a revolt against technology." This observation is an interesting take on the paradox that has troubled critics who found the film hypocritical: Jake could not have participated in the battle that freed Pandora's indigenous people from the apparently evil corporation seeking Unobtanium if said apparently evil corporation had not outfitted the paraplegic Sully with a bioengineered avatar that allowed him to blend in with the Na'vi, become sympathetic to their cause, and ultimately lead them to victory. Der Derian sees Jake's ability to tear down the master's house with the master's tools as liberating and quotes Marcuse's Frankfurt-School-fellow-traveler Walter Benjamin to urge academics to use technology to create compelling critiques of technology, creating, as Benjamin might say, an "uprising on the part of technology" (183).

Yet while Der Derian correctly detects *Avatar*'s participation in a long-running discussion of the impact of technology on the human soul, from a theoretical perspective, the line of argument Cameron pursues in *Avatar* is much closer to Marcuse's. Applying Marcuse's insights about industrial society to Cameron's technologically-enhanced blockbuster allows us to see that underneath the dazzling special effects, Cameron is both warning us about the tendency of industrial society to destroy our souls and making a Marcusian argument about how to transcend the repressive way society uses technology. While a film featuring a protagonist riding on an enormous flying reptile while machine-gunning his enemies would definitely meet the needs of nine-year-old fanboys, it can also participating in a serious critique of the way society sedates its populace by creating false needs. A 10-foot-tall, blue-skinned Rambo who openly critiques advanced industrial society is precisely the technologized and technologizing spokesman that allows Cameron to tell a commercially successful—and therefore broadly influential—tale of how the technology created by a cold, rapacious, and rationalized society can be used to escape from that cold, rapacious, and rationalized society.

To fully appreciate how Cameron's film engages with Marcuse's dilemma, we need to explore the extra elements Cameron adds to existing narratives about white soldiers and indigenous princesses that *Avatar* inherits from films like *Pocahontas*. Studying these additions cannot provide a definitive answer to questions about the progressive or regressive nature of the film's stance on indigenous people, but it does allow us to see more clearly how *Avatar* aligns with Marcuse's discussion of the liberatory promise of technology. We will also need to delineate how Sully's embrace of Na'vi culture illustrates Marcuse's conception of Eros and how Quaritch's desire to destroy everything he cannot control illustrates Marcuse's conception of Thanatos and then turn to the three theoretical pillars of what Marcuse argues in *One-Dimensional Man* are features of industrial society—false needs, repressive de-sublimation, and one-dimensional thought—to explore how similar conceptions inform *Avatar*'s thematics. Then we can fully appreciate how Jake's questioning leads to his revolutionary awakening and in turn understand how the world's most financially successful popcorn film meets Marcuse's test for revolutionary art.

As de Certeau would doubtlessly remind us, however, *Avatar* does not feature a plot or setting that is unheard of in science fiction. In addition to typical filmgoers who would be likely to note the similarities with popular films like *Dances with Wolves*, viewers of *Avatar* who are well-versed in print science fiction would understandably be tempted to see Ursula K. Le Guin's 1972 novella *The Word for World Is Forest* as the "Soldier" to the script for Cameron's latest blockbuster. After all, the director told biographer Rebecca Keegan that the idea for Avatar emerged in the 1970s, and both Le Guin's tale and Cameron's film feature an extractive Earth colony on a planet inhabited by ostensibly primitive people. Both colonies are designed to provide crucial natural resources to what Le Guin's Captain Davidson, foreshadowing Cameron's Jake Sully, describes as a "worn out Earth" (10). Both of these colonies feature scientific advisors who are supposed to gain an understanding of the indigenous people that will make colonial life easier. In both tales, these advisors discover that the indigenous people have cognitive abilities that, in important ways, dwarf those of people from Earth: the planetwide neural network on Pandora and the Athsheans' ability to find insight by controlling their dreams. Both narratives feature antagonists reminiscent of Lt. Colonel Kilgore from 1979's *Apocalypse Now*, though *Word for World*'s Captain Davidson, appearing in an earlier text, would need to be seen as an inspiration or an anticipation of Kilgore while *Avatar*'s Colonel Quaritch could properly be called a descendant. Both texts feature a successful rebellion on the part of the indigenous people that is greatly aided by at least some of the scientific personnel who become, as Le Guin indicates, traitors (125). And both narratives close with the expulsion of the human colonists.

There are, of course, the superficial differences one would expect when dealing with a case of influence and not outright plagiarism. The Athsheans are short and furry, the Pandorans are tall and blue. The Athsheans live in between the roots of large trees, the Pandorans live inside the trees and often use their branches to travel from place to place. And because *The Word for World* is part of what has been called Le Guin's Hainish cycle, the narrative features discussion of events that are far more important in the context of Le Guin's other tales than they are to the plot and theme of the novella—for example, given the narrative's relatively low page count, there is a great deal of attention paid to exposition concerning the creation of the League of Worlds and the place of humans within it.

There are also differences significant differences that illustrate the new dimensions of *Avatar*'s critique. For example, a major thematic shift that occurs between *The Word for World Is Forest* and *Avatar* helps unpack the extra elements Cameron added to this pre-existing speculative narrative: a shift from an expansionist colonialism similar to that practiced by Europeans in the 17th and 18th century on the part of Le Guin's invaders from Earth to an extractive, globally corporate, postcolonial, 21st-century presence on the part of Cameron's apparently evil corporation, the Resource Development Agency. In *The Word for World Is Forest*, the colonists have named Athshe, the planet they are expropriating, New Tahiti in much the same way that, say, Dutch colonists named their North American colony New Amsterdam or that the British, once they took over from the Dutch, named that colony New York. The colonies feature towns and villages and the colonists are excited because a shipment of "breeding females" (7) will let them establish an Earth-like society on New Tahiti. On Pandora, however, RDA personnel live in fortified compounds that are much more like military bases than small towns and dream of rotating back to Earth when their contracts are over. To Le Guin's colonists, New Tahiti is a new home. To the RDA personnel, Pandora is a paycheck. This full commodification of Pandora allows Cameron to downplay links to Earth's actual colonial past—links which were quite apt when Le Guin was writing during the collapse of colonialism—and create a Marcusian critique of industrial society by focusing on the RDA's use of technology to exploit Pandora and the Pandorans—and their human sympathizers—use of technology to liberate themselves.

While Marcuse would probably have been reluctant to see *Avatar*, he would have been comfortable with Cameron's depiction of technology's utopian potential. The theorist, after all, saw no inherent evil in technology Instead, Marcuse saw a great deal of potential freedom in the power technology gives man to escape from alienated labor, and made this argument in several places. In "Liberation from the Affluent Society," Marcuse argues that the "technical and material resources for the realization of freedom are available" (183). In *The Aesthetic Dimension*, the philosopher posits that the "radical possibilities of freedom" are "concretized in the emancipatory potential of technical progress" (27). In *Studies in Critical Philosophy*, Marcuse asserts that because of technological advances "the historical Subject appears capable of building a society in which the imperatives of self-preservation and growth can become the imperatives of freedom: reconciliation of necessity and liberty" (213), though capitalism "undermines" these prospects (215). In the introduction to the 1962 edition of *Eros and Civilization*, Marcuse offers that a non-repressive society is possible, though highly unlikely "as an extension of the achievements of science and technology" (vii).

So while the scholarly discussion reviewed above should make it clear that *Avatar* provides a critique that encompasses environmentalist thematics, a careful viewing reveals that it is not an outright dismissal of technology per se. Indeed, the premise of the film—high-tech toys like Sully's avatar can be a gateway to a critique of advanced industrial society because of the liberatory potential of technology—is founded on this Marcusian dialectic. We should stipulate here that there is plenty of bad technology on display here. As the film opens, audiences see giant earth-moving equipment ripping an enormous open-pit mine into the surface of Pandora. Later, an enormous remote-controlled bulldozer destroys a grove of sacred trees and then Quaritch and RDA security forces use airships to firebomb the tree where Neytiri's clan lives. Yet when paraplegic Jake is allowed to drive the avatar that was designed for his deceased twin brother—a marvelous piece of technology that is so expensive and so complicated that RDA decided that it was better to have the untrained and uneducated Jake replace his brother than build a new avatar from scratch—Cameron takes great pains to depict Jake's joy at being able to run his toes through the dirt once more. The avatar is not merely a plot device; it is a means by which Cameron can contrast the liberatory potential of technology with the destructive use industrial society often puts technology to.

Cameron also infuses the final battle for the Tree of Souls with an abundance of not-so-subtle visual cues that Sully and his comrades have not abandoned the use of technology, but instead use what they need to resist and imply that technology does indeed have an emancipatory potential. Jake, Tsu'tey, Trudy, Norm, and Neytiri all use the same com links that RDA security forces do. Jake brings down the shuttle carrying the daisy cutter bombs with a hand grenade. Rogue pilot Trudy Chacon, flying an SA-2 Samson hovercraft that has been painted a decidedly Na'vi shade of blue, grimly intones, "You're not the only one with a gun, bitch" as she attacks Colonel Quaritch's much larger C-21 Dragon assault ship.

And key Na'vi partisans definitely have guns—and the primary weapon used should be familiar to anyone who has been paying attention to American blockbusters during the last 30 years. During the battle for the tree of souls, Sully is armed not with the Na'vi longbow he needed to master to become part of the clan but instead with the same heavy machine gun he used in the beginning of the film when he was a door gunner for Trudy. But the former recon Marine is not alone in his use of a weapon that can fire over 500 rounds per minute. Scientist Norm Spellman, driving his avatar, uses the same weapon during the battle and at the end of the film Norm and his colleagues from the avatar program are also seen holding this weapon as they eject the surviving RDA personnel from Pandora. According to the Internet Movie Firearms Database, although the script calls it an AVR-30, the live fire props of the weapons used in the film's climactic battle "were built around a fully-functioning M-60"—the American heavy machine gun used during Vietnam and featured prominently in the *Rambo* films—the second of which Cameron wrote. Indeed, the director seems to be so bent on making that link clear that whenever Jake fires this weapon in anger, he makes a grunting scream that sounds very much like Sylvester Stallone's tortured Vietnam Vet did when he fired his M-60.

While on one level the employment of such a problematic icon is grist for the nine-year-old fanboy and aging cold warrior alike, it also aligns Cameron's critique with Marcuse's. When Sully shoots up the master's house with the M-60 he has been issued, he figuratively depicts, however bombastically, the forces that have the potential to break the containment of advanced industrial society. Technology can be liberatory, and even the same military technology that is being used to oppress the indigenous inhabitants of Pandora can also be used for the defensive violence that Marcuse grants may be necessary.

Marcuse did not see the gently coercive power of industrial society being limited to the affective impact of the material goods and living conditions being produced. Marcuse also argued that contemporary consumer society limited the ability to be truly creative and engaged in life by limiting our instinctual drive towards self-fulfillment and altruism. Marcuse put this loss in terms of Eros as *"life instinct"* (21) and notes that Freud called it "the great unifying force that preserves all life" (25) and argued that "the drive toward ever larger unities belongs to the biological-organic nature of Eros itself" (39). Consequently, Marcuse himself could argue that the "sex instincts," broadly considered, "are *life* instincts: the impulse to preserve and enrich life by mastering nature in accordance with the developing vital needs is originally an erotic impulse" (114). Marcuse then notes, as he aims for genuine breadth of sources, that in the New Testament the "message of the Son was the message of liberation: the overthrow of the Law (which is domination) by Agape (which is Eros)" (63). In Marcuse's just society, then, the Law would be overthrown by Eros as people followed their better impulses without interference from industrial society.

Although the connectivity the indigenous flora and fauna of Pandora exhibit have been correctly seen as evocative of computer networks, they also represent an interesting update of Marcuse's "ever-larger" and "biological-organic" unities. Pandora's balanced harmony, even though that balance contains extremely dangerous predators, is Marcusian Eros as a biosphere. All of the beings on Pandora take only what they need to develop life and show loving care for what they do not need. This can be seen when, during his training under Neytiri's direction, Jake kills a game animal with his longbow and recites the Na'vi's ritual prayer: "I see you, brother, and thank you. Your spirit goes with Eywa, your body stays behind to become part of the people." The violence of Pandora is the expected condition of a sustainable natural world. The violence brought by the RDA is exploitative and unsustainable. The expulsion of the RDA contingent from Pandora, then, can also be seen as the overthrow of domination by Eros.

Yet not all of the humans on Avatar are motivated by the fruits of domination. In a move that would have pleased Marcuse—if he could have brought himself to consume such degraded popular entertainment—some of those who find themselves alienated from RDA's attempt to export industrial society to another planet are the intellectuals whom the RDA grudgingly brought along in an attempt to more effectively use soft repression on the Na'vi. Avatar program head Grace Augustine—played by Sigourney Weaver herself—has been on Pandora for decades and literally "wrote the book on Pandoran botany." She has little patience with RDA's priorities, at one point threatening to "kick Selfridge's corporate butt" because she felt he was interfering with her attempts to do science. Consequently, though the film barely implies this, the schools that Grace sets up to teach the Na'vi children English, though ostensibly to win their people over to the presence of the RDA, really were intended to help the Na'vi connect with humanity. Indirect evidence that Grace is motivated by Eros in her dealings with the Na'vi comes when she tells Jake to see the forest through Neytiri's eyes, implying that Grace herself had been able to connect with the indigenous inhabitants of Pandora and see the love of life that permeates that planet. Unsurprisingly, Grace sees the Na'vi rebellion against the RDA as defensive violence designed to help love conquer domination. According to Grace, "the wealth of this world isn't in the ground, it's all around us" in the connections that the beings on Pandora have with one another and the Na'vi are justified because they "are fighting to defend it."

Along with Grace, Jake's fellow avatar driver Norm Spellman is another intellectual who has come to Pandora not to dominate it but to attempt to become part of its erotic community. Understandably, Norm is initially quite jealous of the untrained marine's ability to ingratiate himself with Neytiri and her family. After all, Norm has a PhD and studied the Na'vi for five years, learning their culture and language in preparation for his six-year posting. But Norm quickly forgives Jake his beginner's luck and passes on his knowledge to the marine, quickly recovering from the jealousy his invidious comparison engendered because he can see that Jake is also motivated by an appreciation of life.

Clearly, Jake's presence in the narrative indicates that not all of the humans who see through industrial society are intellectuals. Jake is, or at least was, a special-forces operative with very little in the way of education or training that would make him seek out a great unifying force that preserves all life. However, if we can consider valor at least potentially a kind of sublime love—something that, given a warrior's participation in what Marcuse would call defensive violence, can inspire people to make substantial sacrifices for the greater good, then we can see that Cameron is arguing that not only intellectuals but also warriors can critique industrial society because of their commitment to abstract ideals that would interrogate the assumptions of industrial society and lead individuals to actions that would transcend industrial society. Perhaps the possibility of a martial Eros leading to an appreciation for Pandora's biosystem explains the interest that Neytiri's father and leader of the Omaticaya people Eytukan shows in Jake when he is first brought to Hometree. Eytukan decides not to kill Jake outright but instead see if he can be integrated into the clan because, as he tells Mo'at, "this is the first warrior dreamwalker we have seen. We need to learn more about him." Cameron's film clearly implies that the Na'vi hold warriors in high esteem. Perhaps Eytukan is hoping that a warrior dreamwalker will have some sense of valor and a desire to, for lack of a better phrase, fight for freedom instead of the repression that the RDA's mercenaries are championing.

This thematic preoccupation with the difference between a warrior and a mercenary is announced early in the film. When he first lands on Pandora, Jake sees the battalion of mercenaries that RDA has hired to protect their mining interests and suffers a good deal of verbal abuse at their hands. As Jake rolls off of the transport in his wheelchair, an RDA mercenary in an AMP suit—the armored exoskeleton that allows humans a measure of protection from hostile Pandora—calls him "hot rod." Immediately after that, another RDA mercenary turns to his comrade and calls Jake "meals on wheels." While real men- and women-at-arms often use abusive language, this is not the ideal; militaries around the world spend countless hours and a great deal of money attempting to instill a level of discipline and compassion that would not allow for such language to be casually directed at a disabled civilian. Furthermore, Cameron's generally respectful portrayal of members of the military in previous films combine with his portrayal of the demeanor of RDA forces to suggest that these remarks function symbolically to indicate that the armed RDA personnel have lost any claim to the respect due a warrior.

This is made clear in Jake's narrative aside after he experiences this abuse when the Marine expresses his dismay at what these men and women have become: "Back on Earth, these guys were Army dogs, Marines fighting for freedom. Out here, they are just working for the company, taking the money." Although fighting for freedom is a problematic concept, it contains at least the possibility of unruly human emotions leading to meaningful political commitment. But the RDA has completely commodified the warrior experience, turning valor into a financial transaction. Interestingly, it is not entirely clear at the beginning of the film if Jake himself is not also a mercenary—after all, he is only on Pandora because "the pay is good" for taking his deceased twin's place as an avatar driver and he is easily enlisted in Colonel Quaritch's plan to infiltrate the Na'vi. In a sense, *Avatar* depicts the conversion of Jake from mercenary to warrior because he gains greater respect for life and realizes that he needs to use his skills in the service of life.

Although Jake is clearly the focus of Cameron's exploration of the difference between a mercenary and a warrior, he is not the only member of the RDA's security forces who overcomes the financial lure of being a mercenary and decides to sacrifice for the greater good. Trudy Chacon, the pilot who flew all of the science-related missions and was therefore exposed to Grace's critique of the RDA's motives, eventually comes to help Jake and the avatar scientists escape from RDA custody and to side with the Na'vi partisans in the climactic battle. Her moment of conversion comes when she refuses to participate in the attack on Hometree. When ordered to fire her missiles, Trudy flies away muttering, "I didn't sign up for this" under her breath. While somewhat opaque and cynical, Trudy's utterance nevertheless suggests that she finds firebombing the home of non-combatants fundamentally wrong and longs to use her skills as a pilot for the greater good.

If Cameron's film gives us Grace and Norm as well as Jake and Trudy as examples of humans who form a productive erotic bond with Pandora, he also gives us an ideal type of those in the thrall of Thanatos. Because of the repression of Eros in industrial society, Marcuse sees the growth of Thanatos, the destructive drive that opposes Eros. In *Eros and Civilization*, Marcuse describes Thanatos as the desire to "return to the Nirvana of the womb" (50) and "the regressive impulse for Peace" (69)—of course, "peace" here meaning a general lack of conflict or opposition and not the absence of war. Indeed, Thanatos often leads people to destroy what Eros would have them interact with. Instead of the creative engagement with the world that Eros would engender, then, Thanatos leads to retreat from the world by means of the destruction of the world. And no character in *Avatar* seems to embrace the idea that destroying things leads to a quiet and calm existence than Colonel Quaritch.

There are several scenes in which Quaritch implicitly or explicitly argues that Pandora and the Na'vi should be beaten into submission so that RDA personnel can be kept safe. For example, when he first meets Jake he warns that if he gets soft, "Pandora will shit" him out "dead with zero warning." Quaritch, himself a Recon Marine, then tells Jake that the thought of "a Recon Marine in an avatar" gives him chills because he wants to use Jake to force the Na'vi to cooperate and, if they don't, to help learn how to "hammer them hard." Much later, Quaritch expresses the need to have the Na'vi "by the balls" because he knows that a cataclysmic "shit fight" with the indigenous is all but inevitable. The most obvious and egregious use of the logic of Thanatos comes when Quaritch is preparing his forces for the final battle with the Na'vi, tells the assembled mercenaries that their "only security lies in pre-emptive attack" and that they will "fight terror with terror." Destroying the Tree of Souls will keep RDA personnel safe, according to Quaritch, because that act "will blast a crater so deep within their racial memory that they won't come within 1,000 klicks" ever again.

While Quaritch's words sound very much like the Bush administration's justifications for the 2003 invasion of Iraq and could therefore be seen as more immediate political commentary, the Marcusian implication of his speech is equally clear. Quaritch, obviously the film's villain, is arguing that the way to safety lies through the destruction of life. He is advocating for Thanatos, and he therefore makes an excellent foil for Jake, Grace, and the other characters who advocate for Eros and the engagement with life.

While *Avatar* resonates with Marcuse's thoughts on technology and on the Eros and Thanatos, it also provides a great deal of correspondence with the ideas found in *One-Dimensional Man*. In the introduction, Marcuse openly admits to vacillating between "two contradictory hypotheses: (1) That advanced industrial society is capable of containing qualitative changes for the foreseeable future; (2) that forces and tendencies exist which may break this containment and explode the society" (xlvii). In other words, humanity will either be completely co-opted by a technical and industrial apparatus that appears to provide for all our wants and needs or humanity will overcome that technical and industrial apparatus—but not necessarily physically destroy it—because that apparatus is unsustainable and/or because people have souls after all and will resist. *Avatar* argues that no matter how attractive industrial society may initially appear to be, good, thoughtful people will see through it and eventually side with those whose oppression is the price of industrial society's ability to deliver the goods.

In *One-Dimensional Man*, Marcuse argues that industrial society ensnares its citizens with technology rather than terror, comfort rather than coercion. According to Marcuse, "[h]umanity's repressive subjection to the productive apparatus ... is perpetuated and intensified in the form of many liberties and comforts" (32). While this type of repression may initially seem preferable to more direct and physically coercive forms, is more powerful since, according to Marcuse, all "liberation depends on the consciousness of servitude, and the emergence of this consciousness is always hampered by the predominance of needs and satisfactions which, to a great extent, have become the individual's own" (7). It's easy, in other words, to at least want to fight against someone who has their boot on your throat. It's much more difficult to want to fight against an amorphous industrial system that makes cool things for you.

Cameron integrates the Marcusian concept of false needs into *Avatar* by continually calling attention to the Na'vi's place outside the repressive productive apparatus. Although RDA security forces are not shy about using more direct repression on the Na'vi, RDA administrator—and the film's foremost representative of industrial society—Parker Selfridge longs for the day when the Na'vi become pacified by the bounty of corporatized society and stop preventing RDA from mining unobtanium, which sells for $20 million a kilo and which is the only reason that RDA is on Pandora. For example, when Jake is still secretly working for the security division of RDA, he is told by Selfridge: "Just find out what the blue monkeys want. We've tried to give them education, medicine, roads ... they like mud." This outburst illustrates not only Selfridge's immediate frustration with the Na'vi's recalcitrance but also his industrial-society mindset: they must have a need, and if we supply that need, we will own them. Later, after Sully has become radicalized, Colonel Quaritch uses one of Sully's video diaries to argue that negotiations have become pointless and it is now time to use military force. In the diary, Sully forcefully states that the Na'vi "are not going to give up their home, they are not going to make a deal for lite beer and blue jeans. There is nothing that we have that they want." It would be easy to dismiss Quaritch's use of Sully's analysis as justification for the rocket attack on home tree as the kind of loopy reasoning befitting a cinematic descendant of *Apocalypse Now*'s Lt. Colonel Kilgore, but his conclusions seem to be based on a sophisticated appreciation of the limits of industrial society's soft coercion. If a group can't be bought off with lite beer and blue jeans, after all, then it must be time to use hard repression.

Marcuse also believed that advanced industrial society secured the consent of its citizens by what he termed repressive de-sublimation—the subduing of potentially unruly elements of the human soul like erotic love through commodification of the erotic or other humanizing aspects of existence. According to Marcuse, the mobilization "and administration of libido ... generates submission and weakens the rationality of protest" (75). What could become a gateway to the sublime and therefore a pathway to a critique of advanced industrial society is turned into a pleasurable but minor distraction that is supplied by advanced industrial society. Marcuse's concerns about repressive de-sublimation adds dimension to Jake's interspecies romance with Neytiri, which at first glance could easily be taken as another iteration of narratives featuring a white adventurer going native and having a dalliance with a woman of color. Yet the touchingly chaste way that Sully pursues Neytiri and their apparent status as a life-mated pair suggests that he does not see her as a sexual commodity because she is other but that he instead is experiencing the kind of sublime love that can lead to political radicalization. As Jake tells a very angry Neytiri, who has just found out that he was a spy for RDA security during the time she was falling in love with him, "At first it was just orders. Then I fell in love with the forest and with the Omaticaya people and with you." Although Sully sensibly includes Neytiri, his enumeration of new loves also includes the forest—already site of political resistance to industrial society—and the Omaticaya people—a new political identity for Sully that is, as we have seen earlier, placed in direct opposition to advanced industrial society.

Marcuse believed that false needs and repressive de-sublimation generated one-dimensional thought, a kind of un-dialectical approach to life in which the existence provided by advanced industrial society appears to be the only viable alternative. According to Marcuse, there "is no reason to insist on self-determination if the administered life is the comfortable and even the 'good' life" (OM 425). This type of thinking allows Selfridge to tell Grace that "killing the indigenous looks bad, but there is one think that sharcholders hate more than bad press, and that's a bad quarterly statement" and then defend his profoundly inhumane attitude by observing that he "didn't make up the rules" that he is forced to play by.

Additionally, on Pandora, where advanced industrial society is placed in immediate dialectical opposition to a potentially superior mode of living, RDA officials are keen to portray the indigenous environment as hostile to human life and the artificial world of the base—the well-administered life that RDA has created—as the only place where life is possible. During a security briefing, Colonel Quaritch tells newcomers they must follow "Pandora rules"—which are, of course, his rules—to stay alive. They must fully embrace industrial society because "everything wants to kill you and eat your eyes as jujubes." Quaritch, of course, is not entirely incorrect: humans cannot breathe Pandoran air and there are many predatory animals in the jungle. Yet he is neglecting to mention that the Avatar program has been operating for years and that Dr. Augustine and her colleagues have not only been able to survive but also have at least limited success befriending the Na'vi. Even within the technological apparatus that is the RDA base on Pandora, in other words, there is an alternative to Quaritch's tightly controlled world. Unsurprisingly, Quaritch is greatly annoyed by the Avatar program since, as Marcuse has argued, "the intellectual and emotional refusal to 'go along' appears neurotic and impotent" (OM 9). And Quaritch seems to be channeling Marcuse—albeit in a backhanded way—when he tells Sully that the "Avatar program is a bad joke—a bunch of limp-dick science majors."

Perhaps Quaritch would not have spoken so confidently if he could have seen the box office results of a film where cynical mercenaries, vocalizing support for false needs and embodying the performance principle, are beaten by a group of revolutionaries, including limp-dick science majors, who critique one-dimensional thought and embody Eros. If *Avatar*, in other words, the Hollywood blockbuster that has made more money worldwide than any other film ever released, contains the ability to critiques advanced industrial society, then maybe there is hope. Perhaps people don't want to think like Quaritch, but would rather embrace Sully's ability to see through industrial society even if they often cannot do this in their daily lives.

If *Aliens*, *Titanic*, and *Avatar* can give make people wish they could become questioners like Ripley, Rose, or Sully, then perhaps some blockbuster films can be seen as good examples of revolutionary art, even if they owe their existence to late capitalism and industrial society. Marcuse, arguing against ridged Marxist conceptions of art—think socialist realist novels about tractor factories—noted that

> a work of art can be called revolutionary if, by virtue of the aesthetic transformation, it represents, in the exemplary fate of individuals, the prevailing unfreedom and the rebelling forces, thus breaking through the mystified (and petrified) social reality, and opening the horizon of change…. In this sense, every authentic work of art would be revolutionary, i.e. subversive of perception and understanding, an indictment of the established reality, the appearance of the image of liberation [AD xi].

Some of the critics cited above have implied that *Avatar* is not authentic enough because James Cameron is not a member of the proletariat or that the film is not authentic enough because it cost too much and is too technologically glitzy. Yet Cameron's film, for all the ones and zeros that went into creating it and for all its box office billions, represents not only the prevailing unfreedom, but it also potentially opens a horizon of change—a horizon clearly glimpsed by the third-world protesters who adopted *Avatar*'s images for their own protests—by presenting the appearance of liberation from advanced industrial society.

If we can see *Avatar* as an ideal example of the revolutionary art Marcuse championed, then we can also see *Aliens* and *Titanic* as Cameron's evolutionary steps towards the creation of a fully realized call for revolution against industrial society. Ripley and Rose, after all, are unable to do much to bring down social contexts that create entities like Weyland-Yutani or ideologies like Edwardian gender roles. These are strong women who see through their respective societies, but all they are able to do is survive, with only Rose finding a happy accommodation between her questioning spirit and the social mores that would limit it. Jake, on the other hand, leads a successful revolution. And while Ripley is limited by the world Scott, O'Bannon, and Schusett created and Rose is limited by the historical reality Cameron places her in, Jake and his fellow travelers inhabit an entirely new world, one in which Eros can unambiguously triumph over Thanatos, liberating not only living beings but also technology from industrial society.

# Afterword: The Cultural Half-Life of Subversive Blockbusters

Perhaps we should not pity the blockbuster after all. Not simply because, by definition, they enrich everyone involved in their creation while entertaining millions of people. Instead we should not pity blockbusters because, despite the air of disrepute generated by their association with both the moneychangers and the masses, they contain within them the potential to create a rhetorically efficient cultural critique that can be quickly disseminated into popular memory. Furthermore, as this study has hopefully shown, blockbuster films can actually help transform academic criticism of society into tropes and types of popular culture that, while definitely available for cooptation, nevertheless largely preserve their academic progenitors' initial social critique while at the same time making that critique available far beyond the walls of the academy.

Consequently, in spite of the existence of, say, Michael Bay's *Transformers* movies, we should not be surprised that popular culture can serve as a conduit for popularizations of cultural critiques that would otherwise be confined to the academy. As De Certeau suggests, once an idea become part of popular culture, as Marcuse's critiques of industrial society did in the 1960s, those popularizations are best seen as narratives that are available to be interwoven into other narratives to create the "new" tales storytellers need to appeal to popular audiences. As we have seen, Lucas was indirectly influenced by the popularization of the ideas Marcuse articulated because he inhabited the same social and cultural moment. Scott and Cameron were directly influenced both by the same Marcusian moment in popular culture and by Lucas, and this influence would extend to that director's use of the popularized versions of Marcuse's ideas. Of course, Scott and Cameron added their own extra elements to the existing popular versions of concepts like two-dimensional thought when they created their own narratives.

And while the persistence of Marcusian critique in some of the defining blockbusters of the past forty years illustrates de Certeau's contentions, we should also remember that all three directors made lucrative films that commented on the potentially oppressive relationship between people and industrial society. The success of these films as well as their ability to remain at the forefront of popular culture through adaptations, sequels, and reboots, strongly suggest that the cultural critiques Marcuse articulated both in the classroom and in bestselling books had broken free of both their academic home and the zeitgeist that granted their initial popularity. This transition into the broader popular culture has allowed concepts like one-dimensional thought, Marcuse's conceptualizations of Eros and Thanatos, and false needs to range widely outside the academy. Now, because of the success of the films discussed in this monograph, figurative versions of these critiques will have a long pop-culture half-life as they transcend the post-counterculture moment that so inspired Lucas, Scott, and Cameron.

But just what does that half-life look like? We are, after all, in a different cultural moment than the one that produced *A New Hope*, *Alien*, and *The Terminator*. As this book goes to press, it would be reasonable to argue that films about superheroes have become the dominant form of speculative blockbuster.[1] Yet Given Hollywood's infatuation with reboots, remakes, and sequels, it is likely that we will see the likes of *Terminator Genisys* or *Star Wars: The Force Awakens* for the foreseeable future.[2] Yet subsequent films could not completely jettison the thematic architecture and plot structure of the films they are reworking or the "universe" they are revisiting, so any thematic continuity between an original blockbuster and its rebooted descendant would not indicate that those themes had become ubiquitous popular culture. Additionally, though Lucas has retired, Scott has discussed a sequel to *Prometheus* while Cameron has announced several sequels to *Avatar*. Continued Marcusian thematics in these films, should they appear, would only suggest that their directors had coherent visions of the stories they were telling.

In order to suggest that Marcusian themes have escaped from the cultural moment that inspired Lucas, Scott, and Cameron, we need to explore what happens when other, later directors—directors who did not immediately experience the Marcusian cultural moment—employ thematic conceits based on popularizations of the ideas Marcuse articulated in works that are not an explicit descendant of *Alien* or *The Terminator*.

It is difficult to pin down the exact fate of a given academic critique of society that has been transformed into thematic device(s) employed in science fiction while at the same time claiming those devices have been widely circulated in the broader culture. It's hard, in other words, to look for specific instances of ubiquity. Nevertheless, a brief consideration of two blockbuster science fiction series reveals two possible ways that the Marcusian critiques modified by Lucas, Scott, and Cameron can surface in contemporary popular culture.[3] The first post–Marcusian-moment blockbuster series to be considered will be *The Matrix* films, which were released from 1999 to 2003 and directed by the Wachowski siblings, who were born around the same time Lucas was in film school. Then, we will briefly look at the film adaptations of Suzanne Collins' *The Hunger Games* books, which were released from 2012 to 2015.[4] Collins herself was born in 1962, and while the first film was directed by Gary Ross, who was born in 1956, making him just two years younger than James Cameron, the second and third films were directed by Francis Lawrence, who was born in 1971. The *Matrix* films, though clearly engaged with the task of popularizing other academic critiques of society, seek to update Marcuse's contentions about Eros and Thanatos, and thus illustrate the possibility of other blockbusters carrying on the popularization of the ideas articulated by Marcuse. The *Hunger Games* films, in contrast, treat one-dimensional thought and false needs as givens, as thematic elements that can be deployed with little explanation, demonstrating through their casual employment the cultural penetration and widespread acceptance of those concepts. Before we can delineate the persistence of Marcusian critique in both of these series, however we must first consider their individual financial success and critical reception to fully understand how they are blockbusters in the mold of, say, *A New Hope* or *Terminator 2*. We will then delineate the ways in which each series engages with the Marcusian concepts Lucas, Scott, and Cameron popularized in their films.

It should first be noted here that not discussing the Wachowski siblings' *Matrix* films in a book about blockbuster science fiction films would be a serious omission. After all, 1999's *The Matrix*, winner of four Academy Awards for editing and effects, was that year's fifth most successful film at the box office. Its almost $500 million worldwide gross on a $63 million production budget gives the film a return on investment that easily qualifies it as a blockbuster. And though the first film of the Wachowskis' trilogy has a solid reputation with fans, mainstream critics have given it more guarded praise. Although 87 percent fresh on Rotten Tomatoes, most of the reviews of *The Matrix* tend to praise the film's special effects more than the film's thematic concerns. For example, the *New York Post*'s Rod Dreher offers that it's "very easy to overlook this movie's faults when confronted by the razzle-dazzle visual effects." Critics who were less impressed with the film tended to make their criticism of the film's themes more explicit. According to *The Village Voice*'s Dennis Lim, for example, *The Matrix*'s "mile-a-minute gobbledygook and mystic hogwash" makes the film "tailor-made for [star] Keanu [Reeves'] perpetual look of befuddlement." As we have seen in previous chapters, this is the range of reviews that blockbusters typically generate.

The Matrix's two sequels, both released in 2003, also saw the same mix of financial success and faint critical praise, although the final film has been seen as something of a disappointment. The Matrix Reloaded's worldwide gross of almost $750 million on a production budget of $150 million indicates that it was not quite as lucrative an investment as the first film, but this is common for sequels. The Matrix Revolution's worldwide gross of just under $430 million on a production budget of $150 million suggests that the film was barely profitable when taking into account marketing costs and revenue sharing with theaters. However, both sequels were released in 2003, and if their domestic grosses are combined, the $420 million total—far more than the combined production budgets—is significantly higher than the $337 million earned by that year's domestic box office champion, The Lord of the Rings: The Return of the King. And studio accountants would doubtlessly be pleased by a worldwide take of almost $1.2 billion on a $300 million production budget. The Matrix and its sequels, then, clearly qualify as blockbusters on financial grounds.

Unsurprisingly, reaction to the films on the part of mainstream critics mirrors each film's financial fortune. The Matrix Reloaded has a respectable 73 percent fresh rating on Rotten Tomatoes, though much of the praise is qualified by an admission that a sequel to a groundbreaking film can rarely match the awe produced by the original. For example, the New York Times' Elvis Mitchell argued that the film "has the feel of a holding pattern" though "the 15-minute chase sequence on a multilane highway is alone worth sitting through the picture." Some critics could give the film genuine praise however. Carla Meyer, writing for the San Francisco Chronicle asserts that the "vibrant humanity" of rebels who chose to exit the matrix give the otherwise competent action film more moral heft than its competition.

Like the audiences who waited to watch the third film on DVD, however, mainstream critics appear to be disappointed that the Wachowskis did not ultimately deliver on the promise of the first film. After all, the film is only 36 percent fresh on Rotten Tomatoes, with only nine of the 43 reviews written by those meriting the "Top Critic" designation being fresh. Typical of the disappointed reviewers is the New York Times' A.O. Scott, who complains that while "all" the film's "bombast" might "raise an honest goose bump or two," it "cannot dispel the overall atmosphere of exhaustion." Similarly, Mike Clark, writing in USA Today, argues that among the film's casualties "is the benefit of the doubt that a few deluded types (myself included) gave The Matrix Reloaded." Clearly, The Matrix and its sequels received the kind of critical reaction that blockbusters experience: praise for their entertainment value but guarded concerns or outright criticism of their artistic merits and ability to critique society.

Academic criticism of *The Matrix* and its sequels ranges widely, but it has been far more likely to detect cultural critique than the bulk of the mainstream reviews.[5] Perhaps the two most frequently recurring critical preoccupations are the film's use of religious symbolism—Neo is, after all, the redeemer of Zion who brings lasting peace through sacrificing his life—and the way the film directly or implicitly references critical theory. While the Christology of Neo is both clearly established and not germane to this argument, the trilogy's engagement with critical theory is notable. Understandably, the academic most frequently associated with *The Matrix* is Jean Baudrillard, whom Morpheus appears to be directly referencing when he welcomes Neo to the desert of the real. Further evidence of Baudrillard's influence comes early in the first film when Neo hides the money he earns as a hacker in a hollowed-out copy of *Simulacra and Simulation*. After all, my work here would be much easier if Han Solo had confessed to Princess Leia that he had found his soul in the *Millennium Falcon* until he had met her or if Sarah Connor had a copy of *One-Dimensional Man* in her prison cell. Despite the films' apparent debt to Baudrillard, however, Jaques Lacan, Jaques Derrida, and Frederic Jameson have all been persuasively linked to the Wachowski's trilogy.

But while these arguments delineate the films' primary theoretical debts, *The Matrix* films also engages with Marcusian concepts, providing evidence of the half-life of the thematic elements Lucas, Scott, and Cameron employed. After all, a film about a society in which machines use people for batteries while simultaneously convincing people that they aren't batteries by implanting a false image of the world in their minds—a "computer-generated dream world," according to Morpheus, that has been "pulled over" our eyes—is a pretty good metaphorical presentation of the total capture of humanity by industrial society. Indeed, according to Morpheus, most people are so hopelessly dependent on the system that they will fight to protect it. Evidence of this comes in the act of betrayal committed by Cypher, who was motivated by his desire to return to the Matrix and live what he thought was the good life. *The Matrix* argues that people in industrial society think one-dimensionally, in other words, and are beset by false needs and therefore easily controlled by soft repression. *The Matrix Reloaded* and *The Matrix Revolutions* continue to develop the trilogy's Marcusian arguments by presenting Eros—both traditional romantic love and the kind of self-sacrifice Neo engages in—as the antidote to the Thanatos created by the machines.

Perhaps the best way to investigate the Marcusian elements of *The Matrix* is to explore the parallels between that film and *THX-1138*. There are some interesting surface similarities, yet, as de Certeau would suggest, we should not be surprised that subtly altered elements of a previous tale appear in a popular narrative. It is tempting to suggest that these changes center around a shift from pharmaceuticals as a means of social control—something very appropriate in the early 1970s—to computers as a means of social control—something very appropriate in 1999 at the height of Y2K paranoia. For example, in *THX* education involves giving students IV drips that contain the chemicals that will teach them French, Spanish, or whatever subject is in the lesson plan that day. In *The Matrix*, education involves downloading information via neural link, as when Tank downloads Ju-Jitsu into Neo. The agents that pursue the rebels provide another similarity, as they can be seen as updated versions of the robot police that pursue THX, though Agent Smith sounds an awful lot like Ash admiring the Xenomorph when Smith expresses his admiration for the Matrix. Furthermore, in Lucas' first film the workers in the underground city are either clinic-born clones or birth-born humans who are seen as deviants by the powers that be. In *The Matrix*, the members of the resistance who are born the old fashioned way delight in kidding members who were podborn; incubated by the Matrix in bottles that provide a striking visual quotation of the cloning methods used in *THX*.

These surface similarities are not merely coincidental bits of science fiction trivia, however, but instead point to broader thematic similarities between the two films. After all, LUH helps THX see beyond the structured society he lives in by taking away the pharmaceuticals that dull his senses and replacing them with placebos. Morpheus offers Neo a pill that will let him accept life in the Matrix and a pill that will let him see the Matrix for what it is. And while there is no overt romance between Neo and Morpheus, the romantic relationship between Neo and Trinity functions in the same way as the romantic relationship between THX and LUH precisely because Trinity is also not a vapid beauty but instead an adventurous questioner who helps Neo want to critique his society. Evidence of this comes when Neo meets Trinity for the first time. Neo indicates that he is looking for an answer to a question—in this case, the identity of Morpheus—but Trinity reminds Neo that "it's the question that drives us"; that the act of asking questions and thinking two-dimensionally that leads people to genuine freedom.

Both films are honest enough to portray questioning industrial society as an arduous task. Indeed, after they begin their journeys, both protagonists express regrets: THX asks LUH why she got him involved and Neo tells Morpheus that he wants out. Nevertheless, Neo, like THX, has become a two-dimensional seeker who must follow his questioning of society to its logical conclusion. For THX this involves an ambiguous escape from his underground city and its robot police force because he is able to keep climbing in the face of repeated warnings that he cannot survive outside his city's protective shell. For Neo, this involves defeating the Matrix' agents because he is capable of seeing virtual reality for what it is. Morpheus tells Neo that the agents possess superior strength and speed because they follow specific rules.

The film implies that Neo is stronger and faster than the agents because he can bend those rules. This is illustrated in an exchange with Trinity that takes place as they discuss their frontal assault on a building guarded by military personnel and agents. Trinity worries that no one has ever tried anything like that before, but Neo reassures her by arguing that their plan is going to work precisely because no one has ever tried it before. The one-dimensional agents, in other words, are not prepared for two-dimensional seekers like Trinity and Neo.

*The Matrix* ends with a victorious Neo calling out to other seekers and promising to show them "a world without boundaries" if they would only dare to engage in two-dimensional thought, seeming to provide a more optimistic take on humanity's ability to escape from a technological dystopia than Lucas' first film. In both *The Matrix Reloaded* and *The Matrix Revolutions*, the Wachowskis expand their Marcusian subtext by shifting away from a critique of one-dimensional thought and false needs to a nuanced portrayal of the symbiotic relationship between humans and technology that implicitly echoes Marcuse's contentions that technology can be a great liberator or a great source of enslavement. At the heart of this portrayal is the contention that even though industrial society will attempt to standardize and pacify in the name of Thanatos, the power of Eros—something that, for the Wachowskis, can also exist within machines—will ultimately triumph. If the machines both control humanity and use them as a power source by implanting false images in their minds, then *The Matrix* presents a powerful metaphorical presentation of Thanatos—there should be no conflict because everyone has been captured by a system that literally places them in stasis. Yet that film clearly argues that conflict between the machines and their living power sources is unavoidable, and *Reloaded* and *Revolutions'* depiction of the apparent resolution of this conflict argues that totalizing Thanatos is not possible because Eros always disrupts Thanatos and is ultimately the stronger force.

The final two films in the series ensure that viewers who are paying attention realize that the narratives are not delivering a simplistic message along the lines of "machines bad people good." Instead, the films argue that people can turn the instruments of industrial society towards individual liberation even if the tendency of industrial society is towards Thanatos. In *The Matrix Reloaded* viewers learn that Zion, which is clearly the home of freely-expressed, conventional erotic love, is also highly mechanized and defended in part by what look like weaponized versions of the power loaders from *Aliens*. This visual allusion suggests that the rebellion against the Matrix is just as dependent on technology for their liberation as the rebellion against Emperor Palpatine, Ripley's individual rebellion against Weyland-Yutani, Deckard's escape into nature, the rebellion against Skynet, or the rebellion against the RDA. The film makes this dependence clear when Counselor

Hammond tells Neo, as they look out over the massive devices that provide air and water for Zion, that "these machines are keeping us alive while other machines are coming to kill us." The trick, then, is to use machines to enhance life while limiting machines' ability to turn life into living death.

But how is this to be done? According to *Reloaded* and *Revolutions*, the solution is imminent within the technology itself because technology can be creative and life-affirming and therefore also relies on Eros. Evidence of the machine's need to employ Eros comes in one of the bigger reveals of *Reloaded*. Viewers learn that Neo could not really be "the One" because there have been several "Ones" during the life of the Matrix. During an interview with the Architect, the program that created the Matrix and who, as we learn in *Revolutions*, serves to balance the equation between Thanatos and Eros, Neo learns that there have been several uprisings against the Matrix created by the Matrix. All of these abortive attempts at establishing freedom ended with Zion being smashed by the machines, who then immediately seeded a new Zion. Apparently, the rebellion, Zion, and the One are all a way for the Matrix to use Eros to account for anomalies and is, as Neo remarks, "another system of control." Yet ultimately this system of control fails to contain not only the Eros it uses to balance the equation, but also the Thanatos it must employ to remain operational. After exploring how *Reloaded* and *Revolutions* argue that man-machine symbiosis can be a manifestation of Eros since machines need love too, we will see how the films portray the most powerful threat to the Matrix, Agent Smith, as a personification of Thanatos that must be destroyed by Neo's erotic sacrifice.

If Neo is the One's One, it is because only he fully embraced Eros. Tellingly, the film points out that Neo is the only iteration of the One who has fallen in love and is, implicitly, the only one who can make the sacrifice necessary to bring a measure of freedom to the Matrix. Thus, when he chooses Trinity over restarting Zion—an act of sacrifice that transcends simple sexual attachment and an expression of a wish to live a more human life outside of the Matrix—the Architect remarks that "hope is the greatest human delusion." This sentiment is echoed elsewhere by Agent Smith, who sneeringly opines that only the human mind could invent something as insipid as love. Yet the films make it clear that hope and love, or more precisely the desire to better the world that is inherent in Eros, is not simply a human characteristic, but something that can also be shared by sentient programs. And if even programs can hope, then the universe is not governed by Thanatos-validating cause and effect, as the Architect and the Merovingian, another malevolent program, argue, but is instead ultimately guided by Eros that is best understood as a creative force that both natural and artificial intelligence can use to better the world.

This ability of Eros to transcend the boundaries between man and machines—something that is probably best understood as Marcusian argument modified by extra elements from Donna Haraway's *Cyborg Manifesto*—is clearly illustrated in the first hour of *Revolutions*. In a somewhat disorienting break from the action, Neo spends a great deal of time trapped in a subway station that represents a link between the Matrix and the world inhabited by the machines. There, he meets two programs who are bringing their unauthorized daughter, Seti, to live with the Oracle, a powerful program in the Matrix that supports the rebellion and nurtures the One, therefore advocating for Eros within the equation that the Architect is trying to balance. Seti's parents, even though they are not human, risk deletion from the Matrix because they love their daughter, whose unauthorized function, as the Oracle tells the Architect in *Revolutions*' final scene, is creating vivid sunsets. Here, the films clearly argue that Eros is not the sole property of humanity, but is also easily expressed and vital to technological entities like programs. This argument is reinforced in scenes where the Oracle cares for Seti. The Oracle's grandmotherly demeanor initially appears out of sync with the overall tone of the film—and may partially explain *Revolutions*' poor critical reception and financial performance. But the sight of one of the most powerful programs in the Matrix lovingly nurturing an "illegitimate" program that would have been deactivated in the machine city makes much more sense in the context of an argument about the link between Eros and technology. Consequently, it's not that hard to imagine that when the Oracle tells Seti that cookies need love like everything else does, she is including programs by showing love to Seti while at the same time receiving love from her.

And while programs like the Architect and the Merovingian make persuasive arguments for the necessity of Thanatos, events of the series eventually demonstrate Thanatos' danger even to a society run by machines because of its inherent tendency to enforce a numbing uniformity in the name of peace. This is depicted in the contrast between Neo and his nemesis Agent Smith. In the beginning of *The Matrix*, Neo is a new recruit to the rebellion and Smith is one of the rank and file of the machine's repressive apparatus. By the end of *The Matrix*, however, Neo has begun to question the Matrix and in this questioning has also found new powers that allow him to be a powerful force for Eros. In *Reloaded*, it becomes clear that Neo has set Agent Smith free from the Matrix. Like Neo, Smith can now see through the Matrix and question its workings. But in unplugging him from the system, Neo has created a potent enemy who is motivated by Thanatos. Both are revolutionaries, but while Neo wants to free humanity from the false needs implanted in them by the machines, Smith is so committed to Thanatos that he converts every program and every avatar of an entrapped human he encounters into a copy of himself. Smith's spreading sameness—an excellent visual conceptualization of the false peace of Thanatos—threatens not only the Matrix itself but also the machine metropolis it serves. Yet most of the machines proceed with the plan to destroy and rebuild Zion as if nothing had changed, demonstrating the chief drawbacks of one-dimensional thought.

Not all of the machines underestimate the threat posed by Agent Smith, however. The Oracle warns Neo that Smith will destroy everything if he is not stopped. After attempting to best his nemesis while at the same time prevent the machines from destroying Zion for most of the series, Neo sees beyond the pattern of rebellion and suppression designed by the Architect and realizes that he needs to go to the machine's city and offer to help them defeat Smith. Of course, the machines do not want to admit that they need a human to help them and that, by extension, relying on one-dimensional thought and false needs eventually leads to the destruction of the most rigidly programmed system. Consequently, when Neo confronts the Oz-like personification of the machines in the heart of their city, he is told that he is not needed. Neo confidently replies that if that is the case, the machines should kill him. Instead of dispatching him, and without further comment, the machines proceed to plug him into the Matrix and implicitly bid him to attack their common enemy. Even technology itself, in other words, is aware of the danger of Thanatos.

In many ways, Neo's climactic battle with Agent Smith is just that: the climactic battle at the end of a science fiction trilogy. Neo and Smith soar through the air punching each other, knocking each other into buildings and removing rows of windows or knocking each other into the street and removing yards of asphalt. Yet the thematic underpinnings of this extremely entertaining bit of blockbuster visual excess are never completely hidden. During his battle with Neo, Smith argues that the purpose of life is to end, darkly hinting at the logical conclusion of Thanatos. After all, if Smith wins, everyone will become Smith, everything will be subsumed under his power, and the dynamism that is life will be replaced by a crypt-quiet peace.

The generic demands of the blockbuster combined with the Christological elements of Neo's characterization make his pyrrhic victory over Smith predictable. Yet the end result of Neo's sacrifice is a complete disruption of the pattern of curated rebellion that the Architect has used to keep the machines firmly in control. It is not the end of Thanatos, but instead a move towards the use of technology for human liberation as predicted by Marcuse. Neo's sacrifice in service of the machines comes with an agreement that not only prevents the destruction of the current iteration of Zion, but also allows the inhabitants of Zion to continue their work of removing people from their storage chambers unimpeded. And while this new era of man-machine symbiosis is inflected by a contemporary infatuation with the cyborg, it is nevertheless presented as a cautiously hopeful time. Indeed, even though the Architect dismissively predicts that most people will remain in The Matrix, it is important to note that he is discussing this new reality with the Oracle as they watch one of Seti's sunrises. Unlike the setting sun a hapless THX faces, then, both humanity and machines are greeting the dawn of a new, albeit artificially created, era of diversity and life.

While *The Matrix* trilogy bears less of an impression of popularized Marcusian thought than the films discussed at length in this study, it nevertheless demonstrates that concepts like one-dimensional thought and Thanatos are directly engaged in science fiction blockbusters created by directors whose careers began well after the success of *Star Wars*, the *Alien* films, or *The Terminator* films and who have other thematic fish to fry. Yet blockbusters does not have to engage with a Marcusian critique of society directly in order to demonstrate that the thematic preoccupations of Lucas, Scott, and Cameron are enjoying a robust cultural half-life. Indeed, more casual employment of Marcusian thematics strongly suggests that the theorist's social critique is broadly perceived to be correct. This type of offhand reference to Marcusian thought can be found in the blockbuster films that have been adapted from Suzanne Collins' *Hunger Games* novels.[6]

Like the bestselling books that inspired them, *The Hunger Games* films were definitely blockbusters. The initial film in the series, 2012's *The Hunger Games*, saw a worldwide gross of almost $700 million on a production budget of $78 million. That year, the film's $408 million domestic gross was bested only by *The Avengers* and *The Dark Knight Rises*. Released 18 months later, 2013's *The Hunger Games: Catching Fire* did slightly better at the box office, becoming the highest grossing film in the United States for 2013. In addition to its $425 million domestic take, the first sequel had a worldwide total of $865 million, though the film's $130 million production budget made the difference between the films' profit margins insignificant. One year after *Catching Fire*, *The Hunger Games: Mockingjay—Part 1* was released. Lionsgate chose to split the adaptation of Collins final book into two separate films—a strategy employed on the final installments of both the *Harry Potter* and *Twilight* film adaptation series. In both cases, this decision lead to a slight dip in domestic box office receipts between the film version of the penultimate book and the first part of the film adaptation of the last book.[7] Unsurprisingly, *Mockingjay 1* saw its domestic box office fall slightly to $337 million. Nevertheless, *Mockingjay: Part 1*'s worldwide gross of $752 million on a production budget of $125 million definitely qualifies it as a blockbuster. Furthermore, in a relatively weak year, the film's domestic take was enough to give it second place in 2014's box office sweepstakes behind *American Sniper*. So far, the first three films have grossed $2.3 billion on a combined production budget of $333 million—the kind of return on investment that marks a blockbuster series.

If *The Hunger Games* adaptations have generated box office revenue that places them squarely in blockbuster territory, their reviews from mainstream critics are also typical of the genre: overtly supportive but nevertheless eager to point out that this is, after all, just a big-budget popcorn flick. *The Hunger Games*, for example, is 85 percent fresh on rottentomatoes.com. Many of the reviews are laudatory, with *Rolling Stone*'s Peter Travers praising the film for being "about something pertinent: the mission to define yourself in a world that's spinning off its moral axis." Of course, many reviews simply saw the film as a well-executed blockbuster. The *New York Post*'s Kyle Smith, for example, describes the film as a "cracking adventure of the future" that nevertheless "has problems" plotwise. *The Hunger Games: Catching Fire* is 89 percent fresh on Rotten Tomatoes and received similar reviews with some, like the *New York Daly News*'s Joe Neumaier, finding something of a pop-culture classic. According to Neumaier, the film is "an arrow's breadth from perfect" and has "absolutely outgrown its teen origins. In fact, its dark, satirical action is what the sci-fi of the '70s—*Rollerball*, *A Boy and His Dog*, *Logan's Run*—did best." Other critics, like the *New York Times*' Manohla Dargis, were approving but not quite as enthusiastic. As Dargis notes, *Catching Fire* isn't a great work of art but it's a competent, at times exciting movie and it does something that better, more artistically notable movies often fail to do: It speaks to its moment in time."

*The Hunger Games: Mockingjay Part 1* from 2014 was not as well received as its predecessors.[8] Of course, the film's 65 percent fresh rating on Rotten Tomatoes partially reflects critic's dissatisfaction with the structural deficiencies of a film based on half of a book.[9] *The Hollywood Reporter*'s Todd McCarthy exemplifies this critical disappointment with the studio's divide-and-profit strategy when he argues that from "a dramatic point of view, this would have ideally occupied either the initial third or first half, let's say, of a 140-minute movie, which would have then continued to accelerate toward cathartic action and ultimate resolution." The film as not without its defenders, however. Claudia Puig, writing in *USA Today*, calls the film "a nimbly constructed action-adventure blockbuster with a social conscience." Even the most poorly-reviewed film that has so far been released, then, has seen mainstream critics react in ways typical of blockbusters: praise for the action and dramatic tension, but hand-wringing over evidence that at least some at the studio see the film as little more than lucrative product.

As with *The Matrix* and many of the other films discussed here, academic criticism of *The Hunger Games* has ranged widely yet taken the series far more seriously than critics working in popular media. Understandably, scholars tend to focus on Katniss' status as the female protagonist of a violent and dystopian narrative whose intended audience is adolescent girls. Critics have also explored the texts' relationship to the spectacle and reality television, as well as the series' contributions to young adult literature. What is germane to this discussion, however, is the tendency of some critics to read Panem as a hard dystopia like George Orwell's 1984. While this approach is clearly warranted, however, a closer look at the film reveals that Panem contains a curious mix of hard and soft repression. Broadly speaking, the districts fall under an iron heel that would make the Ministry of Love envious while the Capital is captive to its own prosperity. The focus of the films are on the inhabitants of the districts and audience sympathies are clearly with the districts, and so the film has much more to say about hard repression. Yet since the inhabitants of the capital are themselves captives of a repressive system, the soft repression they undergo is thematically important and its Marcusian overtones represent the persistence of themes made popular by Lucas, Scott, and Cameron in contemporary blockbusters.

Perhaps the best way to conceptualize the split between the different forms of repression and their different literary and theoretical antecedents is to look at the way the first film visually contrasts the Districts and the Capital. Images of District 12 evoke the Great Depression by establishing shots and costumes that seem based on Walker Evans' photographs. Even the Victor's Village, as depicted in *Catching Fire*, features buildings whose exteriors look worn and grimy, even though the interiors are comfortably appointed. If District 12 exists in some kind of eternal 1930s, it should not surprise us that they are subjected to 30s-style totalitarianism. Not only are they watched over by "Peacekeepers" brought in from other districts, but when they mine the coal that is used to keep the Capital's lights on and factories running, they are also essentially doing the kind of forced labor that Hitler used in territory occupied by the Nazis to maintain his war machine and Germany's standard of living.

The uniforms of the Peacekeepers—at least in the first movie, before Katniss' actions in the Games seemingly created the perpetual state of emergency that requires them to dress in full riot gear in almost every scene—provide a visual clue to the kind of totalitarianism experienced in the Capital. The uniforms, though white instead of black, seem to be patterned on the firemen's uniforms in Françoise Truffaut's *Fahrenheit 451*: short helmets with small visors and leather ear flaps, high-collared shirts, jackboots, and leather gloves. Both Truffaut's film and the Ray Bradbury novel it is based on portray mid-century totalitarianism in all its Marcusian glory. The material abundance of society found in *Fahrenheit 451*—e.g., houses with floor-to-ceiling television screens—encourages its citizens to comply with the political insanity of an impending nuclear war and the cultural idiocy of a society that uses its firemen to burn books.

Of course, Panem is based on Ancient Rome, as both its name and the use of violent spectacle to control a restive populace suggests. Yet Rome did not have the manufacturing capability of mid–20th-century industrial society, and could do little more than distribute bread—the "panem" of Collins' allusion—and conduct gladiatorial games and circuses. *The Hunger Games'* Panem, however, could deliver the goods of soft repression, at least to some of its population, and it used these goods both to keep the Capital populace in line and to subvert the anger of the victorious tributes. Indeed, Panem appears to exhibit a spectrum of repression that ranges from the sadistically brutal—witness Gayle's public whipping by the Peacekeepers in *Catching Fire*—to the comfortable entrapment of the parodically fashion-forward Capital lifestyle. And while the hard repression undergone by Katniss and the other residents of District 12 is the focal point of both the rebellion and the thematic concerns of the films, the depiction of soft repression both provides important texture to the films themselves and demonstrates the persistence of Marcuse's contentions about soft repression.

*The Hunger Games* films use soft repression to implicitly explain why the people in the Capital do not protest a political system that annually broadcasts evidence that it is founded on the slaughter of innocents. An interesting byproduct of this televised slaughter is that the surviving innocents become privileged members of the same social system that offered up their lives to the god of social order. The winners of the games, in other words, must then be co-opted by the same culture that recently tried to kill them. Indeed, the seduction of the potential victors begins on the train that takes the tributes to the Capital. In *The Hunger Games*, Effie Trinket, the minder sent from the Capital to District 12 in order to gather tributes for the games, forcefully points out both the luxurious appointments Katniss and Peeta find themselves in and the abundant provisions they are free to indulge in. Once in the Capital, the two tributes find themselves in quarters that make the train look shabby in comparison. The contrast between the hard repression experienced by the Districts and the soft repression found in the Capital comes into sharper focus in the second film when Katniss and Peeta, having been declared co-victors, perform the customary victory tour. Their ritual of public display concludes in the Capital, where they are treated to a party at President Snow's mansion. Here they see well-connected Capital residents consuming outrageous quantities of food, and when they ask how such excess is possible, Peeta and Katniss are offered a drink and told that "it makes you sick so you can go on eating." While the behavior of the Capital citizens is somewhat monstrous, then, it is also quite pleasurable, and we can see this because *Catching Fire* provides us an exterior view of Marcusian soft repression.

The first two films are careful to visually emphasize that the experience of the tributes and the victors are not that unique when compared to the lives of most of the Capital's citizens, however. Beginning with Effie's outrageously festive attire at the reaping in *The Hunger Games*, the films go to great lengths to visually underscore the gulf between the dandified appearance of the residence of the Capital from the hardscrabble attire of the citizens of District

12. In *The Hunger Games* as well as *Catching Fire* there are several establishing shots of Capital street scenes and audience members at Games-related events that feature a menagerie of improbable hairstyles and daring clothing. While Effie, Cinna and the rest of Katniss' prep team all exhibit varying degrees of the Capital's obsession with fashion, its public face is the host of the Hunger Games, Caesar Flickerman, whose ever-changing hairstyle and makeup visually delineate the Capital's ideal man about town. In part, Flickerman, Effie, and the rest of the Capital's inhabitants are another critique of spectacle, but the constant demand for the new that is the hallmark of fashion is one of the many ways false needs manifest themselves in industrial society. After all, a slave to fashion is tied to the supply chain that manufactures and distributes new articles of clothing, new cosmetics, etc. In turn, fashion's slaves are also the slaves of the political system that controls their supply of new looks, even if that system is founded on open and notorious brutality.

Yet the citizens of the Capital are not only addicted to fashion. They are also consumed with the Hunger Games themselves. While the Games are clearly spectacle modeled on the Roman Circus and gladiatorial games—the contestants are introduced in the Capital while riding on chariots, after all—the films also do much to call attention to the manufactured aspect of this spectacle. In both *The Hunger Games* and *Catching Fire*, many scenes are set in the high-tech control room that the Game Maker uses to oversee the slaughter of the tributes. In a sense, we see the factory floor where the spectacle is made, suggesting that it is, at least on a subtextual level, just one more product of industrial society that the Capital uses to instill false needs in its citizens and to discourage them from two-dimensional thought. This depiction also gives a Marcusian subtext to some of the scenes in which the spectacle is critiqued, such as Gayle's suggestion in an early scene of the *Hunger Games* that the Capital's violent spectacle would lose its affective power "if one year they stopped watching." By implying that there is no actual need to watch *The Hunger Games*, Gayle, who is clearly presented as a two-dimensional thinker, is underlining the Games' status as perhaps the only manufactured artifact of soft repression via false needs to be found in all of Panem. Another instance of implicit Marcusian critique comes in *The Hunger Games* when President Snow tells doomed gamemaker Seneca Crane that "hope is stronger than fear." This is both an implicit assertion that Eros is stronger than Thanatos and another admission that the Games' role as product of Panem's industrial apparatus is to convince citizens of the districts that they need to consume fear of the Capital lest they think two-dimensionally about Panem's social structure.

In Collins' third book, *Mockingjay*, the revolution has begun and Katniss and other key characters are either in the militarized spaces of District 13 or, eventually, fighting in the streets of the Capital. The Marcusian elements of

Collins' critique featured in the first two books and their film adaptations, so well-suited for peacetime Panem, diminish as the narrative shifts to a literalist depiction of the use of defensive violence to destroy a violently repressive totalitarian state. Nevertheless, in *Mockingjay Part 1*, the false needs of the former residents of the Capital who have joined the rebellion and fled to District 13 provide comic relief. The inhabitants of 13, the only district to escape from Capital rule, after all, are futuristic Spartans who call each other soldier and live in what is essentially a large bomb shelter. Their clothing consists of drab uniforms and hairstyles that can be charitably described as functional. They eat what the cafeteria serves and do not feel the need to throw up so that they have room for a different flavor of gruel. And since they have been living this way for over 75 years, they have no experience with the material abundance that pervades the lives of the Capital's residents. Although circumstances force them to do so, they are using what technology they have primarily in the service of human liberation.

After Katniss destroyed the dome covering the Games and triggered the revolution at the end of *Catching Fire*, however, Head Gamemaker turned revolutionary Plutarch Heavensbee and a few other rebellious Capitol dwellers escape to District 13 and find themselves without all of the things that Panem's industrial society has taught them to need. While even the residents of the purposefully impoverished District 12 who escaped the Capital's firebombing of their homes by fleeing to 13 struggle with their bare-bones existence, the former inhabitants of the Capital find the instrumentalist society that has taken them in a burden almost too heavy to bear. Heavensbee, the most chipper member of the contingent of Capital exiles, frequently wonders why District 13 does not have coffee. Katniss and Peeta's alcoholic mentor, Haymitch, a victor from District 12 who had long grown use to the excesses of the Capital, dislikes District 13 because it is dry.

Lest the inhabitants of District 13 appear simply puritanical, however, the loudest complaints come from Effie, who frequently and loudly bemoans District 13's lack of clothes and cosmetics. She also wonders why she is not granted access to more fashionable clothes, offering that the "upper ranks" should have privileges. While her complaints are consistent with her portrayal as shallow and out-of-touch and provide a measure of comic relief in what is, for a blockbuster, a downbeat film, they also implicitly underscore District 13's relatively healthier relationship with the fruits of industrial society. Effie, after all, is helping District 13 as it attempts to turn Katniss into The Mockingjay; a potent symbol of the revolution that can be used in propaganda broadcasts. This involves makeup and fancy clothes, albeit imported from the Capital, that demonstrate that District 13 does have fashion—when it needs it—and that while rank does not exactly have privilege, it nevertheless provides some citizens opportunities to use material goods if such use would serve the interests of the commonwealth. That Katniss, Haymitch, and Heavensbee ultimately decide that merely using The Mockingjay as a propaganda symbol is not as effective as actually letting her fight only heightens the film's affinity with Marcuse's views on the fruits of industrial society. Katniss' soul is not in the Mockingjay suit, or in the makeup that Effie artfully applies, but in the struggle to free humanity from the hard and soft repression industrial society is capable of. While the adaptations of Collins' novels are preoccupied with other social critiques, then, Marcusian elements are easily detected, suggesting that popularized versions of the theorist's ideas appear to be enjoying a long half-life.

The persistence of Marcusian themes in *The Matrix* and *The Hunger Games* films strongly suggest that while the mid-century cultural moment that turned a philosophy professor's social critique into the grist for bestselling books and protest movements has passed, the narrative utility of that social critique has not dimmed. Lucas, Scott, and Cameron not only created plots and characters that have been and will continue to be recycled for decades to come, but also devised themes that relied on popularized versions of Marcuse's theories that have been and will continue to be recycled for decades to come. Indeed while the current superhero renaissance in blockbuster film might present thematically dialectical rejoinders to Marcuse's work, the casual reference to soft repression to in *The Hunger Games*—perhaps *The Avengers* films' closest competition—proves that popularizations of Marcuse's critiques have found their place in popular culture's collective unconscious.

And while this study does function on an important level as an argument for Marcuse's continued relevance, it also argues for the critical utility of the Blockbuster. Without apologizing for straightforwardly commercial fare like 2014's reboot of *Teenage Mutant Ninja Turtles*, this study sought to demonstrate, using Marcuse's impact on Lucas, Scott, and Cameron as a case study, that blockbusters could be used to put serious ideas about society in a form that would let them retain most of their critical dynamism while being widely disseminated. Was the critique as thorough as a lecture in one of Marcuse's graduate seminars? Of course not. Yet an intellectual vanguard formulating a social critique that can be appreciated by the masses, at least in the leftist position that Marcuse's reading of society emerged from, is always already part of the plan. So while Hollywood is clearly big business and while the directors discussed are clearly, at this point in their lives, card-carrying members of global capitalism's financial elite, there is nevertheless a utopian quality to their work: the radical idea that popular entertainment just might be one of the opposing forces that helps break the containment of industrial society.

# Chapter Notes

## Chapter 1

1. All financial information about movies under discussion is taken from http://www.boxofficemojo.com unless otherwise noted.

2. With the 2015 release of *Star Wars: The Force Awakens*, all of the directors under consideration have themselves seen at least one of their stories continued or completely remade by others. Lucas, Scott, and Cameron's work is itself not immune to the process de Certeau describes, and this study therefore looks primarily at the historical and cultural moment when these directors were the ones remaking commonplace tales.

3. Stanley Aronowitz argues that Marcuse "never came to terms with film and other forms of popular, especially visual culture, regarding them as instances of the anti-aesthetic" (148). Ben Agger, though arguing that Marcuse embraced "the carnal rock of the Rolling Stones" (337), nevertheless similarly detected a broad bias against mass-market works. According to Agger, the theorist wants to "rescue authentic experience—of hope and sorrow—from the Muzak of popular culture" ("Aesthetic" 333). Marcuse himself made many assertions that would support Aronowitz' and Agger's contentions. In *The Aesthetic Dimension*, Marcuse posited that art cannot "popularize itself without weakening its emancipatory impact" (21). He further asserted that because industrial society delivers the goods not only to the working class but also to most of the middle class in part by means of a soul-deadening mass culture, it is not proper to speak of a mass base for art since "this would only refer to pop art and best sellers" (32). This means that genuinely subversive artists would have difficulty working in popular media and must therefore sometimes "stand against the people" (35).

Similarly, in "Repressive Tolerance," Marcuse argues that the dynamics of the market make it difficult for art to effectively protest the established reality. In *Eros and Civilization* Marcuse frequently suggests that popular culture helped create conformist personalities. For example, Marcuse noted that "the repressive organization of the instincts seems to be *collective*" and as examples of this collective the philosopher cites "gangs, radio, and television" and argue that they "set the pattern for conformity and rebellion" (88). He further observes that in repressive society the "expressions of personality fit and sustain perfectly the socially desired pattern of behavior and thought. This process, which has been completed in the 'mass culture' of late industrial civilization, vitiates the concept of interpersonal relations" (231). So while Marcuse does suggest in *The Aesthetic Dimension* that the discussion of the utopian elements of literature found in that text was "broadly applicable to other texts" (x), there is little in his work that suggests that the theorist himself would see popular science fiction narratives as a place for thematic intervention against repressive society.

4. At this point it should be noted that Marcuse's detractors were not merely the rank and file of the Klan, nervous university administrators, and a governor of California by the name of Ronald Reagan. Many academics, Marxist and otherwise—so many that the official Marcuse website has a "hater's page" cataloging objections raised to his theories—made reasoned and plausible critiques of the philosopher's interpretation of Marx and Freud. These critiques will be overlooked in the present study, however, because it concerns itself with the impact on popular culture of the popularization of Marcuse's ideas and because, typically, popularizations do not even acknowledge critiques of the idea being popularized.

## Chapter 2

1. If space permitted, this chapter could also consider the reconfigurations of Cameron's *Terminator* narratives in the works of later director's films: 2003's *Rise of the Machines*, 2009's *Salvation*, and 2015's *Genisys*. Indeed, *Genisys* uses time travel to reboot Cameron's first film so directly—e.g., it reshoots a key scene from the first film so that Sarah Connor is the one who says "come with me if you live" in an attempt to reflect the relatively more feminist cultural assumptions of 2015—it is as if de Certeau was still alive and working as a script doctor.
2. Unless otherwise noted, all film reviews were taken from online sources linked to www.rottentomatoes.com.
3. For example, Ilsa J. Bick argues that Ripley's assumption of leadership over the convicts on Fury 161, even though she is initially presented as an androgynous simulacrum of a male action hero complete with rippling musculature and a phallic shaved head, gives academic critics the opportunity to shift "the focus of inquiry into what woman contains and" to further explore how "the confusion, fantasies, and fears over what may be found within radically alters the traditional iconography of what constitutes power" (54). Louise Speed also addresses the psychoanalytical and feminist implications of the film when she notes that *Alien³* "explores the dark underbelly of family values" by "addressing profound anxieties over the nature of the female as both phallic mother and monstrous feminine" (137). Speed also finds thematics that are close to Marcuse's concerns, detecting a compelling depiction of what will happen when "technology has left town and turned off the postmodern lights" (125). Furthermore, Speed finds evidence that we are living in "a wasteland of the junked meanings of the postindustrial world" (131) in the film's portrayal of a gradually decaying penal refinery.
4. For example, A. Samuel Kimball finds that the film deconstructs notions of reproduction and contraception because it

> resists the conceptual framework that requires that the alien be represented, precisely at its most reproductive, as threatening the very future and survival of the human species. And yet the film must deploy its strategies of resistance from within the very conceptuality it is attempting to displace. The result is that the film relies on conceptive representations of the future even as it is attempting to move in the direction of contraceptive representations, to develop a counterconceptive image, sense, or apprehension of the future, to a contraceptive of the time to come [97].

Elizabeth Ezra is also impressed by Jenuet's willingness to turn the third sequel to a blockbuster into an art film—she jokingly notes that it "is almost as if the film's target audience were composed of academic viewers, or film critics with a textbook grounding in psychoanalysis under their belts" (58). Ezra, however, is interested in the way that Jenuet uses the film to explore his own status as an outsider in Hollywood. According to Ezra, the "French director's experience of estrangement is evoked in the final words of the film itself, uttered by Ripley when, gazing at earth, Call asks her, 'What happens now?' and she replies, 'I don't know. I'm a stranger here myself'" (56).

## Chapter 3

1. This chapter is a revised version of an article that appeared in *Extrapolation* 50.3 (2009): 417–441.
2. Pollock 246. John Seabrook similarly argues that the auteur "has become the successful, fiscally conservative businessman that his father always wanted him to be" (46).
3. Roger Ebert claimed that "a world that now seems incomparably distant and innocent—was brought back with a rush of feeling that wasn't so much nostalgia as culture shock." Writing in the *New York Times*, Roger Greenspun was more direct, calling *American Graffiti* "a very good movie, funny, tough, unsentimental" and describing it as "full of marvelous performances." Even some academic critics were impressed with Lucas' second film. Michael Dempsey praised the film's "understated but trenchant criticism of nostalgia" and argued approvingly that "Lucas captures the sheer disposability of pop culture and its trappings" (59).
4. By any commercial measure, *American Graffiti* has been a raging success. Within the first year of its release, the film, which cost about $750,000 to make, had done over $21 million at the box office. While that is a return on investment seldom found outside of Ponzi schemes, it is also a respectable figure in its own right. Adjusting the numbers for inflation reveals that Lucas created a genuine hit. Adjusting for inflation, *American Graffiti* would have made $473 million in 2008, while that year's box office champion, *The Dark Knight*, made $531 million.
5. The film found its way onto several best films of 1973 lists, including the *New York Times* and *Time* magazine's ten best lists. And the film's continuing presence on similar lists is a testament to its good standing among the keepers of mainstream cinema tastes. For example, in 1994, *Car and Driver* included the film on its Movies for Motorheads. In 1995, *American Graffiti* was

## Notes. Chapter 3

placed on the National Film Registry. In 2003, *USA Today* included the film in an unnumbered list entitled "The Best of the Big-Cast Classics." In 2006, *Entertainment Weekly* listed at #6 on their list of best high school movies.

6. Others have made similar observations. Lesley Speed argues that *American Graffiti* strives to contain chaotic adolescent experiences by representing them as an ultimately orderly passage into stable adulthood. Similarly, David Shumway, notes that the film "creates a fictional set of memories that ... may actually come to replace the audience's 'original' sense of the past." Consequently, "*American Graffiti* is fundamentally a conservative film that offered its post-Vietnam, post-1960s audience a glimpse of the America it would rather see" (40, 42).

7. Adding the total domestic gross for all six films—including the late 1990s re-release of episodes 4–6 gives a total of $3,443,642,400.

8. *A New Hope* won Academy Awards for Best Art Direction-Set Decoration, Best Costume Design, Best Effects-Visual Effects, Best Film Editing, Best Music-Original Score, and Best Sound. *The Empire Strikes Back* won an Oscar for Best Sound.

9. Lucas told Pollock that he turned to Campbell because "I was trying to get fairy tales, myths, and religion down to a distilled state, studying the pure form to see how and why it worked" (134).

10. Other critics have approached the films by directly employing the Jungian theories that provide the critical infrastructure for Campbell's work. For example, Steven A. Galipeau argues that the series is "a *cultural dream*, one that has meaning for numerous people and symbolically depicts in important aspects the psychological and spiritual shifts taking place in our age" (1–2).

11. David S. Meyer 106. Meyer suggests that the oft-derided Ewok victory illustrates "ultimate irony of technological advantage" (107).

12. Jerold Abrams excuses the rebels for using technology like X-wing fighters and the *Millennium Falcon* because the distinction between ready-to-hand and present-at-hand is not "so much in our various machine products" as in "our basic attitude toward the universe" (110).

13. Answering a question about the poor critical and popular reception of *The Phantom Menace*, Lucas told *Sight and Sound* in 2002 that Episode I had to be made because the "story was written 30 years ago, and I'm trying to be consistent with my story. I couldn't put Harrison Ford in it" (22).

14. Lucas has been involved in many other projects, from the disastrous *Howard the Duck* to the highly profitable *Indiana Jones* series, but the films under consideration are the ones cen-

tral to his career. And while it should be noted that Lucas did not direct *The Empire Strikes Back* or *Return of the Jedi*, he was heavily involved in the writing and production of those films.

15. Roger Ebert supported this possibility in his initial review of *THX* when he speculates that "Warner Bros., having decided to drop" *American Zoetrope*, "didn't back the surviving features very enthusiastically."

16. Kline 4–5. Raymond Cormier has argued that *THX* can be seen as a critique of the "authoritarian 'managerial meritocracy' proposed in Plato's utopian vision" in *The Republic* (193). While this is a responsible reading, in light of Lucas' comments it makes more sense to read the film with a theorist who is attuned to the problematic nature of industrial society.

17. Pye and Myles 118–119. Greenspun also comments on similarities between Lucas' first and second films in his effusive *New York Times* review of *American Graffiti*.

18. Even critics who find Lucas's second film ideologically problematic have found Curt difficult to place within their dismissive treatments of *American Graffiti*. Shumway, for example, offers the backhanded compliment that "Curt seems not to have come from some other representation of the era" (42).

19. Lucas complained, for example, to Pollock about a generation growing up without fairy tales (139) that was in need of "a kids' film that would strengthen contemporary mythology and introduce a basic kind of morality" (144).

20. This reading will focus almost exclusively on the theatrically released live-action films. While there are many related narratives in the expanded universe, they were not created by Lucas and are directed towards a much smaller audience that has greatly different expectations than those of the average theatergoer.

21. According to Pollock, in *A New Hope* "the Tatooine sequences had organic colors, warm shades of gold and brown like C-3PO's burnished parts; as the battle with the Empire neared, the colors changed to black, white, and grey, the shades of evil technology" (161).

22. Han is played by Harrison Ford, who also played Bob Falfa in *American Graffiti*. Interestingly, Falfa crashes his '57 Chevy in the climactic drag race at the end of that film.

23. Elizabeth Cooke has noted that "when a Jedi gets into trouble, he consistently finds himself an ally in the natives of some very natural environments" (88), suggesting that "the natural processes in the biological world can always overcome human creations of technology" (89).

24. The problematic portrayal of the Gungans in general and of JarJar Binks in particular has been widely commented on and Lucas'

broader missteps will not be defended here. Nevertheless, despite any inept portrayals, the events on Naboo still make it clear that the Jedi must rely on species that are outside of the Republic's technological matrix and close to nature.

25. Kornelia Tancheva argues that this scene presents a very "machinelike" library that abounds in knowledge but contains very little wisdom (549).

26. The expanded universe makes a distinction between clone troopers and stormtroopers, who could be clones, birth-born recruits, or conscripts. Since most viewers of the *Star Wars* films would not be aware of this, and since this line of reasoning seems like an apology for Lucas somehow lacking the foresight to have actors with Temuera Morrison's exact measurements play stormtroopers in 1976, this paper will not maintain the distinction.

## *Chapter 4*

1. For example, John L. Cobb cogently argues the sets designed by Swiss artist H.R. Geiger feature "vaginal doorways, cervical mazes on the walls, phallic sculptures on the alien starship" (199). These visual cues indicate that this film is very much about "gestation and birth." (198). Feminist critics have not been universally impressed by the *Nostromo*'s female avenger, however. For example, Vivian Sobchack argues that when Ripley strips down to her underwear in the film's final scene, she "no longer represents a rational and asexual functioning subject, but an irrational, potent, sexual object—a woman, the truly threatening alien" ("Virginity" 107). Judith Newton argues that Ripley's performance before she disrobes is also problematic since Ripley's struggle against the Weyland-Yutani corporation metaphorically represents the fantasy that "white, middle-class women, once integrated into the world of work, will somehow save us from its worst excesses" (83). And Lynda Zwinger finds it interesting that in addition to the xenomorph, Ripley also battles against a malevolent ship's computer called mother. Yet this materfamilias is "a mother," according to Zwinger, "so gothic she will collude with evil capitalists and aliens in the murder of her children" (74–75). For Zwinger, the juxtaposition of this monstrous mother with Ripley's maternal concern for Jonesey the cat at the end of *Alien* strives to "persuade those of us who have had mothers ... that *only* the sentimental qualities" like caring for animals—or young children, as Ripley does in the sequel when she protects Newt from the alien queen—are the mark of a "real" mother.

2. For example, Donald Carveth and Naomi Gold apply the theories of Freud's contemporary and follower Melanie Klein, who was one of the first to use psychoanalysis to study children, and find a parable of sibling rivalry embedded in the film. For Carveth and Gold, when Dallas, Lambert, and Kane enter the Geiger-designed interior of the alien ship on LV-426, "the crew/siblings" penetrate "and explored the mother's body and find—horror of horrors!—another baby, a rival whom they hate and fear" (web). Barbara Creed takes a more traditional Freudian approach when she argues that "*Alien* presents various representations of the primal scene. Behind each of these lurks the figure of the archaic mother [presenting viewers] with a new way of understanding how patriarchal ideology works to deny the 'difference' of woman in her cinematic representation" (129).

3. Of course, *Alien* has been critiqued from Marxist perspectives that would not admit a Marcusian critique. For example, James H. Kavanagh, writing from an Althusserian perspective, argues that "Ripley's concern for the cat functions as a final sign of her recovery for an ideological humanism" (79). However, as this discussion will show, *Alien*'s complex portrayal of the realities of the workplace in industrial society lends itself to the humanist perspective provided by Marcuse.

4. This is not to say that critics have turned their back on the theatrical release. Indeed, Neil Badmington's 2009 argument that the initial theatrical release actually poses more questions about the nature of humanity than the subsequent version concludes by noting that *Blade Runner* outruns its blade runners (487)—that the initial film survives the attacks on it presented by subsequent cuts.

5. Gravett, for example, notes that "in Genesis, God exiles Adam and Eve because they threaten to assume some aspect of the divine" (39) and links this banishment to the rule that forbids replicants from returning to Earth. In keeping with *Blade Runner*'s resistance to neat critical summation, however, Gravett also sees in the paring of Deckard and Batty echoes of the relationship between Jacob and Esau, Isaac's twin sons who were placed into conflict after the younger son tricked the elder out of his birthright. The Bible is not the only ancient text *Blade Runner* draws from; Jane O'Sullivan cogently argues that Rachel is very much like Galatea in Ovid's *Pygmalion*, and when Deckard seduces her, "having broken down her own sense of self, he rebuilds her to suit himself" (153).

6. For example, Joe Abbott, investigating the parallels between Shelly's novel and *Blade Runner*, argues that Scott's film provides a distinctly modern update. According to Abbott, as "cor-

porate executive and replicant creator, Dr. Eldon Tyrell combines the attributes of a corrupt corporate overlord with the traditional Frankenstinein scientist-gone-astray" (344). Tyrell's crime, however is not defying the intentions of an omnipotent god, but instead in refusing to treat his creations as human. Roy Batty is also a more contemporary version of the monster Frankenstein creates, and his "decision to save Deckard signals his transformation from monster to tragic romantic hero, underlining the difference between Dr. Frankenstein and Dr. Tyrell" (346). While there are clear parallels between *Blade Runner* and *Frankenstein*, critics familiar not only with Shelly's novel but also with Romanticism as a whole have found links between the film and texts like Percy Shelly's *Prometheus*. Indeed, Mark Lusser and Kaitlin Gowan argues that *Blade Runner* should be considered a Romantic text since "in general, Scott's modes of representation entangle three prominent aspects of Romanticism—the search for origins, the aesthetics of the gothic and the sublime, and the renunciation of will" (166).

7. Gulianna Bruno's influential article, for example, notes that the "city of *Blade Runner* is not the ultramodern, but the postmodern city" which, for Bruno, is the postindustrial city. *Blade Runner*'s Los Angeles "is not an orderly layout of skyscrapers and ultracomfortable, hypermechanized interiors. Rather, it creates an aesthetic of decay, exposing the dark side of technology, the process of disintegration" (185). It is not only in its setting that *Blade Runner* exemplifies postmodernity, however. As Badmington notes, the film's portrayal of the blurry line between the more human than human replicants and the deeply flawed humans who create or hunt them "frustrates all attempts to limit its depiction of subjectivity to the space of humanism" (472). J.P. Telotte similarly argues that in *Blade Runner* "normal human desire seems practically absent from this future society, as if it had been displaced by a sheer fascination with doubling and its emblems" ("Doubles" 155). The film's relative absence of overt political commentary has even been taken as a deliberate comment on postmodern society. Richard Pope, for example, argues that *Blade Runner* "presents the absence of politics *as such*, and there is something fatal about that" (79).

8. Kramer McLuckie, for example, argues that the "purpose of" *Blade Runner*'s dystopian imagery "is to illustrate late capitalism's devastating effects in the context of a technological, postmodern future" (26). For McLuckie, this allows *Blade Runner* to function as an "indictment of our transnational corporations and their orchestration of our 'reality'" (27). Critics have also looked at the way *Blade Runner* portrays race and citizenship, finding interesting parallels with earlier portrayals of racial tensions and with contemporary concerns over immigration. Brian Locke, comparing the film to nineteenth century slave narratives, argues that *Blade Runner*'s "project of defining humanity through the capacity to feel parallels another literary tradition, the sentimental depiction of blackness and American slavery" (118). After Batty's dying monolog, in other words, we feel sorry for the replicants in the same way 19th-century readers felt sorry for Uncle Tom. Of course, it helps that an Aryan-featured actor who appears to be "an ubermensch," Rutger Hauer, plays Roy Batty. Because his character is a replicant and therefore a virtual slave of the Tyrell Corporation, in other words, he is "a white body in a black subject position" (122–23) and can be productively read as a synthetic reconfiguration of Stowe's character.

9. As Mike Davis notes in his influential study *City of Quartz*, because the growth of Los Angeles is primarily and paradoxically based on the growth of Los Angeles, it will forever remain "largely an entrepôt for megabanks and technology monopolies headquartered elsewhere" (144). Los Angeles' middle and upper classes are thus always in a precarious position. During the early 1980s, when *Blade Runner* was released, much of the city's industrial base departed. Consequently, Anil Narine believes that in Scott's film "the colonial subplot allegorizes middle-class anxieties about vengeful workers rising up and demanding answers from their superiors, and working class fears about being replaced by ambitious immigrants" who come, as do the replicants, illegally" (web).

## Chapter 5

1. Unsurprisingly, the first two *Terminator* films have spawned a universe of sequels, television series, video games, and comic books. Yet while the *Alien* films now seem like individual takes on a common theme, the first two *Terminator* films create a larger narrative whose cohesiveness rivals that of Lucas' *Star Wars* films. Indeed, in 2010 entertainment blogger Peter Sciretta posted clips of a Cameron interview that featured the director offering that he "made a decision to just let" the *Terminator* universe "have its life" because "the soup's been pissed in by other directors" and he no longer wanted to be involved. Interestingly, Cameron had no comment about what graphic novel adaptations like *RoboCop Versus Terminator* had done to the soup.

Cameron's delightfully colloquial charge of soup pissing makes sense when we investigate *T3*'s rejection of Cameron's announced theme as well as his implicit Marcusian take on Quarlo's story. In the audio commentary for the director's cut of *T2*, Cameron informs viewers that when Sarah Connor carves "no fate" on a picnic table, she is writing the theme of the film "in wood." Yet in *T3*, Directed by Jonathan Mostow and written by John D. Brancato and Michael Ferris, Schwarzenegger's terminator tells John Connor that "Judgment Day is inevitable," and Connor himself wonders if "maybe the future is written" after all right before the closing credits. *T3* also negates the humanization of the T-101 that took place in *T2*. This reconfiguration of the *Terminator* narrative not only ignores Ellison's question, posed in "Soldier" of whether or not a soulless soldier can be trained to truly care about those he protects, but it also refutes Cameron's focus on the ability of two-dimensional thought to break the containment of industrial society. *T2*'s two-dimensional cyborg has been replaced by a one-dimensional killing machine who has, fortunately, been programmed to protect Connor. *T3*, however, goes out of its way to underline the difference between the guardian terminators, casting aspersions at the notion that a machine could feel emotions or understand that industrial society would bring only death if it was not overcome. For example, *Rise of the Machines*' version of the T-101 tells John Connor that he is not his father and later tells him that, before he was reprogrammed by Kate Brewster, he assassinated John in the future because John's emotional attachment to his model number allowed him to gain his trust. In another scene, after being partially reprogrammed by the TX and attempting to assassinate John, the T-101 is begged by the future resistance leader to do what it wants to, not what the TX is telling him to. Schwarzenegger curtly responds that "desire is irrelevant" because he is "a machine."

Although it follows the version of events laid out in *T3*, 2009's *Terminator Salvation* seems to walk back some of the refutation of Marcuse's critique found in the penultimate sequel. Directed by McG and written by *T3* scribes John D. Brancato and Michael Ferris, the film features a character representing a return to Marcusian discussions of one-dimensional thought. In *Salvation*, the good terminator is sent forward in time, not by a revolutionary time-travel machine but because Marcus, a condemned murderer, signed his body away to Cyberdyne Systems. After Judgment Day, Skynet turns Marcus into a true human/machine hybrid that doesn't understand that he is not fully human until he sees the exposed metal beneath his flesh. Marcus ultimately sacrifices himself for the resistance, and this version of the company-built man allows McG, Brancato, and Ferris to continue Cameron's critique.

Curiously, although 2015's *Terminator Genisys*, with a script by Laeta Kalogridis and Patrick Lussier—both relatively inexperienced writers who have far more producing or editing credits—does much to literally recreate the events of *The Terminator*, it nevertheless portrays Schwarzenegger's T-101 as a grandfatherly version of the fatherly reformatted company man we meet in *T2*. While this portrayal doubtlessly dovetails with Schwarzenegger's desire to reinvent himself as a mature action star after his stint in politics, it also reiterates Cameron's Marcusian reformulation of the company man that will be discussed in this chapter.

2. For example, Constance Penley calls John Conner "the child who orchestrates his own primal scene" (121). Others have extended their Freudian readings to explore *The Terminator*'s novel take on the heteronormative marriage plot. For example, Goldberg, who suggests that the film features "a quasi-oedipal plot where the son kills the father" (182) and thus could also be read as quietly postulating queer alternatives to heterosexual reproduction. After all, cyborgs like the Terminator represent "a repudiation of biological reproduction" (186) and the way that the Terminator is dressed "is pure Tom of Finland, purveyor of images of bikers and policemen for a gay audience" (191), suggesting that the Terminator is a post-heterosexual being. Additionally, "sensitive type" Kyle Reese may be implicitly depicted as "gay" (183), implying in turn that the soldier's infatuation with Sarah and the act of fathering a child with her are not the act of heterosexual procreation they appear to be. Goldberg supports this contention by noting that "Reese is connected to Sarah by image reproduction, by the photograph. Once again, this aligns him with the cyborg and other than biological modes of reproduction; if these are, even in the imaginary, linked to technologies that exceeded the body, so much the better" (185).

3. For example, Thomas Byers sees in *Terminator 2*'s depiction of the masculine, cyborg surrogate father's beatings at the hands of the relatively slight, ambiguously gendered T1000 fear that the future will bring "the holocaust of the bourgeois heterosexual subject" (8). For Byers, the "the latent content of Sarah Connor's dream of nuclear 'judgment day' in *Terminator 2*" is the fear of the eventual "utter annihilation and dispersal of the subjects of contemporary culture" because these bourgeoisie, heterosexual subjects did not address the obvious threats to their hegemony in time (7). Similarly, James Sey sees the contrast between the two terminators depicting a threat to the heteronormative subject because "the enculturated body requires a zoned sexuality and the operation of taboos" (17). Schwarzenegger's terminator has a clearly

zoned body that is being enculturated, but the liquid metal T1000 can elude the boundaries of human bodies and has little regard for human culture. Consequently, when the T101 defeats the T1000 at the end of the film it suggests that "the only good machine is an oedipalized one, who can be a father and learn the value of human life" (19).

4. Donald Palumbo, for example, employs a Campbellian reading to argue that Sarah transcends "her former self and" accepts "her destiny," becoming "conscious that she is the vehicle of cosmic change" and attaining "the freedom to live" (425). Donna Dominguez, on the other hand, argues that "Ripley's and Connor's characters only achieve a limited success" because they each eventually repudiate the feminine, becoming, in effect, sexless and less 'human' mirrors of male action heroes." Initially, Sarah's martial abilities do not eradicate her status as a woman since "it is clear that Connor would not be a hero if it were not for the son she will bear." Cameron undoes this in *T2*, however, as Sarah becomes "a caricature of man's worst nightmare: a man-hating, physically exaggerated, revenge-minded woman with a gun" (web). Karen B. Mann, while conceding that the film conceives "of ways in which" normative assumptions about sex and gender can be rethought (25), is nevertheless disturbed because the film depicts Kyle Reese's "desire for a woman who possesses the power that time bestows before time has ravaged her." Consequently, audiences cannot truly embrace the "social and sexual optimism" found in the surface portrayal of the pistol packin' mamma that Sarah Connor becomes at the end of the film (24). Similarly, Margaret Goscilo, while also admitting that *The Terminator* may seem feminist when compared to "other contemporary action films" nevertheless feels that on close analysis, the film highly qualifies its female "protagonist's role and unequivocally recuperates "androcentricity on a grand scale" (37). J. P. Telotte provides support for Goscilo's assertions when he notes that Sarah "is a character who moves between self-determination and objectification, who seems easy prey precisely because she lacks a clear self-image, as if she already embodied the sort of manipulation that a technological hegemony seems to promise" ("Exposed," web).

5. For example, Victoria Warren, comparing the film to John Dryden's restoration play *Conquest of Granada*, first performed in 1670, notes that both Dryden's protagonist "Almanzor and the Terminator are bigger, stronger, more ultra-manly than other men" (21). Yet while the ultra-manly Terminator made an excellent villain in the first film, the kinder, gentler Terminator of the sequel led some to argue that Cameron was commenting on a crisis in notions of masculinity. Anne-Marie Harvey, noting that *Terminator 2* was filmed during the early 1990s, a time of "contradictions and problems" for those trying to define desirable masculinity, posits that the "reformed" Terminator creates a "paternal masculinity" that is "both humanly impossible to attain and ultimately impossible to sustain" since the ideal-father Terminator must be destroyed to save the world (27).

6. J. P. Telotte, working from a Baudrillardian perspective to elucidate the film's commentary on the human condition in a technological age, argues that the "manufactured bodies of these cyborgs become not simply sites of special effects displays, but measures of our own human level of 'manufacture,' our own constructedness." Indeed, for Telotte, the Terminator's human appearance represents "how easy it is to 'pass' in this world." The sequel's T1000, which "seems to be all surface, with no real 'inside'" gives viewers "a sense of how complex the problem has become" ("Exposed," web). Similarly, Mark Jancovich argues that *The Terminator* "investigates the way in which humanity is regulated and controlled by scientific rationalization in an attempt to identify that which is truly human" (3). For Jancovich, Cameron's films depict, in the image of the "good" and "bad" terminators, how machines have become "an image of both pleasure and horror" in modernity, promising "to free labor from 'machinelike' operations and to open up the possibility of a utopian space beyond the realm of necessity" but also threatening to "degrade the labor process and transform human activity into mere mechanistic components" (6).

Carl Freedman's discussion of thematic concerns with the nature of humanity in Cameron's films becomes more explicitly political when he identifies a disturbing anti-humanism in Arnold Schwarzenegger's decision to identify himself with the Terminator during his successful 2003 bid to become governor of California. Although understanding why Schwarzenegger would want to trade on his fame, Freedman argues that "what the Terminator *enacts*, what he allows the viewer to relish vicariously, is an all-too human rage against the human body" (543). Consequently, when voters choose to elect Schwarzenegger to "terminate" California's problems, it reflects "a more advanced stage of political despair" (545). Similarly, Doran Larson finds battle between Schwarzenegger's Terminator and the T1000 as a coded reenactment of the culture wars of the early 1990s. For Larson, "as a vision of the body politic, the" liquid metal T1000 "is dissolution into anarchy, a nightmare image of continually overturning hierarchy" (63), and the reformed and domesticated T101 is the fascistic means of containing that anarchy.

7. For example, Fran Pheasant-Kelly argues that the cyborgs in films like *Terminator 2* signal "ambivalence regarding medicine" and "therefore perpetuate the theme of science careening out of control" (62). Byers similarly argues that the liquid metal T1000's attributes are comparable to those of electronic, information-age technologies (10) and the new Terminator therefore allows Cameron to play on his audience's fears of the cultural impact of those technologies. Mark Duckenfield addresses American manufacturing when he argues that the Terminator movies are an allegorical representation of the "struggle between declining industries in the United States and the rising high-technology ones of an economically vibrant Japan" (2). Duckenfield posits that in *Terminator 2*, "the reprogrammed Terminator" is a "kinder, gentler, domesticated heavy industry; still big and powerful but losing its competitive edge" (3), while the stoic and shape-shifting "evil Terminator personifies the Japanese economy and its alleged threat to America's future economic prosperity" (4). Robert F. Arnold, providing a similar though more specific argument than Duckenfield, discusses the changes that were occurring in the U.S. automotive industry while the two *Terminator* films were in production and concludes that "the perception that industrial robots would replace human workers may have contributed" to the popularity of *The Terminator* (24). And while not disputing the notion that "technology is good so long as it remains within human control," the first film nevertheless provides "the substitute satisfaction of terminating the robot terminator" (25).

8. Although Ellison's lawsuit also claimed that Cameron plagiarized "Demon with a Glass Hand," this episode seems to provide more of a basis for the plot device of the doomed romance between Kyle Reese and Sarah Connor than any extended Marcusian commentary. In Ellison's narrative, a cyborg named Mr. Trent has been sent back from the far future to protect a computer—Trent's glass hand—that holds the key to the location of the inhabitants of the Earth after they fled an alien invasion. At the beginning of the episode, Trent does not clearly understand any of this, however, and is only dimly aware of what it means to be a cyborg. He is being pursued by the Kyban, members of the race that attacked the earth in the future, and almost all of the story takes place in the office building where the Kyban have hidden their time machine. As he battles the alien assassins, Trent receives help from a woman named Consuela and they begin to fall in love. After the defeat of the Kyban and the destruction of their time portal, however, Consuela realizes that she cannot love a cyborg and leaves Trent to be alone, presumably for the entirety of the 1,200 years it will take for him to be able to use his computer hand to defeat all of the Kyban and return the vanquished people of Earth to their homes. Thematically, then, "Demon with a Glass Hand" does not contribute as much to *The Terminator*'s Marcusian critique of one-dimensional thought as does "Soldier," but it definitely gave Cameron material to rework into his own tale of time-crossed lovers who could not be together because of the need to save humanity in the future. Interestingly, however, *Terminator Genisys*' depiction of Schwarzenegger's grandfatherly terminator patiently waiting from 1984 to 2015 for the arrival of Sarah Connor and Kyle Reese to begin what is depicted as the final battle with Skynet seems to revisit Trent's lonely vigil.

9. Curiously, themes and plot elements similar to those of "Soldier" emerge in early episodes of the James Cameron–produced television series *Dark Angel*, which ran from the fall of 2000 to the spring of 2002. A knowledgeable viewer of the show, however, would realize that *Dark Angel* had components of other speculative tales. For example, the show's premise of genetic vivisection—Max, the protagonist, has feline DNA—echoes that of H.G. Wells' *The Island of Dr. Moreau*. The pilot features hovering police drones and hacked cable signals that visually reference John Carpenter's *They Live*. Furthermore, Carlos Megila and Carlos Trillo, creators of the early–1990s Spanish-language graphic novel *Cybersix*, threatened Cameron and his collaborators with legal action after claiming that *Dark Angel* borrowed heavily from *Cybersix*'s plot, characters, and themes. Yet there remain several important parallels between the pilot for *Dark Angel*—the series underwent several changes during its brief run as the producers sought to keep it on the air—and "Soldier." Both narratives feature a supersoldier created in a government lab. Both narratives feature that supersoldier encountering the domestic sphere and grudgingly defending it. Max, *Dark Angel*'s protagonist, for example, rescues a young girl from the gangsters who have kidnapped her and Quarlo protects the Kagan family. Indeed, *Dark Angel*'s pilot seems to imply an answer to "Soldier"'s speculation that Quarlo had actually begun to care for the people he protects. And finally, both Max and Quarlo are chased by federal agencies who want to incarcerate and study them.

10. Shapiro, however, claims that Cameron admitted to borrowing from "a couple of Harlan Ellison *Outer Limits* episodes" (98). Cameron has also given alternate explanations for the postapocalyptic hellscape he depicts in the opening scenes of his first two films. In the

audio commentary on the director's cut of *T2*, the director indicates that he viewed the film's theme as specifically anti-nuclear and more generally a meditation on whether technology will overwhelm us or we will learn how to control technology. In support of his contentions, the director indicates that the opening sequence that features nuclear explosions obliterating Los Angeles is a riff on the "duck and cover" civil defense films the director watched in his childhood. Interestingly, in addition to the implicit nod to Marcusian thinking in his formulation about technology, Cameron also notes that he became aware of the possibility that a nuclear holocaust might destroy the earth around his tenth year—close in time to the original air date of "Soldier."

## Chapter 6

1. Aubrey Solomon, *Twentieth Century Fox: A Corporate and Financial History* (Metuchen, N.J.: Scarecrow Press, 1989), 260.
2. Appreciative critics include Peter Kramer, who argues that *Aliens* sets "up the world and action of the film as an extension of the female protagonist's subjectivity" ("Women First," web). Susan Yunis and Tammy Ostrander find Ripley's maternal bent somewhat more problematic, contrasting the alien queen's "image of mindless motherhood—reproduction gone berserk" and therefore "a projection of the overpopulation, speciesism, and parasitic imperialism" which represent humanity's death drive with Ripley's adoption of Newt, which "represents an alternative to monstrous motherhood" (69–71). Other arguments merely concede that the film offers a glimpse of utopian feminism before reverting to more reactionary thematics, however. Janice Hocker Rushing, for example, believes that *Aliens* is a retelling of the myth of the frontier in which "traditional patriarchal values are ultimately reaffirmed" (10) and therefore participates in the revisionist and conservative mood of the mid–1980s, but admits that Ripley's "determination to rescue Newt from the clutches of the monster recalls Demeter's rage at Hades for the theft of Persephone" (17). Steve Nolan finds a similar mixed message, arguing that Ripley moves "between masculine and feminine identification" fluidly, as evidenced by her suiting up in the power loader to become "a fully masculinized mother" in order to fight the alien queen (207). Critics troubled by Cameron's depiction of the maternal include Chad Hermann, who claims Ripley asserts a "productive, protective, intimate maternal power" (42) though her reconstructed family with Newt "excludes her from" biological reproduction so that she can "act like a man" and fight the alien queen (44). Margaret Goscilo similarly argues that "Cameron's" most prominent depiction of "female heroism" in *Aliens* is "a maternity theme that manages to qualify even the remarkable Ripley" (50). And Krin Gabbard further posits that "*Aliens* found ingenious ways of reconstructing the bourgeois family" typical of "Reagan Age cinema" (30), giving Cameron's film a "reactionary ideology" (33) enabled by Ripley's "surrogate marriage to Hicks" (37). Other critics find Cameron's maternal elements commenting on American colonialism in ways that seem to justify it. In addition to Rushing's arguments, Thomas Vaughn argues that in *Aliens*, the "frontier has not grown into a place of fertility, but through the reversal of the womb metaphor, becomes hungry and savage. That which once produced, now consumes" (430) and, therefore, must be nuked from space.
3. Fred A. Holliday, II, interviewing Cameron for *Creative Screenwriting*, argues that the director "was able to turn the conventions of the war film genre"—conventions like Gorman's "ineffectual commanding officer" on their ear by infusing them with elements from the science fiction and horror genres" (45, 48). Cameron, noting that the drop ships are "a sci-fi variant on the Huey" helicopters that transported American troops in Vietnam" (47), eagerly supports Holliday's contentions, saying that he was "taking the kind of *Platoon* movie, the classic ground-pounders in war situation, and making an alloy out of that with the film *Aliens*, which is a very different kind of film, gave it a hybrid vigor" (46).
4. Joe Abbott, for example, admits that an initial critique can be found in the inability of the corporate/military apparatus to save Hadley's Hope, suggesting that "in 1986 and in the wake of Vietnam," the military-industrial complex "is defeated by its own buffoonery" (23). Yet Abbott nevertheless sees Ripley's seizing command of the surviving marines and her suggestion to nuke Hadley's Hope from orbit as right-wing extremism because these actions elevate "the individual above the community for the community's own good," pandering to audience's "attitude of rising mistrust aimed at the monolithic structures considered essential to its capitalist ideology" (24, 25). Harvey R. Greenburg similarly argues that Cameron's revisions overturn Scott's depiction of the "inhuman exploitativeness" of Weyland-Yutani that "evolved out of earlier terrestrial capitalist excess," in a film informed by a "stripped-down rightish populism" that blames "one bad apple in the corporate barrel" for the company's excesses ("Fembo" 165, 166, 169).
5. Zani notes that George Bernard Shaw as-

serted that the band did not play "Nearer My God, to Thee" (127).

6. For example, the film often looks very much like Cameron's 1989 box-office-disappointment *The Abyss*. *Titanic*'s opening, after all, features high-tech submersibles and underwater robots, and Cameron's decision to drag out this exotic technology gives an interesting science-fiction cast to a tale that, while it is definitely concerned with the limits of technology, is anchored in a relatively well-known past event and consequently features the now-outmoded machines of 1912. The submersibles also look like they had been removed from the warehouse that stored unused props from *The Abyss*, foreshadowing several links to a film that audiences had probably forgotten Cameron made. After all, both films contain scenes of main characters fleeing flooded compartments on a high-tech, one-of-a-kind oceangoing vessel and shivering in cold seawater. Furthermore, both films share a surface thematic that can be loosely translated as "love is stronger than death." Both films feature lovers in problematic relationships—*Titanic*'s Jack and Rose are star-crossed because of class differences, *The Abyss*' Bud and Lindsay are about to finalize their divorce—who go through an ordeal in dangerous waters that bonds them, literally or figuratively, for life. In both couples, the man saves his love from death twice. Jack saves Rose from committing suicide by jumping off the *Titanic*'s fantail and Bud saves Lindsay from a sinking submersible before drowning himself. Jack also saves Rose by giving her the piece of flotsam that keeps Rose alive after the *Titanic* goes down. Bud saves Lindsay again by performing a two-mile-deep dive and defusing a nuclear warhead. Jack and Rose's love goes on and on because Rose keeps Jack's memory alive; Bud and Lindsay's love goes on and on because angelic aliens save him from the adverse impacts of making a two-mile-deep dive without enough oxygen. One could argue that on some levels *Titanic* appears to be a successful reboot of Cameron's first oceangoing love story.

## *Afterword*

1. While Marvel's Avengers-based "universe" appears poised to rule the box office for the next several years and DC hopes to challenge their longtime rival with a filmic version of the Justice League, the ascendency of the superhero film that has taken place over the past fifteen years starkly contrasts with the 20 lean years that came before. From 1980 to 1999—perhaps the peak years of Lucas, Scott, and Cameron's influence—there were only six superhero films that made it into the top ten in terms of domestic gross for the year they were released. And while 1989's *Batman* was #1, 1992's *Batman Returns* was #3, and 1995's *Batman Forever* was #2, the other films include 1990's *Teenage Mutant Ninja Turtles* and 1994's *The Mask*, which is arguably a spoof of the genre. From 2000 to 2014, there were 21 superhero films that made it into the top ten in terms of domestic gross for the year they were released. Perhaps more impressively, nine of those films—almost half—took first or second place. Even though this number includes curiosities like Will Smith's portrayal of an alcoholic superhero in 2008's *Hancock*, 2004's *The Incredibles*, Disney's animated film about a family of superheroes, and 2014's science fiction film *Guardians of the Galaxy*—included because it is officially part of the Marvel Cinematic Universe—the clearly evident increase in the popularity of superhero blockbusters indicates an important cultural shift.

Though risking oversimplification, it could reasonably be argued that superhero films involve a reaction to the workaday worlds and protagonists of *Alien* or *The Terminator* or even the catch-as-can appearance of the rebel forces in the first three theatrically released *Star Wars* films. After all, there is no evil corporation in sight, and nothing like the potentially democratic and Eros-symbolizing force. Instead, there are alien gods or demi-gods—Thor, Superman—or wealthy industrialists who use their fortunes to fight crime—Iron Man, Batman. Spider Man's powers come from being bitten by a radioactive spider in what, regardless of the version of the origin story one considers, is essentially an industrial accident involving nuclear radiation. It could easily be argued that the source of his web-slinging ability provides an implicit apology for the excesses of industrial society. And a scientifically engineered supersoldier like Captain America's most recent, filmic iteration seems to be, if I may be permitted to mix my Marvel and DC metaphors, a Bizzaro World version of not only Quarlo but of Cameron's reformulations of him in the *Terminator* films. Furthermore, though Captain America's initial creation at the outset of American involvement in World War II clearly participated in its immediate historical moment's necessary drive to convince citizens to participate in the war effort, the 2011 Paramount/Marvel film provides an interesting counterpoint to Weyland-Yutani's desire to weaponize the xenomorphs. This turn away from a Marcusian emphasis on helping contemporary citizens process the meaning of industrial society and towards narratives about superhuman or remarkable individuals saving the world indicates a movement within a cultural dialectic that is beyond the scope of the present study.

2. After all, as this manuscript heads to the publisher *Jurassic World*, a fourth sequel to 1993's *Jurassic Park*, has generated almost $400 million at the domestic box office. This an impressive feat for a late sequel—even when taking inflation into consideration—since the total domestic box office for *Jurassic Park* was $410 million.

3. This is not to say that more direct manifestations of the popularization of Marcuse's critiques cannot be found in current popular culture. After all, Cameron 2009 *Avatar* and Scott's 2012 *Prometheus* are relatively recent works, and both directors have promised sequels. Reboots, like 2015's *Terminator Genysis*, and sequels like *Star Wars Episode VII: The Force Awakens*, though created by different directors and writers, could also owe a thematic debt to the ideas first popularized by Marcuse. At this point in this study, however, it is important to ask what happens when younger directors working with new material incorporate Marcusian critique into their blockbusters.

4. An investigation of the text of Collins' novels would doubtless reveal the employment of themes related to the ideas Marcuse popularized. But because of the scope of this monograph—none of the films by Lucas, Scott, or Cameron discussed here are direct adaptations of successful novels—this afterword will only look at the big-screen versions of Collins' texts.

5. Because of the relatively brief discussions of both the *Matrix* films and the *Hunger Games* films in this afterword, the relevant academic criticism for these films will not receive the same extensive treatment as the relevant criticism of the films discussed in the preceding chapters.

6. Because this project focuses on blockbuster films and not bestselling novels, this afterword will not examine Collins' books. And while the films under consideration here are largely faithful to the books that they are based on, it is important to note that while Collins cowrote the screenplay for *The Hunger Games*, she was not as involved in the scripts for the subsequent films.

7. The domestic box office for 2009's *Harry Potter and the Half-Blood Prince* was $301 million. The domestic box office for 2010's *Harry Potter and the Deathly Hallows Part 1* was $295 million. The domestic box office for 2010's *The Twilight Saga: Eclipse* was $300 million, while the domestic box office for 2011's *The Twilight Saga: Breaking Dawn Part 1* was $281 million.

8. As this book goes to press, *Mockingjay Part 2* has not yet been released. Given that the Marcusian elements are largely found in the first two films—when Panem is not at war and when the action is not largely set in either the Spartan interiors of District 13 or the war-torn streets of the Capital—a discussion of the events of the final film would add little to the central argument of this Afterword.

9. Although their individual scores vary widely from each other—*Breaking Dawn Part 1* is 24 percent fresh and *Harry Potter and the Deathly Hallows Part 1* is 78 percent fresh—both were the lowest rated films in their respective series.

# Bibliography

Abbott, Joe. "The 'Monster' Reconsidered: *Blade Runner*'s Replicant as Epic Hero." *Extrapolation* 34.4 (1993): 340–350. Print.

\_\_\_\_\_. "They Came from Beyond the Center: Ideology and Political Textuality in the Radical Science Fiction Films of James Cameron." *Literature/Film Quarterly* 22.1 (1994): 21–27. Print.

Abrams, Jerold J. "A Technological Galaxy: Heidegger and the Philosophy of Technology in *Star Wars*." In Kevin Decker and Jason T. Eberl, eds., *Star Wars and Philosophy: More Powerful Than You Can Possibly Imagine*. Chicago: Open Court, 2005. Print.

Academy of Achievement. "A Drive of Titanic Proportions." *James Cameron: Interviews* 110–132. Print.

Adamson, Joni. "Indigenous Literatures, Multinaturalism, and *Avatar*: The Emergence of Indigenous Cosmopolitics." *American Literary History* 24.1 (2012): 143–162. Print.

Adorno, Theodor, and Herbert Marcuse. "Correspondence on the German Student Movement." Trans. Esther Leslie. *New Left Review* 233 (1999): 123–136. Print.

Agger, Ben. "Marcuse's Aesthetic Politics: Ideology-Critique and Socialist Ontology." *Dialectical Anthropology* 12.3 (1987): 329–341. Print.

\_\_\_\_\_. "Work and Authority in Marcuse and Habermas." *Human Studies* 2.3 (July 1979): 191–208. Print.

Andersen, Paul W. S., dir. *Alien Vs. Predator*. Perf. Sanaa Lathan, Lance Henriksen. Twentieth Century-Fox, 2004. DVD.

Antal, Nimrod, dir. *Predators*. Perf. Adrian Brody, Topher Grace. Twentieth Century-Fox, 2010. DVD.

Arcudi, John, and Mike Willis. *Aliens Genocide*. Milwaukie, OR: Dark Horse Comics, 1992. Print.

Arnold, Robert F. "Termination or Transformation: The *Terminator* Films and Recent Changes in the U.S. Auto Industry." *Film Quarterly* 52.1 (1998): 20–30. Print.

Aron, Raymond. "Student Rebellion: Vision of the Future or Echo from the Past?" *Political Science Quarterly* 84.2 (June 1969): 289–310. Print.

Aronowitz, Stanley. "The Unknown Herbert Marcuse." *Social Text* 58 (Spring 1999): 133–154. Print.

Arroyo, Jose, and Edward Lawrenson, "Massive Attack." *Sight and Sound* 8.2 (February 1998): 16–19. Web.

*Avatar*. Internet Movie Firearms Database. January 6, 2011. Web.

Badmington, Neil. "*Blade Runner*'s Blade Runners." *Semiotica* 173.1 (2009): 471–489. Print.

Beck, Bernard. "The Overdeveloped Society: *THX-1138*." *Trans-Action* 8.11 (September 1971): 60–64. Print.

Begor, David. "Defense of the Clones." *Bright Lights Film Journal* 38 (2002). August 31, 2009. Web.

Bergenthaler, Hannes. "A Sense of No-Place: *Avatar* and the Pitfalls of Ecocentric Identification." *European Journal of English Studies* 16.2 (2012): 151–162. Print.

Bernardoni, James. *The New Hollywood: What the Movies Did with the New Freedoms of the Seventies*. Jefferson, NC: McFarland, 1991. Print.

Beyers, Thomas B. "Terminating the Postmodern: Masculinity and Pomophobia." *Modern Fiction Studies* 41.1 (1995): 5–33. Print.

Bick, Ilsa J. "'Well, I Guess I Must Make You Nervous': Women and the Space of Alien[3]." *Post Script: Essays in Film and the Humanities* 14.1–2 (1994): 45–58. Print.

Bourne, Tom. "Herbert Marcuse: Grandfather of the New Left." *Change* 11.6 (September 1979): 36 37, 64. Print.

Briones, Claudia. "Scientific Avatars or Doing Anthropology of (and Against) Our Modern Discontent." *Postcolonial Studies* 14.3 (2011): 313–329. Print.

Brown, William. "Contemporary Mainstream Cinema Is Good for You: Connections Between Surrealism and Today's Digital Blockbusters." *Studies in European Cinema* 6.1 (2009): 17–29. Print.

Bruno, Giuliana. "Ramble City: Postmodernism and *Blade Runner*." *Alien Zone* 183–195. Print.

Byer, Thomas B. "Commodity Futures." *Alien Zone* 39–50. Print.

Cahn, Edward L., dir. *It! The Terror from Beyond Space*. Perf. Marshall Thompson, Shirley Patterson. Robert E. Kent Productions, 1958. DVD.

Callenbach, Ernest. "Short Notices." *Film Quarterly* 24.4 (1971): 63–4. Print.

Cameron, James, dir. *The Abyss*. Perf. Ed Harris, Mary Elizabeth Mastrantonio, Michael Biehn. Twentieth Century–Fox, 1989. DVD.

———. *Aliens*. Perf. Sigourney Weaver, Carrie Henn, Michel Biehn. Twentieth Century–Fox, 1986. DVD.

———. *Avatar*. Perf. Sam Worthington, Zoe Saldana, Sigourney Weaver. Twentieth Century–Fox, 2009. DVD.

———. *Piranha Part Two: The Spawning*. Perf. Tricia O'Neil, Steve Marachuk, Lance Henriksen. Brouwersgracht Investments, 1982. DVD.

———. *The Terminator*. Perf. Arnold Schwarzenegger, Linda Hamilton, Michel Biehn. Orion, 1984. DVD.

———. *Terminator 2: Judgment Day*. Perf. Arnold Schwarzenegger, Linda Hamilton, Edward Furlong. Twentieth Century–Fox, 1991. DVD.

———. *Titanic*. Perf. Leonardo DiCaprio, Kate Winslet, Billy Zane. Twentieth Century–Fox/Paramount, 1997. DVD.

———. *True Lies*. Perf. Arnold Schwarzenegger, Jamie Lee Curtis, Tom Arnold. Twentieth Century–Fox, 1994. DVD.

Cameron, James, writ. *Rambo: First Blood Part II*. Perf. Sylvester Stallone, Richard Crenna, Charles Napier. Anabasis N.V., 1985. DVD.

———. *Strange Days*. Perf. Ralph Fiennes, Angela Bassett, Juliette Lewis. Twentieth Century–Fox, 1996. DVD.

Canby, Vincent. "*Alien* Brings Chills from the Far Galaxy: A Gothic Set in Space." *New York Times* May 25, 1979. Web.

———. "*Alien*[3]; Hal, If You Are Still Out There, Here's a Computer-Friendly Sequel." *New York Times* May 22, 1992. Web.

———. Rev. of *Rambo: First Blood, Part II*. *New York Times* May 22, 1985. Web.

Carveth, Donald L., and Gold, Naomi. "The Pre-Oedipalizing of Klein in (North) America: Ridley Scott's *Alien* Re-Analyzed." *PSYART: A Hyperlink Journal for the Psychological Study of the Arts* 3 (1999). Web.

Chambers, L. "Jim Cameron's Titanic Adventure." *Written by* 2 (Dec 1998): 34–40. Print.

Chute, David. "The 1984 Movie Review: James Cameron Interviewed by David Chute." *James Cameron: Interviews* 8–14. Print.

Clark, Bruce D., dir. *Galaxy of Terror*. Perf. Edward Albert, Erin Moran, Ray Walston. New World Cinema, 1981. DVD.

Clark, Mike. "*The Matrix Revolutions*: This Big Finish Isn't the One." *USA Today* November 4, 2003. Web.

Cleaver, Thomas McKelvey. "How to Direct a Terminator." *James Cameron: Interviews* 3–7. Print.

Clifford, James. "Response to Orin Starn: Here Comes the Anthros (Again): The Strange Marriage of Anthropology and Native America." *Cultural Anthropology* 26.2 (2011): 218–224. Print.

Clover, Joshua. "The Struggle for Space." *Film Quarterly* 63.3 (Spring 2010): 6–7. Print.

Cobbs, John L. "*Alien* as an Abortion Parable." *Literature/Film Quarterly* 18 (1990): 198–201. Print.

Cooke, Elizabeth F. "Be Mindful of the Living Force: Environmental Ethics in *Star Wars*." In Kevin Decker and Jason T. Eberl, eds., *Star Wars and Philosophy: More Powerful Than You Can Possibly Imagine*. Chicago: Open Court, 2005. Print.

Cooley, Charles Horton. *Social Organization: A Study of the Larger Mind*. New York: Charles Scribner's Sons, 1909. Print.

Cormier, Raymond. "The Closed Society and Its Friends: Plato's *Republic* and Lucas' *THX-1138*." *Literature and Film Quarterly* 18.3 (1990): 193–197. Print.

Covert, Colin. "It's Not Nice to Play with Your Prey." *Minneapolis Star-Tribune* July 8, 2010. Web.

Creed, Barbara. "*Alien* and the Monstrous-Feminine." *Alien Zone* 128–141. Print.

Dante, Joe, dir. *Piranha*. Perf. Bradford Dilman, Heather Menzies-Urich, Kevin McCarthy. New World Pictures, 1978. DVD.

Dargis, Manohla. "A New Eden, Both Cosmic and Cinematic." Rev. of *Avatar*, dir. James Cameron. *New York Times* 18 December 2009. Web.

———. "Striking Where Myth Meets Moment." Rev. of *The Hunger Games: Catching Fire*. *New York Times* 21 November 2013. Web.

Davis, Mike. *City of Quartz: Excavating the Future in Los Angeles*. 1990. New York: Verso, 2006. Print.

Davis, Todd F., and Kenneth Womack. "The

Ethics of Sentimentality in James Cameron's *Titanic*." *Journal of Popular Film and Television* 29.1 (2001): 42–48. Print.
de Certeau, Michel. *The Practice of Everyday Life*. Trans. Steven Rendall. 1984. Berkeley: California University Press, 1988. Print.
Delson, James. "*Alien* from the Inside Out: Part II." *Ridley Scott: Interviews* 11–30. Print.
"Demon with a Glass Hand." *The Outer Limits*. Writ. Harlan Ellison. Dir. Byron Haskin. 1964. Web.
Dempsy, Michael. Rev. of *American Graffiti*. *Film Quarterly* 27.1 (Autumn 1973): 58–60. Print.
Der Derian, James. "Now We Are All Avatars." *Millennium: Journal of International Studies* 39.1: 181–86. Print.
Dominguez, Diana. "'It's Not Easy Being a Cast-Iron Bitch': Sexual Difference and the Female Action Hero." *Reconstructions* 5.4 (Fall 2005). Web.
Dreher, Rod. "*Matrix a* Treat for Sci-Fi Fans." *New York Post* March 31, 1999. Web.
Duckenfield, Mark. "Terminator 2: An Economic Call to Arms?" *Studies in Popular Culture* 17.1 (1994): 1–16. Print.
Durham, Brent. *James Cameron: Interviews*. Jackson: Mississippi University Press, 2011. Print.
Ebert, Roger. Rev. of *Alien*. *Chicago Sun-Times* October 26, 2003. Web.
\_\_\_\_. Rev. of *Aliens*. *Chicago Sun-Times* July 18, 1986. Web.
\_\_\_\_. Rev. of *Alien Resurrection*. *Chicago Sun-Times* November 26, 1997. Web.
\_\_\_\_. Review of *American Graffiti*. *Chicago Sun-Times* March 2, 2009. Web.
\_\_\_\_. "*Avatar*" Exceeds the Hype; Cameron Remains King of the World with Triumphant, Effect-Filled Masterpiece of a Fantasy Film." Rev. of *Avatar*, dir. James Cameron. *Chicago Sun-Times* December 12, 2009: 5. Lexis-Nexis. Web.
\_\_\_\_. Review of *Blade Runner*. *Chicago Sun-Times* November 23, 2007. Web.
\_\_\_\_. Review of *Predator*. *Chicago Sun-Times* June 12, 1987. Web.
\_\_\_\_. Review of *Terminator 2: Judgment Day*. *Chicago Sun-Times* July 3, 1991. Web.
\_\_\_\_. Review of *THX-1138*. *Chicago Sun-Times* February 4, 2009. Web.
\_\_\_\_. Review of *Titanic*. *Chicago Sun-Times* December 19, 1997. Web.
Edgette, Joseph J. "*RMS Titanic*: Memorialized in Popular Literature and Culture." *Studies in the Literary Imagination* 39.1 (2006): 119–142. Print.
Elsaesser, Thomas. "James Cameron's *Avatar*: Access for All." *New Review of Film and Television Studies* 9.3 (2011): 247–264. Print.

Ezra, Elizabeth. "Resurrecting the Alien Director: Jean-Pierre Jeunet in Hollywood." *New Cinemas: Journal of Contemporary Film* 1.1 (2002): 54–60. Print.
Farber, Stephen. "George Lucas: The Stinky Kid Hits the Big Time." *Film Quarterly* 27.3 (1974): 2–9. Print.
Fincher, David. *Alien³*. Perf. Sigourney Weaver, Charles S. Dutton, Charles Dance. Twentieth Century–Fox, 1992. DVD.
Fitting, Peter. "Futurecop: The Neutralization of Revolt in *Blade Runner*." *Science Fiction Studies* 14 (1987): 340–354. Print.
Floyd, Nigel. "*Aliens*: James Cameron Interview." *James Cameron: Interviews* 35–40. Print.
Frank, Kevin. "'Whether Beast or Human': The Cultural Legacies of Dread, Locks, and Dystopia." *Small Axe: A Caribbean Journal of Criticism* 23 (2007): 46–62. Print.
Frauenfelder, David. "Popular Culture and Classical Mythology." *The Classical World* 98.2 (Winter 2005): 210–213. Print.
Freedman, Carl. "Polemical Afterword: Some Brief Reflections on Arnold Schwarzenegger and on Science Fiction in Contemporary American Culture." *PMLA* 119.3 (2004): 539–546. Print.
Friedman, Norman L. "*The Terminator*: Changes in Critical Evaluations of Cultural Productions." *Journal of Popular Culture* 28.1 (1994): 73–80. Print.
Galipeau, Steven A. *The Journey of Luke Skywalker: An Analysis of Modern Myth and Symbol*. Chicago: Open Court, 2001. Print.
Gates, Charlie. "Epic, Jaw-Dropping Suspense." Rev. of *Avatar*, dir. James Cameron. *The Press* (Christchurch, New Zealand) December 19, 2009: 4. Lexis-Nexis. Web.
Goldberg, Jonathan. "Recalling Totalties: The Mirrored Stages of Arnold Schwarzenegger." *Differences* 4.1 (1992): 172–204. Print.
Goldsmith, Jeff. "The Terminator Versus the Hollywood Cyborgs." *Creative Screenwriting* 10.4 (2003): 69–73. Print.
Goodman, Walter. Review of *Aliens*. *New York Times* July 18, 1986. Web.
Gordon, Andrew. "The Power of the Force: Sex in the Star Wars Trilogy." In Donald Palumbo, ed., *Eros in the Mind's Eye: Sexuality and the Fantastic in Art and Film*. Westport, CT: Greenwood Press, 1986. 181–198.
\_\_\_\_. "Star Wars: A Myth for Our Time." In Joel W. Martin and Conrad E. Ostwalt, eds., *Screening the Sacred: Religion, Myth, and Ideology in Popular American Film*. Boulder, CO: Westview Press, 1995. 71–84.
Goscilo, Margaret. "Deconstructing the *Terminator*." *Film Criticism* 12.2 (1987): 37–52. Print.
Graham, Pat. Review of *Predator*. July 25, 2013. Web.

Grabbard, Krin. "*Aliens* and the New Family Romance." *Post Script* 8.1 (1988): 29–42. Print.

Gravett, Sharon L. "The Sacred and the Profane: Examining the Religious Subtext of Ridley Scott's *Blade Runner*." *Literature/Film Quarterly* 26.1 (1998): 38–45. Print.

Greene, Ray. "Rich and Strange." *James Cameron: Interviews* 71–76. Print.

Greenburg, Harvey R. "Fembo: *Aliens*' Intentions." *Journal of Popular Film and Television* 15.4 (1988): 146–171. Print.

_____. "Reimagining the Gargoyle: Psychoanalytic Notes on *Alien*" *Camera Obscura* 5.3 (1986): 86–109. Print.

Greenspun, Roger. Review of *American Graffiti*. *New York Times* August 1973. Web.

_____. "March 12, 1971, Lucas's 'THX1138': Love Is a Punishable Crime in Future." *New York Times* February 4, 2009. Web.

Guerif, Francois, and Alain Garel. "Ridley Scott." *Ridley Scott: Interviews* 56–63. Print.

Guynes, Sean A. "Do Androids Dream of Proto-Indo-European Fables About Sheep?" *The Vocabula Review* 14.7 (July 2012). Web.

Halter, Ed. "Slime Pickings." *Village Voice* August 10, 2004. Web.

Hammer, Espen. "Marcuse's Critical Theory of Modernity." *Philosophy and Social Criticism* 34.9 (November 2008): 1071–93. Print.

Harvey, Anne-Marie. "Terminating the Father: Technology, Paternity, and Patriarchy in *Terminator 2*." *Masculinities* 3.2 (1995): 25–42. Print.

Henthorne, Tom. "Boys to Men: Medievalism and Masculinity in *Star Wars* and *E.T. the Extraterrestrial*." In *The Medieval Hero on Screen: Representations from Beowulf to Buffy*. Jefferson, NC: McFarland, 2004. 73–90. Print.

Herman, Chad. "'Some Horrible Dream About (S)Mothering': Sexuality, Gender, and Family in the *Alien* Trilogy." *Post Script* 16.3 (1997): 36–50. Print.

Hillis, Ken. "From Capital to Karma: James Cameron's *Avatar*." *Postmodern Culture* 19.3 (May 2009). Project Muse. Web.

Hinson, Hal. Rev. of *Alien³*. *Washington Post*, May 22, 1992. Web.

Holliday, Fred A. "Hybrid Vigor: Generic Transformations in James Cameron's *Aliens*." *Creative Screenwriting* 5.4 (1998): 45–49. Print.

Holte, Jim. "Puritans in Space: Puritan Ideology and the American Science Fiction Film." In Donald Palumbo, ed., *Eros in the Mind's Eye: Sexuality and the Fantastic in Art and Film*. Westport, CT: Greenwood Press, 1986. 181–192. Print.

Hopkins, Stephen, dir. *Predator 2*. Perf. Kevin Peter Hall, Danny Glover. Twentieth Century-Fox, 1990. DVD.

Horowitz, Michael G. "Portrait of the Marxist as an Old Trouper." *Playboy* September 1970: 174ff, 228, 231ff. Print.

Howe, Desson. "Review of *Predator 2*." *Washington Post* November 23, 1990. Web.

Howells, Richard. "One Hundred Years of the *Titanic* on Film." *Historical Journal of Film, Radio, and Television* 32.1 (2012): 73–93. Print.

Hunter, Stephen. "*Alien Resurrection*: Birth of the Ooze." *Washington Post* November 28, 1997. Web.

Hurley, James S. "*Titanic* Allegories: The Blockbuster as Art Film." *Strategies* 14.1 (2001): 91 120. Print.

Jackson, Sandra. "Terrans, Extraterrestrials, Warriors, and the Last (Wo)Man Standing." *African Identities* 7.2 (May 2009): 237–253. Print.

Jameson, Frederic. "Herbert Marcuse: Towards a Marxist Hermeneutic." *Salmagundi* 20 (Summer/Fall 1972): 126–133. Print.

_____. *Postmodernism: Or, the Cultural Logic of Late Capitalism*. Durham: Duke University Press, 1991. Print.

_____. "Reification and Utopia in Mass Culture." *Social Text* 1 (1979): 130–148. Print.

Jankovich, Mark. "Modernity and Subjectivity in the *Terminator*: The Machine as Monster in Contemporary American Culture." *The Velvet Light Trap* 30 (1992): 3–17. Print.

Jeunet, Jean Paul, dir. *Alien Resurrection*. Perf. Sigourney Weaver, Winona Ryder. Twentieth Century-Fox, 1997. DVD.

Julka, K. L. "Herbert Marcuse's Messianic Humanism: Politics of the New Left." *Social Scientist* 7.12 (July 1979): 13–23. Print.

Katsiaficas, George. "Marcuse as an Activist: Reminiscences of His Theory and Practice." *New Political Science* 36.7 (Summer/Fall 1996). Web.

Katz, Barry M. "Praxis and Poiesis: Toward an Intellectual Biography of Herbert Marcuse." *New German Critique* 18 (Autumn 1979): 12–18. Print.

Kavanagh, James H. "Feminism, Humanism, and Science in *Alien*." *Alien Zone* 73–81. Print.

Keegan, Rebecca. *The Futurist: The Life and Films of James Cameron*. New York: Crown, 2009. Print.

Keen, Sam, and John Raser. "A Conversation with Herbert Marcuse: Revolutionary Eroticism, the Tactics of Terror, the Young, Psychotherapy, the Environment, Technology, Reich." *Psychology Today* 4.2 (February 1971): 35–40, 60–66. Print.

Kellner, Douglas. "Marcuse, Liberation, and Radical Ecology." *Capitalism, Nature, Socialism* 3.3 (September 1992) Web.

Kendrick, James. "Marxist Overtones in Three Films by James Cameron." *Journal of Popular Film and Television* 27.3 (1999): 36–44. Print.

Kennedy, Harlan. "Twenty-First Century Nervous Breakdown." *Ridley Scott: Interviews* 31–41. Print.

Kershner, Irvin, dir. *The Empire Strikes Back*. Perf. Mark Hamill, Carrie Fisher, Harrison Ford. Twentieth Century-Fox, 1980. DVD.

Kimball, A. Samuel. "Conceptions and Contraceptions of the Future: *Terminator 2, The Matrix*, and *Alien Resurrection*." *Camera Obscura* 17.2 (2002): 68–107. Print.

Kline, Sally. *George Lucas: Interviews*. Jackson: Mississippi University Press, 1999. Print.

Knapp, Laurence F., and Andrea F. Kulas. *Ridley Scott: Interviews*. Jackson: Mississippi University Press, 2005. Print.

Kramer, Peter. "Big Pictures: Studying Contemporary Hollywood Cinema Through Its Greatest Hits." In Jacqueline Furby and Karen Randell, eds., *Screen Methods: Comparative Readings in Film Studies*. London: Wallflower, 2005. 124–132.

_____. "Women First: *Titanic* (1997), Action-Adventure Films, and Hollywood's Female Audience." *Historical Journal of Film, Radio and Television* 18.4 (October 1998). Web.

Kuhn, Annette. *Alien Zone: Cultural Theory and Contemporary Science Fiction Cinema*. New York: Verso, 1990. Print.

Kuiper, Koenraad. "Star Wars: An Imperial Myth." *Journal of Popular Culture* 21.4 (1988): 77–86. Print.

Lancashire, Anne. "*Attack of the Clones* and the Politics of Star Wars." *Dalhousie Review* 82.2 (2002): 235–53. Print.

Larson, Doran. "Machine as Messiah: Cyborgs, Morphs, and the American Body Politic." *Cinema Journal* 36.4 (1997): 57–75. Print.

Larsen, Ernst. "*Alien. Dawn of the Dead*. High-Tech Horror." *Jump Cut* 21 (November 1979). Web.

Latour, Bruno. "An Attempt at a 'Compositionist' Manifesto." *New Literary History* 41.3 (Summer 2010). Print.

Lawrence, Francis. *The Hunger Games: Catching Fire*. Perf. Jennifer Lawrence, Josh Hutcherson, Liam Hemsworth. Lionsgate, 2013. DVD.

_____. *The Hunger Games—Mockingjay Part 1*. Perf. Jennifer Lawrence, Josh Hutcherson, Liam Hemsworth. Lionsgate, 2014. DVD.

Le Guin, Ursula K. *The Word for World Is Forest*. New York: Berkeley, 1972. Print.

Lev, Peter. "Whose Future? *Star Wars, Alien, and Blade Runner*." *Literature/Film Quarterly* 26.1 (1998): 30–37. Print.

Levy, Shawn. "Send in the Clones." *Sight and Sound* 12.7 (July 2002): 20–22. Print.

Lewis, Jon. "The Perfect Money Machine(S)." In Jon lewis and Eric Smoodin, ed., *Looking Past the Screen: Case Studies in American Film History and Method*. Durham: Duke University Press, 2007. Print.

Leydon, Joe. Rev. of *AVP Requiem*. *Variety* December 26, 2007. Web.

Lim, Dennis. "Grand Allusions." *Village Voice* April 6, 1999. Web

Lioi, Anthony. "The Triumph of Eywa: *Avatar*, Pantheism, and the Sign of a Green Ecumene." *Ecozon@* 2.2 (2011): 40–59. Print.

Littau, Karin. "Media, Mythology, and Morphogenesis: *Aliens*." *Convergence: The International Journal of Research into New Media Technologies* 17.1 (2011): 19–36. Print.

Locke, Brian. "White and 'Black" versus Yellow: Metaphor and *Blade Runner*'s Racial Politics." *Arizona Quarterly* 65.4 (2009): 113–138. Print.

Lucas, George, dir. *American Graffiti*. Perf. Ronnie Howard, Richard Dreyfuss, Paul LeMat. Universal, 1973. DVD.

_____. *Attack of the Clones*. Perf. Hayden Christensen, Natalie Portman, Ewan McGregor. Twentieth Century-Fox, 2002. DVD.

_____. *A New Hope*. Perf. Mark Hamill, Carrie Fisher, Harrison Ford. Twentieth Century-Fox, 1977. DVD.

_____. *The Phantom Menace*. Perf. Liam Neeson, Natalie Portman, Ewan McGregor, Jake Lloyd. Twentieth Century-Fox 1999. DVD.

_____. *Revenge of the Sith*. Perf. Hayden Christensen, Natalie Portman, Ewan McGregor. Twentieth Century-Fox, 2005. DVD.

_____. *THX-1138*. Perf. Robert Duvall, Maggie McOmie, Donald Pleasence. American Zoetrope, 1971. DVD.

Lumenick, Lou. "In *Predators* Its Shoot First, Prey Later." *New York Post* July 9, 2010. Web.

Lusser, Mark, and Kaitlin Gowan. "The Romantic Roots of *Blade Runner*." *Wordsworth Circle* 43.3 (2012): 165–172. Print.

Malinovich, Myriam Miedzian. "On Herbert Marcuse and the Concept of Psychological Freedom." *Social Research* 49.1 (Spring 1982): 158–180. Print.

Mann, Karen B. "Narrative Entanglements: The *Terminator*." *Film Quarterly* 43.2 (1989): 17 27. Print.

Marcuse, Herbert. *The Aesthetic Dimension: Toward a Critique of Marxist Aesthetics*. 1977. Boston: Beacon Press, 1978. Print.

_____. "Ecology and the Critique of Modern Society." *Capitalism, Nature, Socialism* 3.3 (1992): 29–37. Print.

_____. *Eros and Civilization: A Philosophical Inquiry Into Freud*. 1955. New York: Vintage, 1962. Print.

_____. "Failure of the New Left?" *New German Critique* 18 (1979): 3–11. Print.

_____. "Letters to Chicago Surrealists, October 1971—March 1973." *Arsenal* 4 (1979): 31–38, 39–47. Print.

_____. "Liberation from the Affluent Society." In David Cooper, ed., *The Dialectics of Liberation*. Harmondsworth: Penguin, 1968: 175–192. Print.

_____. "Marxism and Feminism." *Women's Studies* 2.3 (1974): 279–288. Print.

_____. "The Movement in a New Era of Repression." *Berkeley Journal of Sociology* 16 (1971–72): 1–14. Print.

_____. *One-Dimensional Man: Studies in the Ideology of Advanced Industrial Society.* 1964. Boston: Beacon Press, 1991. Print.

_____. "Protosocialism and Late Capitalism: Toward a Theoretical Synthesis Based on Bahro's Analysis." Trans. Michael Vale et al. *International Journal of Politics* 10.2/3 (Summer/Fall 1980): 25–48. Print.

_____. "The Realm of Freedom and the Realm of Necessity: A Reconsideration." *Praxis* 5.1 (1969): (20–25). Print.

_____. *Studies in Critical Philosophy*. Trans. Joris De Bres. Boston: Beacon, 1973. Print.

Marquand, Richard, dir. *Return of the Jedi*. Perf. Mark Hamill, Carrie Fisher, Harrison Ford. Twentieth Century-Fox, 1983. DVD.

Maslin, Janet. "Film Review: A Spectacle as Sweeping as the Sea." *New York Times* December 19, 1997. Web.

_____. "*Predator 2: The Quarry—Humans.*" *New York Times* November 21, 1990. Web.

_____. Rev. of *Blade Runner*. *New York Times* June 25, 1982. Web.

_____. "'Terminator': Suspense Tale." *New York Times* October 26, 1984. Web.

Matheson, T. J. "Marcuse, Ellul, and the Science-Fiction Film: Negative Responses to Technology." *Science Fiction Studies* 19.3 (1992): 326–339. Print.

McAllister, Matthew, Ian Gordon, and Mark Jancovich. "Block Buster Art House: Meets Superhero Comic, or Meets Graphic Novel? The Contradictory Relationship Between Film and Comic Art." *Journal of Popular Film and Television* 34.3 (2006): 108–115. Print.

McCarthy, Todd. Rev. of *The Hunger Games—Mockingjay Part 1*. the Hollywood Reporter November 10, 2014. Web.

McGee, Patrick. "Terrible Beauties: Messianic Time and the Image of Social Redemption in James Cameron's *Titanic*." *Postmodern Culture* 10.1 (1999): Web.

McIntyre, Dan. "Prototypical Characteristics of Blockbuster Movie Dialog: A Corpus Stylistic Analysis." *Texas Studies in Language and Literature* 54.3 (2012): 402–425. Print.

McLuckie, Kramer. "'The Scream Instead of the Statement?' Two Landmark Films in Science Fiction's Meandering Path to Critical Relevance." *Film Matters* (Winter 2011): 24–29. Print.

McTiernan, John, dir. *Predator*. Perf. Arnold Schwarzenegger, Carl Weathers, Elpidia Carrillo. Twentieth Century-Fox, 1987. DVD.

Menand, Lois. "Gross Points: Is the Blockbuster the End of Cinema?" *New Yorker* 80.45 (February 7, 2005): 82–89. Web.

Meyer, Carla. "The Second One Rocks in *Reloaded*." SFGate.com, October 17, 2003. Web.

Meyer, David S. "*Star Wars, Star Wars*, and American Political Culture." *Journal of Popular Culture* 26.1 (1992): 99–115. Print.

Mitchell, Elvis. "Film Review: "An Idealized World and a Troubled Hero." *New York Times* May 14, 2003. Web.

Mosely, Bill. "20,000 Leagues Under the Sea: The Movie Director as Capitan Nemo." *James Cameron: Interviews* 77–109. Print.

Mostow, Jonathan, dir. *Terminator 3: Rise of the Machines*. Perf. Arnold Schwarzenegger, Nick Stahl, Kristanna Loken. Warner Bros., 2003. DVD.

Mulrooney, Jonathan. "The Sadness of *Avatar*." *Wordsworth Circle* 42.3 (2011): 201–04. Print.

Murakami, Jimmy, dir. *Battle Beyond the Stars*. Perf. George Peppard, Robert Vaughn, Richard Thomas. New World Cinema, 1980. DVD.

Narine, Anil. "Policing Traumatized Boundaries of Self and Nation: Undocumented Labor in *Blade Runner*." *Americana* 5.2 (2006). Web.

Nashawaty, Chris. "American Graffiti." *Entertainment Weekly* January 3, 1999: 94–98. Print.

_____. "AVP Requiem." *Entertainment Weekly* January 9, 2008. Web.

Neumaier, Joe. Rev. of *The Hunger Games: Catching Fire*. *New York Daily News* 18 November 2013. Web.

Newman, Kim. "Prometheus Unbound (Ridley Scott's *Prometheus*)." *Sight and Sound* 22.7. Web.

Newton, Judith. "Feminism and Anxiety in *Alien*." *Alien Zone* 82–87. Print.

Nolan, Steve. "Worshipping (Wo)Men: Liturgical Representation and Feminist Film Theory: An *Alien/S* Identification." *Bulletin of the John Rhylands University Library of Manchester* 80.3 (1998): 195–213. Print.

O'Heir, Andrew. "The Horror, the Horror." Rev. of *Alien* Salon.com. Web.

Osmond, Andrew. Rev. of *Aliens Vs. Predator: Requiem*. *Sight and Sound* 18.3 (2008): 54. Print.

O'Sullivan, Jane. "Virtual Metamorphosis: Cosmetic and Cybernetic Revisions of Pygmalion's 'Living Doll.'" *Arethusa* 41.1 (2008): 133–156. Print.

Palumbo, Donald. "The Monomyth in James Cameron's the *Terminator*: Sarah as Monomythic Heroine." *The Journal of Popular Culture* 41.3 (2008): 413–427. Print.

Peary, Danny. "Directing *Alien* and *Blade Runner*: An Interview with Ridley Scott." *Ridley Scott: Interviews* 42–55. Print.

Penley, Constance. "Time Travel, Primal Scene, and the Critical Dystopia." *Alien Zone* 116–127. Print.

Perren, Alisa. "Sex, Lies, and Marketing: Miramax and the Development of the Quality Blockbuster." *Film Quarterly* 55.2 (2001): 30–39. Print.

Phesant-Kelly, Fran. "Cinematic Cyborgs, Abject Bodies: Post-Human Hybridity in *T2* and *Robocop*." *Film International* 9.5 (2011): 54–63. Print.

"Pilot." *Dark Angel.* Writ. James Cameron. Dir. David Nutter. 2000. DVD.

Pollock, Dale. *Skywalking: The Life and Films of George Lucas.* 1983. New York: Da Capo, 1999. Print.

Pope, Richard. "Affects of the Gaze: Post Oedipal Desire and the Traversal of Fantasy in *Blade Runner*." *Camera Obscura* 25.1 (2010): 68–95. Print.

Post, Mike, dir. *Good Guys Wear Black.* Perfs. Chuck Norris, Anne Archer, James Franciscus. Mar Vista Productions, 1978. DVD.

Puig, Claudia. "*Mockingjay* Is Best Games Yet." *USA Today* November 23, 2014. Web.

Pye, Michael, and Lynda Myles. *The Movie Brats: How the Film Generation Took Over Hollywood.* New York: Holt, Reinhart, & Winston, 1979. Print.

Rainer, Peter. Rev. of *Avatar*, dir. James Cameron. *Christian Science Monitor* December 17, 2009. *Lexis-Nexis.* Web. 21 December 2010.

Reitz, Charles. "Marcuse in America—Exile as Educator: Deprovincializing One-Dimensional Culture in the U.S.A." *Fast Capitalism* 5.2 (2009). Web.

Review: *The Terminator. Variety* December 31, 1983. Web.

Rhetts, JoAnne. "Writer-Director Shows the Special Effects Energy Can Radiate" *James Cameron: Interviews* 15–18. Print.

Richardson, John H. "Iron Jim." *James Cameron: Interviews* 57–70. Print.

Rieder, John "Race and Revenge Fantasies in *Avatar*, *District 9*, and *Inglorious Basterds*." *Science Fiction Film and Television* 4.1 (2011): 41–56. Print.

Robb, Brian J. *Ridley Scott: The Pocket Essential Guide.* Harpenden: Pocket Essentials, 2005. Print.

Ronge, Darry. "Paradise Found and Exploited." Rev. of *Avatar*, dir. James Cameron. *Sunday Times* (South Africa) December 20, 2009. Web.

Rose, Brad. "The Triumph of Social Control: A Look at Herbert Marcuse's *One Dimensional Man* 25 Years Later." *Berkeley Journal of Sociology* 35 (1990): 55–68. Print.

Ross, Gary, dir. *The Hunger Games.* Perf. Jennifer Lawrence, Josh Hutcherson, Liam Hemsworth. Lionsgate, 2012. DVD.

Rushing, Janice Hocker. "Evolution of the 'New Frontier' in *Alien* and *Aliens*: Patriarchal Co-Optation of the Feminine Archetype." *The Quarterly Journal of Speech* 75.1 (1989): 1–24. Print.

Rushing, Janice Hocker, and Thomas S. Frentz. "Singing Over the Bones: James Cameron's *Titanic*." *Critical Studies in Media Communication* 17.1 (2000): 1–27. Print.

Russell, John G. "Don't It Make My Black Face Blue: Race, Avatars, Albescence, and the Transnational Imaginary." *Journal of Popular Culture* 46.1 (2013): 193–217. Print.

Ryan, Michael, and Douglas Kelner. "Technophobia." *Alien Zone* 58–65. Print.

Sammon, Paul M. "Interview with Ridley Scott." *Ridley Scott: Interviews* 89–115. Print.

Sargent, Joseph, dir. *Colossus: The Forbin Project.* Perf. Eric Braeden, Susan Clark, Gordon Pinset. Universal, 1970. DVD.

Scheide, Frank. "Fredrick Jackson Turner's 'Frontier Thesis,' *Avatar* (2009), and the Representation of Native Americans in Hollywood Film." *The International Journal of the Arts in Society* 5.6 (2011): 197–210. Print.

Schoolman, Morton. "Marcuse's Aesthetics and the Displacement of Critical Theory." *New German Critique* 8 (Spring 1976): 54–79. Print.

Sciretta, Peter. "James Cameron Talks Avatar 2, Terminator 5 & 6, Spiderman Reboot, Batman Movies, How Hollywood Is Getting 3D Wrong, and His Oscar Chances." Slashfilm.com. Blog post. January 10, 2014.

Scott, A.O. "The Game Concludes with Light and Noise." Rev. of *The Matrix Revolutions. The New York Times* 5 November 2003. Web.

\_\_\_\_\_. "Once More Unto the Galactic Void." Rev. of *Prometheus. New York Times* June 7, 2012. Web.

Scott, Ridley, dir. *Alien.* Perf. Sigourney Weaver, Tom Skerritt, John Hurt. Twentieth Century-Fox, 1979. DVD.

\_\_\_\_\_. *Blade Runner.* Perf. Harrison Ford, Rutger Hauer, Sean Young. Twentieth Century-Fox, 1982. DVD.

\_\_\_\_\_. *Prometheus.* Perf. Noomi Rapace, Logan Marshall-Green, Michael Fassbender. Twentieth Century-Fox, 2010. DVD.

Seabrook, John. "Why Is the Force Still with Us?" *New Yorker* January 6, 1997: 40–53. Print.

Seegert, Alf. "Till We Have [Inter]Faces: The Cybercultural Ecologies of *Avatar*." *Western Humanities Review* 64.2 (2010): 112–31. Print.

Sey, James. "The Terminator Syndrome: Science Fiction, Cinema, and Contemporary Culture." *Literator* 13.3 (1992): 13–19. Print.

Shapiro, Marc. *James Cameron: An Unauthor-*

ized Biography. Los Angeles: Renaissance, 2000. Print.

Shumway, David R. "Rock 'n' Roll Sound Tracks and the Production of Nostalgia." *Cinema Journal* 38.2 (Winter 1999): 36–51. Print.

Silvio, Carl, and Tony M. Vinci. *Culture, Identities, and Technology in the Star Wars Films.* Jefferson, NC: McFarland, 2007. Print.

Smiley, Tavis. "James Cameron." *James Cameron: Interviews* 189–99. Print.

Smith, Kyle. "Let the Games Begin." Rev. of *The Hunger Games. New York Post* 21 March 2012. Web.

\_\_\_\_\_. "Out of This World." Rev. of *Prometheus. New York Post* 8 June 2012.

Snider, Mike. "The Future Is Now for Lucas' *THX-1138*." *USA Today* May 21, 2004: E1. Print.

Sobchack, Vivian. "Between a Rock and a Hard Place: How Ridley Scott's *Prometheus* Deals with Impossible Expectations and Mythological Baggage." *Film Comment* July 1, 2012: 30–34. Print.

\_\_\_\_\_. "The Virginity of Astronauts: Sex and the Science Fiction Film." *Alien Zone* 103–115.

"Soldier." *The Outer Limits.* Writ. Harlan Ellison. Dir. Gerd Oswald. 1964. Web.

Speed, Lesley. "Tuesday's Gone: The Nostalgic Teen Film." *Journal of Popular Film and Television* 26.1 (1998): 24–32. Print.

Speed, Louise. "*Alien³*: A Postmodern Encounter with the Abject." *Arizona Quarterly* 54.1 (1998): 125–151. Print.

Stabile, Donald. "The New Class and Capitalism: A Three-And-Three Thirds Class Model." *Review of Radical Political Economics* 15.4 (1983): 45–70. Print.

Stahl, Roger. "Why We 'Support the Troops': Rhetorical Evaluations." *Rhetoric and Public Affairs* 12.4 (2009): 533–570. Print.

Starin, Orin. "Here Come the Anthros (Again): The Strange Marriage of Anthropology and Native Americans." *Cultural Anthropology* 26.2 (2011): 179–204. Print.

Starosielski, Nicole "'Movements That Are Drawn': A History of Environmental Animation from the *Lorax* to *FernGully* to *Avatar*." *International Communication Gazette* 73.1–2 (2011): 145–163. Print.

Stradley, Randy, writ., and Phillip Norwood ct al. (art). *Aliens vs. Predator* 1.1 (June 1990): Milwaukie, OR: Dark Horse Comics. Print.

Strause, Colin, and Greg Strause, dirs. *Aliens Vs. Predator: Requiem.* Perf. Reiko Aylesworth, Steven Pasquale. Twentieth Century–Fox, 2007. DVD.

Tancheva, Kornelia. "Recasting the Debate: The Sign of the Library in Popular Culture." *Libraries and Culture* 40.4 (Fall 2005): 530–46. Print.

Tang, Yong. "*Avatar*: A Marxist Saga on a Far Distant Planet." *TripleC* 9.2 (2011): 657–667. Print.

Taylor, Alan, dir. *Terminator Genisys.* Perf. Arnold Schwarzenegger, Emelia Clarke, Jason Clarke. Paramount, 2015. DVD.

Telotte, J.P. "The Doubles of Fantasy and the Space of Desire." *Alien Zone* 152–159. Print.

\_\_\_\_\_. *Science Fiction Film.* New York: Cambridge University Press, 2001. Print.

\_\_\_\_\_. "*The Terminator, Terminator 2*, and the Exposed Body." *Journal of Popular Film and Television* 20.2 (1992): Web.

Travers, Peter. Rev. of *The Hunger Games. Rolling Stone* March 21, 2012. Web.

Turan, Kenneth. "He Said He'd Be Back: Arnold and *Terminator 2* Return with a Vengeance." *Los Angeles Times* July 3, 1991. Web.

van Vogt, A. E. *The Voyage of the Space Beagle.* 1950. New York: Pocket Books, 1977. Print.

"Vatican Critical of *Avatar*'s Spiritual Message." CBC News January 13, 2010. *Lexis-Nexis.* Web. 21 Dec. 2010.

Vaughn, Thomas. "Voices of Sexual Distortion: Rape, Birth, and Self-Annihilation Metaphors in the *Alien* Trilogy." *Quarterly Journal of Speech* 81.4 (1995): 423–435. Print.

Verheiden, Mark (script), Ron Randall and Chris Warner (art). *Predator* 1.4 (March 1990). Milwaukie, OR: Dark Horse Comics. Print.

Vivas, Eliseo. "Marcuse on Art." *Modern Age* 14.2 (Spring 1970): 140–149. Print.

Voskuil, Caryn. "Philosophy, Gender, and Popular Fictions: Classical Gender Constructs in the Film *Titanic*." *Critical Engagements* 1.1 (2007): 102–116. Print.

Wachowski, Andy, and Lana Wachowski, dirs. *The Matrix.* Perf. Keanu Reeves, Laurence Fishburne, Carrie-Anne Moss, Hugo Weaving. Warner Bros., 1999. DVD.

\_\_\_\_\_, and \_\_\_\_\_. *The Matrix Reloaded.* Perf. Keanu Reeves, Laurence Fishburne, Carrie-Anne Moss, Hugo Weaving. Warner Bros., 2003. DVD.

\_\_\_\_\_, and \_\_\_\_\_. *The Matrix Revolutions.* Perf. Keanu Reeves, Laurence Fishburne, Carrie-Anne Moss, Hugo Weaving. Warner Bros., 2003. DVD.

Warren, Victoria. "From the Restoration to Hollywood: John Dryden's *Conquest of Grenada* to James Cameron's *Terminator* Films." *Restoration: Studies in English Literary Culture, 1660–1700* 27.2 (2003): 17–40. Print.

White, Rob. "Only Connect." *Film Quarterly* 63.3 (Spring 2010): 4–5. Print.

Williams, Douglas E. "Ideology as Dystopia: An Interpretation of *Blade Runner*." *International Political Science Review* 9.4 (1988): 381–394. Print.

Williams, Raymond. *The Sociology of Culture.* New York: Shocken, 1982. Print.

Wolf, Richard Paul, Barrington Moore, Jr., and Herbert Marcuse. *A Critique of Pure Tolerance*. Boston: Beacon Press, 1969. Print.

Wotton, Adrian. "James Cameron." *James Cameron: Interviews* 147–168. Print.

Wright, David A. "The Advanced Commandos of Some Invading Force: *Deliverance* and *Predator*: An (Un)Likely Comparison." *James Dickey Newsletter* 25 (2009): 17–35. Print.

Wright, Will. "The Empire Bites the Dust." *Social Text* 6 (Autumn 1982): 120–25. Print.

York, Ashley Elaine. "From Chick Flicks to Millennial Blockbusters: Spinning Female-Driven Narratives into Franchises." *Journal of Popular Culture* 43.1 (2010): 3–25. Print.

Yunis, Susan, and Tammy Ostrander. "Tales Your Mother Never Told You: Aliens and the Horrors of Motherhood." *Journal of the Fantastic in the Arts* 14.1 (2003): 68–76. Print.

Zani, Stephen. "*Titanic*: Traumatic Disaster and Recuperation." *Journal of Popular Film and Television* 31.3 (2003): 125–131. Print.

Žižek, Slavoj. "*Avatar*: Return of the Natives." *New Statesman* March 2010. Web.

Zwinger, Lynda. "Blood Relations: Feminist Theory Meets the Uncanny Alien Bug Mother." *Hypatia* 7.2 (Spring 1992): 74–90. Print.

# Index

*The Aesthetic Dimension* 15, 16, 23, 63, 159
*Alien* (film) 2, 8–9, 31, 35, 37, 45, 77–85, 90, 102–104
*Alien* (franchise/universe) 30, 36, 99, 124–125
*Alien Apocalypse* 41–42
*Alien Resurrection* 32, 38–40
*Alien³* 32, 36–38
*Alien Versus Predator Eternal* 42
*Alien vs. Predator: Requiem* 43, 48–49
*Aliens* 32, 35, 37, 135–142
*Aliens vs. Predators* (graphic novel) 42–43
*American Graffiti* 11, 61–63, 143
*Attack of the Clones* 71–72
*Avatar* 1, 152–168
*AVP: Alien vs. Predator* (film) 43, 47–48

*Battle Beyond the Stars* 115
*Blade Runner* 25, 32, 85–98, 104–106, 108–109

Cameron, James 8, 14, 29, 31, 32, 112–119, 125–126
*Colossus: The Forbin Project* 56, 120–121

Dark Horse Comics 40–41, 42
de Certeau, Michel 10, 27–28, 30, 52, 55

Ellison, Harlan 31; "Demon with a Glass Hand" 31, 194n8; "I Have No Mouth and I Must Scream" 122; "Soldier" 31, 122–124, 130
*The Empire Strikes Back* 66–67, 68
*Eros and Civilization* 13, 16, 19–20, 21, 22, 23, 36, 60, 64, 68, 89, 94, 159, 164
*An Essay on Liberation* 88

Frankfurt School 12, 24
Freud, Sigmund 17, 20

*Galaxy of Terror* 115
*Good Guys Wear Black* 114

*The Hero with a Thousand Faces* 9, 54
*The Hunger Games* (trilogy) 179–185

*It! The Terror from Beyond Space* 31, 32, 34, 101

Jameson, Frederic 7, 53
*Jaws* 1, 7, 116
Jeunet, Jean-Pierre 6, 38–40

Lucas, George 9, 11, 14, 27, 28, 30, 52–55, 57, 58, 64, 74, 112

Marcuse, Herbert (background) 2, 11–13, 30, 35, 40, 44, 55, 57, 80
Marcuse, Herbert (concepts): defensive violence 17, 22; Eros 19–20, 60, 68, 94–97, 108–111, 126–133, 141–142, 148–150, 161, 168, 176–179; false needs 18, 60, 72, 89–90, 173, 183; industrial society 23; one-dimensional thought 18, 61, 65, 66, 70, 81–83, 132; performance principle 21, 37–38, 39–40, 41–51, 76, 85, 127, 129, 139–141; refusal 68; repressive de-sublimation 20, 60, 166; soft repression 18, 181–182; surplus repression 20; Thanatos 21, 59, 61, 72, 94–95, 97, 105, 108–111, 120, 131, 164, 175, 177–178; two-dimensional thought 64, 71, 83–84, 92–94, 103–104, 132, 174–175; unfreedom 19, 58, 72
Marcuse, Herbert (shorter works): "Ecology and the Critique of Modern Society" 24; "Failure of the New Left?" 17; "Letters to Chicago Surrealists" 15, 16, 18; "Liberation from the Affluent Society" 15, 23, 63, 159; "Marxism and Feminism" 22; "The

Movement in a New Era of Repression" 16, 18, 89; "Protosocialism and Late Capitalism" 13, 24; "The Realms of Freedom" 66; *see also The Aesthetic Dimension; Eros and Civilization; An Essay on Liberation; One-Dimensional Man; Studies in Critical Philosophy*
Marx, Karl 9
*The Matrix* (trilogy) 171–179

*A New Hope* 1, 11, 14, 65–66
New Left 12

*One-Dimensional Man* 13, 18, 55, 58, 59, 60, 61, 62, 81, 84, 98, 139, 164–165

*The Phantom Menace* 70–71
*Piranha* 116
*Piranha Part Two: The Spawning* 115–117
*Planet of the Vampires* 77–78
*The Practice of Everyday Life* 27
*Predator* 44–45
*Predator 2* 45–46
*Predators* 49–50, 100
*Prometheus* 77, 98–111

*Rambo* 44
*Rambo II* 32, 118, 136–139
*Return of the Jedi* 2, 67–70

*Revenge of the Sith* 72–73

Scott, Ridley 8–9, 14, 73–77, 100–102
Spielberg, Steven 7
*Star Wars* franchise (Lucas) 54
*Strange Days* 114
*Studies in Critical Philosophy* 23, 63, 65, 68, 159

*The Terminator* 25, 29, 113, 118, 121, 124, 126–129
*Terminator Genisys* 29
*Terminator Salvation* 29
*Terminator 3: Rise of the Machines* 29
*Terminator 2: Judgement Day* 2, 29, 113, 121–122, 124, 129–133
*THX-1138* 11, 25, 56–61, 71, 173
*Titanic* 8, 142–151
*True Lies* 114

van Vogt, A.E. 31, 34, 115; "Black Destroyer" 31, 33; "Discord in Scarlet" 31
*The Voyage of the Space Beagle* 32–33, 77

Williams, Raymond 28
*The Word for World Is Forest* 157–159

*The X-Files* 40

www.ingramcontent.com/pod-product-compliance
Ingram Content Group UK Ltd.
Pitfield, Milton Keynes, MK11 3LW, UK
UKHW042001140426
5217IPUK00015B/912